MASTURBATION

MASTURBATION

THE HISTORY OF A GREAT TERROR

JEAN STENGERS

ANNE VAN NECK

TRANSLATED BY

KATHRYN A. HOFFMANN

palgrave

MASTURBATION: THE HISTORY OF A GREAT TERROR
This translation © Kathryn Hoffmann, 2001
All rights reserved. No part of this book may be used or reproduced in
any manner whatsoever without written permission except in the case of
brief quotations embodied in critical articles or reviews.

First published 2001 by
PALGRAVE
175 Fifth Avenue, New York, N.Y.10010 and
Houndmills, Basingstoke, Hampshire RG21 6XS.
Companies and representatives throughout the world

Originally published in French as *Histoire d'une grande peur, la
masturbation*, by Jean Stengers et Anne Van Neck. © Institut Synthélabo
pour le progrès de la connaissance, 1998.

PALGRAVE is the new global publishing imprint of St. Martin's Press
LLC Scholarly and Reference Division and Palgrave Publishers Ltd
(formerly Macmillan Press Ltd).

ISBN 0–312–22443–5 (hardback)

Library of Congress Cataloging-in-Publication Data
Stengers, Jean.
[Histoire d'une grande peur, la masturbation. English]
Masturbation : the history of a great terror / Jean Stengers, Anne Van
Neck ; translated by Kathryn A. Hoffmann.
    p. cm.
Includes bibliographical references and index.
ISBN 0–312–22443–5
    1. Masturbation—History. 2. Masturbation—Moral and ethical
aspects—History. I. Neck, Anne van, d. 1982.
HQ447.S75 2001
306.77'2'09—dc21   2001019450

A catalogue record for this book is available
from the British Library.

Design by Letra Libre, Inc.

First edition: July 2001
10 9 8 7 6 5 4 3 2 1

Printed in the United States of America.

CONTENTS

INTRODUCTION

JEAN STENGERS

This book will perhaps seem provocative. That provocation does not reside in the topic, which unquestionably merits serious investigation. The fear of masturbation constituted, in terms of both its breadth and its duration, a true social phenomenon. What will doubtless shock some, however, is the approach to the topic, which might appear unorthodox. When one analyzes a social phenomenon, it is customary, one might even say obligatory, to search for—and find—its roots largely within society itself. In this book, we will attempt to show how certain ideas, seemingly inexplicable in terms of social context, were launched by several men, and how those ideas triumphed without that social context serving as the key to their success. It is an illustration of the force of ideas as well as an illustration of the role the individual can play within phenomena reputed to be collective. It is better to show our colors at the outset; that way, the critics can hone their weapons.

A second source of surprise and criticism will doubtless be our decision to restrict our analysis to the Occident. Would it not have been better to broaden our perspectives and take into account ways of thinking about masturbation in other civilizations? Wasn't this the ideal occasion to apply the methods of social anthropology?

Truthfully, we would have liked to take that route. Yet one insurmountable obstacle unfortunately stood in our way: the state of our knowledge. Our competence in areas beyond Europe or the Western world is mediocre at best. As a noted expert has said: "most information about masturbation in non-European societies and cultures is either anecdotal or stereotypic."[1] Anecdotes and stereotypes did not seem to us sufficient basis for a serious study. We preferred to forgo the attempt.

This book bears two names, the introduction only one. Anne Van Neck passed on in January 1982. She was only 41 years old.

A word on the genesis of the book and the roles of the two authors. I took up the topic in 1976–1977, in a contemporary history seminar I was teaching at the Free University of Brussels. I found it presented certain analogies—particularly in terms of conceptions of sexuality—with a theme that I had previously looked at, and that had resulted in the publication of a lengthy article: "Les pratiques anticonceptionnelles dans le mariage au XIXe et au XXe siècles: problèmes humains et attitudes religieuses" (in *Revue Belge de Philologie et d'Histoire*, vol. XLIX, 1971, pp. 403–81 and 1119–1174). The work for the seminar was interesting. The undergraduate history students who participated contributed much. I thank them warmly.

I had appointed Anne Van Neck, Ph.D., research assistant in the university's Institute of History, as a reader for the seminar. This was admittedly not at all her area of historical specialization. Yet she took the subject to heart and, beyond her work for the seminar, she undertook, as I was doing myself, more advanced research on the subject. This research was to result in a book that we had decided to write together. The project was never entirely completed, but even in its partially completed state, it testifies to Anne Van Neck's courage. She began writing the first draft of the book, based on our joint notes, when she was already seriously ill and aware of that fact. She saw that draft through the sixth chapter prior to her death. This was a draft we had planned to rework together.

Left with sole responsibility for the project, I gave it, in a new draft, the shape I felt appropriate. Any criticisms of the form or the content should therefore be directed toward myself. I would like, on the other hand, that whatever there is of positive value in this work serve as an homage to Anne Van Neck, an homage to her memory and also to her admirable talent. This young historian, who initially began her studies in medieval history, eventually specialized in areas of contemporary history demanding exacting scholarship. She published articles that were fresh and very well documented on public finances in Belgium in the nineteenth and twentieth centuries, particularly on urban finances (in *Acta Historica Bruxellensia. Travaux de l'Institut d'Histoire de l'Université Libre de Bruxelles*, vol. I, II, and III, Bruxelles, 1967 to 1974). She left us with a doctoral thesis that is a monumental work and one of considerable importance: *Les débuts de la machine à vapeur dans l'industrie belge, 1800–1850* (Brussels, Académie Royale de Belgique, 1979, 898 pages; winner of the Academy's Suzanne Tassier Prize). Those who would like to know what conclusions she reached will find them readily accessible in a posthumous overview of her book published under the same title in the *Bulletin de la Classe des Lettres et des Sciences morales et politiques de l'Académie* (1982, no. 6, pp. 245–265). Also of note among her publications is a basic study, written in collaboration with Eliane Gubin, of the distribution of professions in the mid-nineteenth-century population of Belgium (in *Histoire et Méthode = Acta Historica Bruxellensia*, vol. IV, Brussels, 1981, pp. 269–365). A fine capacity for research and a rigor of thought shone through all her research. Our loss, in January 1982—it is her former thesis director who testifies to this—was great.

Chapter One

"A Shameful Vice Which Decimates Youth"

(Proudhon)[1]

"There is no need for us to describe here an act which is unfortunately as well known as it is shameful": it is with these words that the entry *Masturbation* begins in the *Grand Dictionnaire universel du XIX*ᵉ *siècle* by Pierre Larousse. This article is of a length proportionate to the importance of the subject—more than a page of text in extremely small typeface. Masturbation is not described here (except by the simple definition: "Solitary act of pleasure performed by touching the sexual parts"), but the "fatal results" are detailed at length.

"All physicians agree that masturbation predisposes to a great number of illnesses. Those individuals who abandon themselves to it unchecked are thrown before long into a state of general weakness. . . . Its overall result is the development of phthisis accompanied by consumption and the appearance of various troubles of the nervous system. . . . In the realm of the intellect, the disorders are, if possible, even more pronounced." As for the masturbator, "both feeling and the imagination are blunted. Everything fatigues him, right up to the smallest mental exercise. He becomes incapable of the slightest intellectual work. He notices his physical and moral degeneration, but his will has lost the energy needed to remedy it. . . . The most profound melancholy and hypochondria overcome him. The memory of what he was, the thought of what he could have been throw him at times into a state of sadness filled with disgust for all the joys of life and can lead him to suicide."

The tremolos continue at length, in dramatic perfection.[2]

This is a text from 1873.[3] From the outset, a question arises: is it representative? Is this portrait of masturbation a faithful reflection of the conceptions of the time?

In an attempt to answer that question, we will limit ourselves, to begin, to the period stretching from around 1815 to just a bit beyond 1873, and to ideas that could be found in France or in texts in French. Within this chronological and geographical frame, the answer is unequivocal: the Larousse of 1873 was perfectly—one might almost be tempted to say admirably—representative.

The period opened, in 1819, with a *Dictionnaire des sciences médicales* in which we find: "The terrible effects of the . . . deadly habit of masturbation have been the topic of studies by the most famous physicians of all time. . . . According to them, the continual excitation of the genital organs is liable to give rise to almost all the acute or chronic illnesses which can disturb the harmony of our functions."[4]

From 1819 to 1873 and beyond, that was the only refrain to be heard.

"Almost all the acute or chronic illnesses," we've just read. Combining all the different studies on the subject, as well as medical treatises and hygiene manuals, we end up with an extraordinarily broad, varied, and horrific spectrum of the diverse ills liable to strike the masturbator. Troubles of the cerebrospinal system (here we are following the medical classifications of the period): cephalalgias, vertigo, cerebral congestion, and in general "all the illnesses of the brain and the spinal column." Nervous troubles: asthenia, melancholia, hysteria, convulsions, stupidity, imbecility, and insanity. Sense organs and phonation: weakening or total loss of sight and hearing; progressive loss of smell and taste; phonation disorders. Skeletal system: rachitis, gibbosities, stunting of growth, articular rheumatism, and gout. Muscular and adipose system: weight loss, etiolation, paralysis. Cardiovascular system: palpitations, syncope, lesions of the heart and the large blood vessels, aneurysmal rupture. Respiratory system: chronic catarrh, phthisis, tubercular consumption, scrofula. Digestive system: chronic gastralgia, dyspepsia, colic. Genitourinary system: spermatorrhea, prostatitis, impotence, sterility. And the final prognosis, for the incurable masturbator: death.

The above list, representing only a selection, was compiled from various texts by different authors. No author predicted all these ills at the same time. Each author had, as it were, his favorite ills; that was the mark of his originality. But the overall tone of the medical predictions for the masturbator was always the same: it was uniformly somber, even tragic.

Death: this word, evoking the final outcome, resonates in the literature of the time. "The victims of genital ardor, . . . each day, take a step closer to the tomb," wrote A. Debay in his *Hygiène et physiologie du mariage.*[5] Réveillé-Parise in 1828 viewed masturbation as the harbinger of the end, not only of the individual, but of the race itself. "Masturbation is one of those scourges which secretly attack and destroy humanity. In my opinion, neither the plague, nor war, nor the pox, nor a host of similar evils, have more disastrous results for humanity than this fatal habit. It is the destroyer of civilization, and all the more redoutable in that it works continually, undermining the generations bit by bit."[6] Dr. De Bourge expressed the same idea in 1860: "This abominable practice has put to death more individuals than all the great wars, joined to the most depopulating epidemics."[7] And Dr. Fonssagrives wrote in turn: "What the perverted habits of the child, prolonged into adolescence, take away from the shared patrimony of a country's forces, is incalculable, and one could almost assert that universal domination would belong to he who would extirpate this shameful leprosy from his breast." "It cannot be repeated often enough," Fonssagrives adds, "it is one of the most serious causes of the degeneration of the species."[8]

What gave these pervasive ideas weight in the nineteenth century is that they were defended at the same time by physicians, hygienists, moralists, and educators, who formed a common front. Masturbation simultaneously took on the horrifying image of sin, vice, and self-destruction. It was attacked vigorously and unsparingly for its supposed moral as well as physical ravages. Moralists and physicians backed each other up. Moral and medical notions were mixed in the vocabulary of the period: lethal vice, destructive, shameful and pernicious pleasure; and fatal aberration.

Debreyne, who was both a physician and a moral theologian, placed the physical and moral "degradation" of the masturbator on the same footing. His description is, for the period, classic: "Youth who are victims of this unhappy and shameful passion more or less lose memory, intelligence; they become stupid, foolish, imbecilic, somber, sad, melancholic, hypochondriacal, timid, indolent, cowardly, lazy." The masturbator "ends up by falling into a hideous marasmus and a disgusting decrepitude." And Debreyne inveighed: "Consider him now this mindless and degraded being; look at him, bent under the weight of crime and infamy, dragging the scraps of material and animal life through the shadows. The unhappy man! he sinned against God, against nature, and against himself. He violated the laws of the Creator, disfigured the image of God in his person, and changed it into that of a beast."[9] Dr. Devay almost as energetically wrote that the inveterate masturbator "is dead to feelings for family, country and humanity."[10] Monsignor Dupanloup was not a physician and spoke purely as an educator: when this evil spreads, he wrote, it is "like the plague." "Professors, Directors, Superiors, open your eyes and be vigilant! for there is the enemy, the formidable enemy: if it penetrates, if it enters, it will devastate your house, it will destroy everything, it will pile victims upon victims, dead bodies upon dead bodies!"

When a culprit has been caught, for Dupanloup, "an immediate and merciless repression is necessary; and this repression, is exclusion, . . . immediate." The case must be treated like a cancer. "Extirpate, and quickly, or the horrible wound will spread and ravage everything. . . . One must be merciless on this point, and throughout the term, from beginning to end. . . . I once had to advise the head of an establishment that the evil had invaded, to send home sixty-nine students; he did it, and saved his house; and it is today one of the largest and most prosperous educational establishments in France."[11]

Scholars and popularizers, generalists and specialists, authors of weighty treatises and of books designed for the general public joined forces on the front of medicine and hygiene—all were fighting the same battle.

The works dedicated specifically to masturbation—or, to use a common synonym of the time—"onanism"—are numerous. Tissot's *Onanisme,* an eighteenth-century classic, continued to be reedited through the next century. "It continues to be reprinted daily," noted the Larousse in 1876.[12] The lengthy series of Tissot's emulators opened with Dr. Doussin-Dubreuil, who published his *Lettres sur les dangers de l'onanisme* in 1813.[13] Listing all the subsequent works and authors would be tedious. Translations drew upon the foreign repertory. One of the most widely read works was the English *Self-Preservation,* translated into French as *La conservation de soi-même.* It is a medical treatise on weakening and disorders of the genital organs resulting from solitary habits, by Samuel La'Mert. Published for the first time in French translation in 1847, the book was already in its thirtieth edition in 1860. "Masturbation," wrote La'Mert, "is the most certain, though not always the most immediate and direct avenue to destruction." He placed particular emphasis—a feature of the English works—on the effects of "that destestable practice" on mental health. "It is a remarkable fact, that the miserable victims of sensual excess, more especially those addicted to self-pollution . . . are especially prone to insanity."[14]

The authors of hygiene manuals who, like La'Mert, addressed the general public, were no less eloquent. Take for example Auguste Debay's *L'Hygiène et physiologie du mariage*, already mentioned. It was a bestseller in France. In 40 years, from 1848 to 1888, it would appear in 172 editions, with a total of nearly 200,000 copies.[15] By the tens of thousands, Debay's readers were thus warned of the "ravages" wrought by the "fatal habit of solitary pleasures." When the malady becomes acute, Debay wrote, "the victims are hideous to look at; they inspire digust and pity."[16]

Even though—in the realm of ideas—there have often been two Frances, here there is but one: no difference between conservatives and republicans, Catholics and freethinkers is apparent. The names of Proudhon and Pierre Larousse, which appear at the beginning of this chapter, were found alongside that of Monsignor Dupanloup. Littré, shining star of the positivist school, changed not a word of the definition of masturbation when, in 1855, he published a "completely revised" edition of Nysten's *Dictionnaire de médecine* : "shameful habit, all the more dangerous in that the opportunities to indulge in it are always present. Wasting, marasmus, degradation are the normal consequences."[17] The perfect example of the republican physician in the nineteenth century was François Raspail. His *Manuel annuaire de la santé* would be a prodigious success.[18] He too denounced the "scourge of onanism." Since Raspail's panacea, which he prescribed for anything and everything, was camphor, it is camphor that he recommended to combat this scourge. "The precaution" should be taken "to wrap the genital organs in a heavy layer of camphor powder. . . . Every evening, take care to sprinkle camphor powder on the sheets, or even better, put some between the mattress and the sheets." It is also useful to "adopt, in the case of children, the use [understood: nighttime use] of bathing suits equipped with a bag of camphor at the perineum."[19]

Pictures came to the aid of the written word in putting youth on its guard and inspiring it with salutary fear. The *Livre sans titre,* published in Paris in 1830 and subsequently reedited, has an introductory quote from Tissot: "This deadly habit kills more youth than all diseases combined." This is followed by 16 colored engravings representing the successive stages of the evil's evolution. The first portrait is that of a pink and spruce young man with an abundance of curly hair. From plate to plate, he deteriorates in ever more tragic fashion. The last plate is "the tomb": "At the age of seventeen, he expires, and in horrible agony."[20]

The *Livre sans titre*—whose engravings are reproduced following chapter five—inspired imitations. One of them was published by Casterman in Tournai, Belgium, around 1835. Here we again find the case of the young man who, after horrible suffering, dies at the age of 17. But for good measure, we also find the case of a woman. The woman does not die; she loses her nose. The text reads: "Sauvages reports that a peasant woman, as a result of indecent acts, lost her nose. In its place there remained only a small bump barely the size of a pea; her lips had nearly disappeared, and the opening of her mouth was so shrunken that it was difficult to insert one's small finger in it." The engraving accompanying the text shows a woman with a bandage over the spot where her nose would be, with the caption: "She lost her nose through a shameful vice! . . ."[21]

If one was not able to slip a young man a copy of the *Livre sans titre*, one could take him to an anatomical museum: to the Paris office of Dr. Bertrand, for example, at the beginning of the nineteenth century. Here, an entire room was devoted to onanism, with wax figures representing:

1. A young man reduced to mortal agony and in the last stages of emaciation by masturbation.
2. A young man with an interesting face, enjoying perfect health.
3. The same man, become hideous through masturbation.
4. A young woman of great beauty, enjoying perfect health.
5. The same woman, six months later, become very ugly, thin and exhausted from having succumbed to solitary vices, of which she was lucky to have rid herself through marriage,

as well as other figures representing various illnesses suffered by the masturbator.[22] A visit was highly recommended: "This very curious office," wrote Doussin-Dubreuil, "had a much greater effect on the masturbators who visited it, than all that has been written on the dangers of masturbation."[23]

A great fear of masturbation thus truly existed in the nineteenth century. The texts just quoted are unquestionably heavyhanded; they were designed to grab public attention. In all likelihood, the overall atmosphere of the period was less tense than these documents lead us to believe. It is also true that alongside what was openly said and written, there was much that was toned down, insinuated, implied—for, let us not forget, we are dealing with a "shameful" vice of which decency does not always permit one to speak. Yet despite all that, the very existence of a pervading fear felt by parents, educators, and young people themselves was incontrovertible.

Revelations of concrete cases fed that fear. The authors knew the victims of the evil. They pointed them out, especially those who had perished from it. The young Gaétan Viaris, in a letter addressed to his father in August 1832, explained that one of his schoolmates has just died from masturbation. "Having developed a taste for it, he did it so often and in so few days, that this previously big and round-faced boy, became thin, bony, and worn and finally died in horrible agony." Gaétan Viaris is a clever boy, having invoked this "fearful example" in order to ask his father for money so that he can purchase normal sex.[24] The Goncourt brothers, who indefatigably collected Parisian gossip, recorded Sainte-Beuve's merciless attack on poor Augustin Thierry, who has gone blind: "This blindness, which led so often to his being compared to Homer, was not even the result of the pox, but simply of masturbation."[25] Later, the Goncourts told the story of a widow and her son. A perverse friend took pleasure in "trying out the power of erotic books and obscene pictures" on the young boy, with so much success that the latter "died of exhaustion from masturbation."[26] Novels, like life itself, also provided examples. Paul

Bonnetain, in *Charlot s'amuse,* told the sad story of a young man who, victim of his vice, falls into a stupor before throwing himself into the water.[27] Prosecuted for obscenity, Bonnetain defended himself by claiming to have written a "scientific novel." He was acquitted, in any event.[28]

The result of fear was an arsenal of measures taken to combat the evil. The watchwords that dominated the combat were: *prevention, restraint, supervision, cure.*

Prevention came first. It was a question, in all cases, of forestalling not only masturbation, but also nocturnal emissions, which were also judged to be highly dangerous.

One of the principal weapons in the battle for prevention was gymnastics, physical exercise. There was nothing like it for the healthy fatiguing of children's bodies and for bringing them to the brink of a profoundly refreshing sleep. "Gymnastic exercises, pushed to the point of fatigue," wrote Debay, "have the effect of transferring the excess of vitality fixed in the genital organs to the skeletal and muscular systems; they must be practiced twice a day, and particularly in the evening. The masturbator, fatigued by his exercises, falls asleep naturally almost before his head touches the pillow, without indulging his vice."[29] A good method consisted in "rewarding exercise practiced before bedtime; for example, drawing water from a well, grinding coffee, or turning a spinning wheel until the point of fatigue; when the subject says he is tired, urge him to turn more by doubling the reward. The extreme lassitude into which the child falls will not permit him to think about his vice."[30]

All sports and outdoor games were recommended. Certain authors, however, expressed reservations. For example, girls were to be prevented from playing on hobbyhorses, and boys from sliding down bannisters.[31] Also banned "for reasons easy to imagine" was "the climbing rope," which "could even be counterproductive to the goal of preservation."[32] Dr. Londe advised also that "country outings and hunting" should be practiced only under continual surveillance. "In fact," he clarifies, "without that, the young man

disappears into the woods and finds within several minutes of that
solitude all that is capable of intoxicating his imagination and
leading him to satisfy his deplorable penchant."[33]

But the sport endorsed by all without reservation was swim-
ming. It was, along with baths and cold or warm water ablutions
of the genital organs, considered an excellent preventative as well
as a remedy, offering the double benefit of muscular fatigue and
cleanliness. Rozier furnished on this point a "scientific" explanation: "Bathwater, by dissolving and carrying away the saline,
earthy and alkaline molecules which perspiration deposits in the
pores and the exhaling and absorbing orifices of the skin, elimi-
nates a source of irritation which can sympathetically excite the
other organs. Considered in this light, the bath is as much a pre-
server of chastity as it is one of the first cosmetics."[34] A rigorous
hygiene would also prevent the appearance of Ascaridae worms
and, with them, dangerous itching.

The child, clean and tired, would throw himself on the bed and
fall deeply asleep. This would not eliminate the need, however, for
vigilance in regard to his surroundings. The bed, first of all, must
be hard: feather mattresses and soft blankets that incite lethargy
were to be banned. The same goes for children's chairs: seats of
straw or of wood were preferable and, in serious cases, benches of
stone or marble. Nightclothes were to be selected with caution.
Certain writers advocated a long shirt enveloping the feet and
equipped with a seat flap "that must be tightly fastened in the
evening after the excretory needs have been satisfied."[35]

The position to be adopted by the sleeper was regulated: several authors advised against sleeping on the back or the left side.
"If his penchant is too pronounced," some proposed putting the
child to bed "with an adult person of the same sex."[36] "According
to the case," suggested Dr. Crommelinck, "choose a male or female bed companion of a reasonable age and who is not unaware
of the problem. It is not a teacher who is needed here, but a trust-
worthy friend."[37] In the case of older individuals, this Belgian
doctor came up with an imaginative solution that is particularly

reliable in the event that the "fatal desire overcomes you in bed": "Keep a set of parallel bars in your room: they don't take up much space and won't even wake up your neighbor, no matter how violent the exercises which you should practice enthusiastically for half an hour or longer, as needed."[38]

Diet was another aspect of bodily hygiene. Here too, there was unanimity, at least on the basic principle: sobriety was the rule. Simple but fortifying foods were prescribed and all exciting foods were to be avoided. The list of recommended and non-recommended foods is too long to detail here. Spices, rich meats, and venison were generally banned. Salted fish was also sometimes suspect; considered as "having very marked aphrodisiacal properties." "It has been observed," wrote Dr. Pavet de Courteille in his *Hygiène des collèges et des maisons d'éducation,* "that peoples who live only on fish are much more precocious in puberty than others, and far more inclined to overindulgence."[39] Wine, too, was often suspect.

Last, it was important to limit the amount of liquid consumed. "Abundant urine retained too long in the bladder . . . draws too much blood to the very part from which we want to draw it away," explained Friedlander.[40] Crommelinck shares his opinion and adds prudently: "Urinate quickly, do not shake your penis, even if it means having several drops of urine drip into your pants," so as to "scrupulously avoid touching the genitals."[41]

An imperative naturally accompanies this encyclopedia of diets: it is mental hygiene, completely indissociable from bodily hygiene. Here, the imagination, the "madwoman in the attic," was the great enemy. The mind is to be occupied with "objects which banish any thought of sensual pleasure."[42] The study of the natural sciences, "requiring by nature a great effort," was often recommended: it had the advantage of not exciting any passion.[43] Commelinck gives his practical advice: "Keep a collection of the best poets at hand, and as soon as the desire to masturbate overcomes you, give yourself fifty or a hundred verses to learn by heart, giving preference to selections on morals, philosophy or history. The more difficult the piece, the better."[44] Dances and the theater were pernicious, as were conversations upon light or ambiguous topics. Books, brochures, newspapers, and paintings to which children have access were to be carefully chosen. Even in the case of the Bible, Friedlander emphasizes, only selections were to be read.[45]

If, despite all these preventive measures, the danger persisted, additional steps would need to be contemplated: appropriate measures would have to be taken to prohibit the child from committing the shameless act.

The most simple method, during the night, was to tie the child's hands to the bed rails. Several physicians—for example, Dr. Simon in his *Traité d'hygiène appliquée à l'éducation de la jeunesse* (1827)—recommended this rudimentary practice.[46] Accounts confirm that this became common practice rather quickly. There were also variations on the procedure. Doussin-Dubreuil was familiar with the case of an "unfortunate young man" who "had had the courage during the last year of his life to spend his nights in a chair, a collar around his neck and his two hands tied with two ropes attached to both sides of his chair."[47]

Instruments represented another level of sophistication. "In our time," a medical dictionary of 1881 read, "a great number of instruments have been conceived for boys or girls. These instruments must all fill the same prescription: to imprison the genital organs of the child or the adult, in such a way that he is unable to reach them, while still permitting menstrual flow and micturition. It is easy to see what a variety of forms these appliances might take."[48]

At the beginning of the nineteenth century, we find reports of a "very skilled mechanic" in Paris who "has invented several instruments as ingenious as they are efficacious in combatting the furor of onanism in children of both sexes" and of a "hernial surgeon" who "is the inventor of an undergarment that is to be worn day and night, and which serves the same purpose."[49] The "hernial surgeon" in question, Jalade-Lafond, had moreover invented something better than an undergarment: it was an extremely complicated bandage that permitted the child "full liberty of all his limbs," but which worked like an abdominal straitjacket from which he was incapable of liberating himself.[50] The ingenuity of later manufacturers would focus on the development of an entire series of belts. A "surgical bazaar" in Paris in 1860 offered an entire range. "These instruments," a handbill said, "are an insurmountable barrier against those solitary habits which religion and society have condemned." They "are worn without the slightest sensation of discomfort, as they have no metal fittings."[51] The list of such sometimes rather extraordinary inventions is long.

All of this was not the fruit of the wild imaginings of a few obsessed souls. The Larousse—again the Larousse—endorsed the methods in 1873: "One can even resort to varied mechanical instruments designed to prevent the child from abusing himself."[52] It must be noted, however, that the unanimity of the medical corps, often so striking on the question of masturbation, was missing on this point. A number of doctors were partisans of the devices, especially in serious cases, but others opposed them. The instruments risked, some said, either attenuating the child's sense of responsibility or provoking feelings of revolt. Their efficacity, moreover, was questionable. "The ingenuity of the researchers seems to have cooled after a host of unsuccesful endeavors," Fonssagrives wrote in 1870.[53]

What is clear is that the instruments were well-known in the nineteenth century. Literary works alluded to them. In 1848, Flaubert derided "the Gentleman who has invented, for the statues in the Nantes Museum, tin plate fig leaves that look like antionanism instruments," that is to say, he added, "like shameful metallic underpants shining like polished saucepans."[54] The theme appears again more than thirty years later in *Bouvard et Pécuchet*.[55] The two heroes, who are raising young Victor, suspect him of a "bad habit." Pécuchet "questioned his disciple in such a way as to give him ideas, and before long, he had no doubts. Then he called him a criminal, believing all was lost."[56] (That nineteenth-century expression would have worked just as well as the quote from Proudhon as the epigraph of this chapter.) "Buy him an appliance," Bouvard advised. Eventually, the two friends decided to tire young Victor out with exercise and take up "cross-country races."

Even if recourse to instruments must have been relatively rare—they were often, incidentally, expensive—the notion was certainly present throughout the century. [57] A teacher from Anvers, in Belgium, introduced his new invention, an anti-masturbatory school bench, as late as 1873. This bench "prevents schoolboys from crossing or closing their legs." "Thus both the rubbing and the heating of the genital parts are avoided, and one of the causes of masturbation is thus eliminated, a malady that could have wrought the greatest of havoc will have been banished from the school."[58]

Constant surveillance was as necessary as prevention and restraint. Parents and educators were instructed and enjoined to be incessantly on their guard throughout children's early years and adolescence, to be vigilant for the slightest suspicious sign, to keep a lookout for the smallest clue to the presence of the evil. Clues might have included a hint of pallor or a slightly drawn look, abnormal sweats, any tendency toward weariness, and, of course, a stain on nightshirt or sheets. A rigorous investigation was required, from the moment suspicion arose. "The investigation is laborious, it is sad," Fonssagrives declared, "but it must be conducted forcefully, until the end. What matter of greater importance could there be for the family?"[59]

Remaining vigilant for even the smallest clue was all the more important in that it would permit energetic intervention from the very start of the malady, since once the vice was established, the cure was often exceedingly delicate and difficult. There was no true remedy that was readily applicable. The malady could be arrested only by energetically applying a series of converging techniques, both psychological and physical. On the psychological level, moral and religious sermons were designed to make the masturbator, gripped with fear and shame for his behavior, envisage the calamities that awaited him. On the physical level, the same measures that had been prescribed for preventing or restraining the child's behavior were to be continued; fatiguing him was particularly recommended. Prescribed too were various medicinal products, for example, calming herbal teas made from various plants: orange flowers, centaury, violets, marsh mallow, couch grass, purslane, lettuce, water lily. In the event of weakening, however—and weakening, alas! occurred quickly—vigorous tonics were to be administered. Each doctor had his favorite products and procedures, but none dared to promise a sure cure: the malady was perverse.

If masturbation was a serious problem for physicians, it was no less a thorny one for confessors. Monsignor Bouvier wrote in his *Dissertatio in sextum Decalogi praeceptum:* "The execrable habit of masturbation, when it is inveterate, drags confessors into a sort of dispair. It is difficult to prudently determine if one can, if one must allow penitents who have surrendered to this vice to partake of the sacraments of penitence and of communion. It is to be feared that they will stray from the confessional and become even more immoral if they are harshly treated; if they are treated indulgently, they will continue to wallow in the mire of the vice."[60]

Bouvier recommended making a distinction between the sinner inspired by "malice or indolence" and the sinner who succumbed to "the violence of temptation": "In the first case, absolution must be put off until the sinner has truly mended his ways; but in the second, one must, through the grace of absolution and by the holy Eucharist, seek to aid the unfortunate penitent who is fighting against a tyrannical passion and who is contrite." In this way, there remained hope for a mending of the ways that would be extinguished were the sacraments to be withheld.

Monsignor Bouvier's grand finale is particularly interesting. "Sometimes," he wrote, "marriage must be recommended, to those capable of entering into it, as the sole, or at least the most effective, remedy." Marriage was in fact—it was often repeated during this period—the only cure that could be considered radical, to be imposed, of course, at the first instant that age permitted. Dr. Rozier spoke of "immolating vice at nature's most cherished altar, the altar of marriage,"[61] and Dr. Crommelink spoke of a "radical, definitive cure."[62] The Larousse called it a "heroic remedy" that "has truly cured more than one unfortunate who would otherwise have been lost without this option."[63]

Nineteenth-century families could not fail to hear the warnings and take them into consideration in their marriage decisions. In his correspondence with Queen Victoria in 1853, King Léopold I of Belgium explained why he was anxious to marry off his eldest son, who was only 18 (the future Léopold II). One of the reasons, he said, was that "young men often fall into a habit destructive of health, mind, spirit, in short everything," a habit, the king added, for which marriage is often the "only" method of salvation. For further information on this delicate topic, Léopold referred Victoria to her husband, "dear Albert."[64]

The various elements outlined above allow us to draw one sure conclusion: the fear of masturbation during the period we've considered—and that stretches, let us recall, from around 1815 until a bit beyond 1875—was truly a social phenomenon.

The obvious question: "in what society?" is a legitimate one. Most of the texts that we have quoted have more than a hint of the bourgeoisie, and the upper bourgeoisie at that, about them. The dietary prescriptions, which mention simple "but succulent" dishes, and the exhortations to study the natural sciences are not addressed to the popular classes. There is hardly anything except Raspail's camphor that is frankly democratic. One can certainly imagine that once the ideas eventually filtered down into the popular classes, the methods were far more rudimentary. The anti-masturbatory belts were quite expensive, but a couple of bandages solid enough to imprison the hands could be cheaply fashioned. Yet this is pure speculation: we have no idea to what depths and across what strata of French society the fear of masturbation penetrated. The sources are mute. It is one of the great sources of consternation for the historian and an invitation to his or her modesty: at a distance of barely a little more than a century, the dimensions of a social phenomenon of this magnitude have faded into the distance and elude the historian's grasp.

Even if the depth of its hold cannot be fully known, the term "social phenomenon" is nonetheless justified. Two questions naturally arise: where did this phenomenena come from, and when did it begin?

Chapter Two

Before the Fear

In order to understand the psychology of an even more distant past, let us first turn to the Church and its doctrines, to religious theology.

We'll start with the end of the sixteenth century and the *Somme des péchez* of the Franciscan Benedicti.[1] Here, masturbation is clearly described and no less clearly condemned:

"Whoever engages in voluntary pollution outside of marriage, which is termed *mollities* by the theologians, sins against the natural order. . . . Voluntary pollution that is procured while awake, either by touching, by cogitation and delectation, by locution or conversation with women or men, by the reading of immodest books, or by whatever other means, is a mortal sin."[2]

In pronouncing this condemnation, Benedicti is following Church tradition. From the beginning of the Middle Ages, the penitentials contained the list of penances imposed upon masturbators. The severity in the Middle Ages varied widely from one penitential to another—just as it did for a number of sins—but the degree of severity indicated most often that what was being punished was truly considered to be a grievous sin.[3]

In the thirteenth century, a particularly pronounced religious condemnation of masturbation appeared in a collection of pious anecdotes written by Thomas of Cantimpré, the *Bonum universale de apibus*.[4] Thomas told two stories in which God punished the guilty with death.[5] One of these unfortunates died while screaming, "May God's vengeance be upon me! May God's vengeance be upon me!" God's anger, in the face of this abject sin, manifested itself not only through divine retribution but through miracles, which functioned as so many warnings. It is thus, he told us, that a masturbator, having tried, with guilty intentions, to grasp his penis, suddenly felt a snake in his hand.[6] Thomas abominated "the heinousness of this sin."[7]

In the fifteenth century, Gerson concerned himself with the manner of confessing youthful offenders. How, he wondered, is one "to extract from their heart the abominable pus of this foul sin that is called *mollities*" (*saniem abominabilem peccati illius detestabilis quod dicitur mollities*)? Gerson cited approvingly a classic questioning style that was the fruit of the long experience of a theology instructor in Paris. In fact, if the confessor wished to arrive at a result, he must appear to be "skillful and circumspect." The questioning began with an innocuous question: "Friend, do you remember, during your childhood, around the age of 10 or 12, that your penis became erect?" From there, the questioner moved on to the subjects touching and ejaculation. The instructor cited by Gerson also indicated remedies that were both spiritual and physical: prayers, acts of contrition, moderate diet, and cold water.[8]

"Sin against nature": the expression was employed forcefully in the thirteenth century by Thomas Aquinas (there is, he wrote, *vitium contra naturam* if "without carnal union, pollution is provoked to obtain sexual pleasure"),[9] in the fifteenth century by Saint Antoninus (*De vicio contra naturum: mollicies*),[10] and in the sixteenth century by Cajetan ("voluntary pollution" is a "mortal sin" and "one of the sins against nature," *unum de peccatis contra naturam*).[11]

Benedicti, at the end of the sixteenth century, inherited the traditional view. The form of his account was nonetheless innovative:

it is in the *Somme des péchez* that we find, for the first time, solidly and systematically elaborated, the moral theology that would remain largely unchanged in the centuries to follow.

Three principal elements of his account are striking:

1. The radical qualification of masturbation as a mortal sin.

The thoughts that fed the masturbator's imagination at the moment of committing the act may have further aggravated his case. Cajetan had already stated this.[12] Benedicti wrote: "If while committing this sin, someone imagines himself with, or desires a married woman, beyond the sin of *mollities*, it is a sin of adultery; if he desires a virgin, it is debauchery; if he desires a nun, it is sacrilege."[13] Monsignor Bouvier, in the nineteenth century, added to this enumeration the case in which the Virgin Mary is the object of desire: "horrible sacrilege," *horrendum sacrilegium.*[14]

2. The condemnation of masturbation was not based solely on the notion that it was an unnatural act. It was also supported by divine word—that is to say, by biblical text and essentially by two passages: the first from the Old and the second from the New Testament.

The first passage was the tale, in Genesis, of the crime of Onan (Gen., 38, 6–10). Judah, the Bible says, had three sons, the eldest of whom were Er and Onan. Er married Tamar, but he "offended Yahweh greatly, so Yahweh brought about his death. Then Judah said to Onan, *take your brother's wife, and do your duty as her brother-in-law, to produce a child for your brother.* But Onan, knowing the child would not be his, spilt his seed on the ground every time he slept with his brother's wife, to avoid providing a child for his brother. What he did was offensive to Yahweh, so he brought about his death also."[15]

What had Onan done that merited death? The theologians formed two schools of opinion, it must be noted, on this point. For some—and this is Benedicti's opinion—Onan had masturbated, thus avoiding his conjugal duties; for others, he had practiced something that was also a crime: *coitus interruptus.* Calvin, for example, was a partisan of the second interpretation in his commentary on Genesis: "To withdrawal on purpose from woman, so that the seed falls to the ground, is doubly monstrous: for it is the extinguishing of all hopes for posterity, as well as the murder of the anticipated child before his birth."[16] The two equations, Onan's crime = masturbation, and Onan's crime = *coitus interruptus*, are thus in competition.[17] We will be discussing only the former here.

The second text cited by Benedicti was a passage from Saint Paul, in the first Epistle to the Corinthians (6, 9–10), which he translated thus: "Do not be mistaken: for fornicators, adulterers, *mols*, sodomites, thieves . . . will never inherit the kingdom of God."[18] *Mols*, for Benedicti, are those who are guilty of *mollities*.

These constituted the two principal and long-standing scriptural bases for the condemnation of masturbation.

It should be noted that both bases were unstable. Modern exegetes occasionally differ on the precise interpretation of the passage on Onan's crime in Genesis, but almost all share the opinion that the crime, punished by death, was neither masturbation nor *coitus interruptus*. It was Onan's refusal, contrary to his duty, to furnish descendants for his brother that merited divine retribution.[19] In Saint Paul, on the other hand, the "mols" of Corinth— *molles* in the Latin of the Vulgate—are in fact, according to the Greek text, "degenerates," weak and effeminate, which takes us rather far from masturbation.[20] But the importance of these texts, in this instance, lies not in their intrinsic content: it is in the use to which they have been put.

3. When it came to "nocturnal pollutions," discussion was more difficult and delicate. Saint Thomas had already taken up the problem with a surprisingly indulgent outlook. He thought that nocturnal pollutions were never sinful, for even if they were the result of lascivious thoughts entertained before sleep, it was these thoughts that constituted the sin, not the emissions themselves.[21] Alexander de Hales, also in the thirteenth century, was far more severe. If the pollutions are the product of drunkenness or of unhealthy thoughts *(ex crapula vel ex immunda cogitatione)*, they are

certainly sinful.[22] Cajetan, in the fifteenth century, shared these views, and even criticized Saint Thomas.[23]

All this leads to clear distinctions on Benedicti's part. "He who pollutes himself during sleep," he wrote, "sometimes sins mortally, sometimes venially, and sometimes not at all," and sometimes, on the contrary, is "commendable."

All depended, in point of fact, on the causes of the emission. If it is a question of "lascivious thoughts and preceding cogitations, still fresh in the mind" during sleep, since "the preceding cogitation was a mortal sin, so will be the pollution resulting from it." Similarly, if the pollution "comes from gluttony or drunkenness, it is also a mortal sin." Once again, if it "comes from having eaten spicy and lust-inducing meats, it is also a mortal sin when one has eaten them . . . in order to induce the pollution when one is asleep at night."

Again in the case of "spicy and lust-inducing meats," it was necessary to clarify the intention. "If someone eats them just for the pleasures of the palate (that is to say, has given into temptation), and not to that end (the pollution), it is not a mortal offense: since the pleasures of the palate are not necessarily mortal sins." In other terms, if "the cause of the pollution is venial," the pollution itself will only be a venial sin.

There is no sin at all if the pollution "arises from a natural debility," or if it is "induced by the action of evil spirits which trouble our imagination during sleep, by filling it with various impressions and phantasms."

Benedicti comes back here to an idea dear to Saint Thomas, that the devil can play a great role in nocturnal emissions by inspiring the ideas that provoke them. The devil's goal is primarily to act in such a way that his victim, finding himself to be defiled, cannot partake of communion when he awakes the following day.[24] The pollution is thus "provoked through diabolical illusion in order to prevent worship," wrote Benedicti, who judged this to be "a customary practice of these evil spirits."[25]

The final case was that of pollution "produced by too great abstinence": in this case, Benedicti emphasized, "it is praiseworthy."[26]

The type of moral theological reasoning that we've just encountered in the writings of Benedicti would reappear in later
centuries. Despite some expected alterations and additions, its
basic structure remained intact. There is an entire lineage that can
be followed: Sanchez, Laymann, Bonacina, Tamburini, Sporer,
Habert, the theologians of Salamanca, Lacroix, Roncaglia, Collet,
Saint Alfonsus de Ligorio.[27] Across the writings of these seven-
teenth- and eighteenth-century authors, it is easy to see to what
extent theological reasoning remained essentially stable.

Stability meant the condemnation would remain unswervingly
harsh. But this sin that moral theology condemned so energetically—was it pursued with equal energy in the daily life of the
Church? Here is the true problem and here, it must be admitted,
is the enigma. Evidence is lacking. But certain silences, certain
gaps, can be telling. Following Gerson in the fifteenth century,
there was practically no work, significant or insignificant, that
sought to guide confessors by indicating the best way of unmask-
ing the masturbator.[28] This testifies, one might conclude, to a certain lack of interest in this priestly activity. Priests who spoke of
their activities in this realm were moreover extremely rare.[29] The
interpretation of silence is clearly tricky, but we are likely not risk-
ing too much in concluding that the pursuit of masturbation did
not appear high on the list of priorities until the second half of the
eighteenth century. It was not, apparently, one of the real preoc-
cupations of the clergy.

A parallel comes to mind here: it is the comparison with penal
law. Like all other crimes and sexual offenses, masturbation could
also be pursued in the courts. The repression, in principle, was severe. *Mollities* could be punished with "banishment or other extraordinary sentences," wrote the great Flemish jurist Wielant at
the beginning of the sixteenth century.[30] Joost de Damhoudere,
another Flemish jurist who, a little later in the sixteenth century,
took Wielant as his model, specified too that the *mastrupatores,*
because of the "awful enormity" of their offense *(propter foedam
enormitatem),* should be condemned to exile or other extraordi-

nary punishment.[31] "An extraordinary punishment" was the verdict of the public prosecutor of Artois, Pierre Desmasures.[32] "When the crime is discovered, it must be punished by banishment, or considerable fines," wrote Le Brun de la Rochette in the seventeenth century.[33]

All this seems extraordinarily harsh, but Wielant, Damhouder, Desmasures, and Le Brun de la Rochette were in agreement: the verdicts were theoretical since in practice they were rarely pronounced. The crime of *mollities* has to "be brought to the attention of the judicial system, which only rarely happens," Wielant wrote.[34] Damhouder stressed the same point: the crime is "horrible and execrable" *(horribilis et execranda)* and it will be punished by God, but since it occurs in secret, it rarely comes to the attention of the judge.[35] After having said, "When this crime is revealed," Le Brun de la Rochette immediately added, "which occurs but rarely since it is committed in secret." Punishment is in truth in God's hands, even if "the wretches who revel in it elude man's justice, they will not escape that of God."[36] Pierre Desmasures was the clearest of all: "in such cases," he emphasized, "investigations are neither common nor practiced."[37] There are thus no prosecutions.

Could this passivity of the secular law, explicable by the difficulty of uncovering the facts, also have been at least partially the product of a certain lack of zeal on the part of the Church? The notion is not implausible.

But leaving the realm of hypothesis, there is one essential and absolutely certain point that can be made: among those jurists or theologians who, before the second half of the eighteenth century, forcefully condemned masturbation as a sin against nature, not a single one is to be found who based his verdict on medical grounds, on the physical harm that masturbation could cause. The physical aspect never came into play.

Or perhaps more correctly, the physical aspect did come into play and so did medicine, but the other way around: some authors felt obliged to refute the ideas of certain physicians who viewed the voluntary emission of sperm as beneficial.

The principal, and striking, lesson that can be drawn from the theologians of the fifteenth, sixteenth, and seventeenth centuries is that the medical science that can be glimpsed, just below the surface of the texts and sometimes barely veiled at all, appears sometimes to view masturbation in a favorable light, within certain limits, and under certain circumstances, to be sure.

The series of texts opened in the fifteenth century with Saint Antoninus. To provoke nocturnal pollution through gluttony or drink is a mortal sin, he wrote, "even if one has done it, not for the purpose of pleasure, but for that of relieving the needs of nature and health." *Etiam si faceret non ob delectationem sed ad allevationem naturae et sanitatem:* the terms are clear. Moreover, Antoninus added, he who while awake pollutes himself voluntarily "only for his health" *(ob sanitatem solum)* will not avoid the state of mortal sin.[38]

At the end of the seventeenth century, the Spanish Jesuit Toledo gives us the clearest text. To induce pollution is always a mortal sin, *quamvis propter sanitatem fiat,* "even if it is done for the sake of health." *Mollities* "is against nature, and is not permitted for health, the saving of life, or any other possible reason. Consequently, physicians who recommend such an act for reasons of health commit an extremely grave sin." *Unde gravissime peccant medici, qui talem actum consulunt ob sanitatem.*[39]

Rebellus, a Portuguese Jesuit, enlightens us several years later on the logic underpinning the physicians' advice: for them it was a matter of evacuating in this manner contaminated and thus harmful sperm. Rebellus's condemnation was the same as Toledo's: "We must condemn the claim that it is permissible to use the hand and stroking in order to evacuate contaminated and harmful sperm, for reasons of health."[40]

Thomas Sanchez took up the problem of corrupt semen in his famous treatise on marriage. No self-induced evacuation of semen, even if that semen is believed to be harmful, can possibly be permitted, he emphasizes. It cannot be done even to save one's life *(ad vitam tuendam).* In fact, the emission of sperm induces such a violent pleasure in man that authorizing that emission in certain situations is risky. Men, caught in the throes of pleasure, might at every turn find cause to rationalize the spilling of their sperm. It would be a general debauchery. The ban must thus be absolute.[41]

Laymann repeated it in 1630, in his *Théorie morale:* it is always a mortal sin and a sin against nature, even if the goal is to "recover one's health or to conserve one's life."[42] That is, Beyerlink wrote, the *communis opinio* of the theologians, and it is not to be contravened.[43]

Bonacina, during the same period, was particularly verbose on this topic. He forcefully enunciated the principle: "It is not permissible to provoke pollution for reasons of health *(propter sanitatem),* and a physician may not prescribe any medicine whose only effect would be to induce pollution."[44] But Bonacina was primarily concerned with refuting possible objections. One will object, for example, he said, that if it is permissible to amputate a limb to safeguard one's health, it must *a fortiori* be permissible to evacuate sperm when that evacuation is recommended for the health of the body. Answer: those are two different things, for amputation produces an intense physical pain, and there is thus no risk of opening the door to more amputations, while—and here Bonacina agreed with Sanchez—there is a risk of opening the door to an infinity of pleasures if pollution, a source of pleasure rather than of pain, is authorized. Bonacina's conclusion was strictly heroic: it is better to sacrifice life for the love of chastity.[45] The logic is revealing: it shows that for him, health might very well be found in the realm of unchastity.

Sporer, a particularly indulgent moralist, adopted a slightly less rigorous attitude in 1690: for the evacuation of corrupt and harmful semen, he condemned all masturbation but permitted medicines.[46] Roncaglia, in 1736, continued to follow the more severe line of thought: even if the semen was unquestionably contaminated and had placed the life of the individual in grave danger, all processes of evacuation were forbidden, including medicines.[47]

It is against this backdrop of medical notions favorably disposed to the evacuation of corrupt sperm that a minor but characteristic controversy should be situated. It would divide theologians from the fifteenth century on. When it is a question of health, is it permissible simply to desire a nocturnal emission, without doing anything to induce it? Saint Antoninus responded affirmatively: there is no sin.[48] Navarrus, in the sixteenth century, goes in the same direction, stating: "It is not a mortal sin to feel the desire that a pollution occur during your sleep in order that nature might be relieved."[49] One of Navarrus's supporting arguments was that the physician may wish for his patient to have a pollution, because he believes this will contribute significantly to the well-being of his client—*quam credit saluti eius plurimum conductam iri.*[50] Toledo (with some reservations)[51] and Tamburini[52] share his opinion. Other theologians however considered that even the simple desire—even for reasons of health, let us repeat—constituted a sin. It is this harsher reasoning that would tend to dominate.[53]

The most remarkable case, however, in this interplay between medicine and moral theology, was that of Caramuel, who was, in any event, a rather colorful character.[54] Juan Caramuel, born in Madrid in 1606, had entered the Cistercian order in Spain, and his succeeding career took him across Europe. His contemporaries admired him for his skill and his prodigious erudition but were often perplexed by his paradoxical thought. In his *Théologia moralis fundamentalis,* on pollution, he provided a rather stunning example.

Is the voluntary shedding of semen a mortal sin? Caramuel asked. Unquestionably yes. But is it a sin because it is intrinsically bad? Absolutely not. What, in fact, is semen? It was an unresolvable topic of scholarly debate. Some stated it was sweat, others saliva, some claimed it was milk and the majority insisted that it was blood. Now no one could dare to maintain that it was not possible, for good reason, to rid the body of sweat, saliva, blood, or milk. Nor could it have been suggested that the difference was that semen is made for generation, for women's milk is made to feed the future of the race, and blood to feed the individual, and one may relieve oneself of the last two without committing any sin.

The evil of voluntary pollution thus lay not in its unnaturalness. It lay merely in the divine interdiction. If God had not forbidden it, things would have been different.

And here the paradoxical audacity of Caramuel is fully apparent. "If God had not forbidden masturbation," he wrote, "it would never be bad, it would often be good, and it might occasionally even be obligatory, under pain of mortal sin." Why obligatory?

Without God's interdiction, the fact that man might be required to masturbate, under pain of mortal sin, is clearly demonstrable. A sick man is in fact required to take whatever remedies are necessary for the conservation of his health, and we know that there are illnesses which are linked to the quantity and the quality of semen, that these illnesses are life-threatening, and that they can only be cured by the emission of semen. Thus, had there been no divine obstacle, the emission of semen would, in such a case, have been a required act, an indispensable remedy.

All of that obviously reads even better in the original Latin.[55]

Caramuel was by no means laxist: the divine interdiction being what it was, death is preferable to the remedy of masturbation: *potius mori*. But this was solely due to the divine interdiction. If tomorrow, he said, God forbade bleeding, which is a useful procedure in the fight against illness, he who today is required to be bled to save his life, tomorrow would be required to die rather than to let himself be bled.[56]

All this has a bit of a defiant air about it. It is not surprising that Rome intervened with a condemnation of Caramuel. In March 1679, we find proposition number XLIX among the 65 propositions solemnly condemned by Innocent XI: "Natural law does not prohibit masturbation. Consequently, if God had not forbidden it, it would often be good and might occasionally be obligatory, under pain of mortal sin." *(Mollities jure naturae prohibita non est. Unde si Deus eam non interdixisset, saepe esset bona, et aliquando obligatoria sub mortali).*[57] So much for Caramuel.

Caramuel's tale may seem anecdotal. But it has the merit of revealing, through the lens of theology, a medical science that prescribes masturbation for the sake of health in certain cases. Caramuel's text does this better than any other.

What exactly is this medical science? It is Galenic medicine, still extremely influential in the sixteenth and seventeenth centuries. In his work, Galen emphasized the dangers of the retention of sperm, especially when it was abundant. Speaking only of the benefits of normal sexual relations, Galen did not go so far as to conclude that masturbation may have beneficial effects, but what he wrote certainly goes implicitly in that direction. He cited rather pointedly the case of Diogenes the Cynic. Diogenes, it was commonly known, masturbated in public.[58] Galen offers a medical interpretation of his case. "Diogenes the Cynic philosopher," he wrote,

> is known to have been the most self-controlled of all people in regard to every act which required abstinence and endurance. However, he indulged in sexual relations, since he wanted to get rid of the inconvenience caused by the retention of sperm, but he did it not for the pleasure associated with this elimination. Once he made an arrangement with a courtesan. But, as the story goes, when she came to him after some delay, he already has discharged the sperm by manual friction of his genitalia. After arrival he sent her away with the words: "My hand was faster than you in celebrating the bridal night." It is evident that a chaste person does not indulge in sexual intercourse for pleasure, but with the intention to relieve this urge, as if this were not associated with pleasure.[59]

Commentators have often been struck by this passage on Diogenes.[60] It would not be hard to see it as a barely dissimulated invitation to masturbation. But what was essential, in Galenic medicine, was the notion of the disadvantages of sperm retention.

Unfortunately, accounts of medical practices based on this theory are almost entirely lacking—and this is one of the greatest lacunae in our knowledge. At the very most, there was the case of a patient with congested testicles cited in England, at the beginning of the eighteenth century. Purges and bleedings having had no effect, "mastupration was allowed." The patient, we are told, was cured.[61]

Galenic medicine did not, of course, represent the only medical approach, but in none, at least until the seventeenth century, do we find the slightest denunciation of any potential health risks of masturbation.

Here is a most interesting test case: medical literature of the Middle Ages devoted to child care has been studied in detail. No matter what the sources of inspiration—Galenic or other—of this literature, not the slightest allusion to masturbation and *a fortiori* to its eventual risks is to be found.[62]

The illustrious sixteenth-century Italian anatomist Fallopius strayed somewhat from Galen's theory,[63] but what does he teach us? That a good method for strengthening the penis of young boys, in order to develop their procreative powers, is to pull on the penis vigorously and repeatedly in order to stretch it out *(multam et frequentem extensionem)*.[64] One can well imagine with what horror such advice would have been received three centuries later.

Recommendations for combating nocturnal emissions are also to be found. These can in fact be extremely disagreeable. Some of the most intriguing recommendations are those of Vettori, in the sixteenth century. Vettori recommended various medicines but also pointed out a procedure successfully used to cure a man who had suffered from nocturnal pollution uninterruptedly for four months: when he went to bed, one end of a string or cord was tied around his penis and the other end around his neck. If, during the night, his penis swelled and became erect, the string produced enough pain to wake him up. He was thus cured.[65] The Dutch physician Pieter van Foreest, at the end of the sixteenth century, cited this method approvingly.[66] It is understandable that physicians sought to eliminate the troubles caused by nocturnal emissions.

Pieter van Foreest—or Foretus—went even further, however: he energetically condemned the loathsome conduct of Diogenes the Cynic, and therefore masturbation. The condemnation in itself, however, is quite revealing. Foretus, despite the fact that he was a physician, did not condemn masturbation on medical grounds; we must condemn this conduct, he wrote, "because we are Christians" *(cum Christiani summus)* and because we follow the teachings of Saint Paul in his Epistle to the Corinthians.[67] The reference is religious, not medical.[68]

We spoke of nocturnal emissions above. The verdict on them was far from universally negative. It was sometimes positive, and when it was, we find ourselves again in the pathways of Galenic medicine. The most extraordinary text on this subject was that of a physician from La Rochelle, Nicolas Venette, who extols man's superiority over woman.[69] This superiority, he said, resides notably in the fact that man pollutes himself and thus rids himself of superfluous seed, while woman, lacking this advantage, retains her corrupt seed. To quote Venette:

> Woman does not have the ability to pollute herself, as does man, or to discharge her superfluous seed. She sometimes retains it lengthily in her testicles or in the horns of her uterus, where it becomes tainted and turns yellow, murky, or foul smelling, instead of white and clear as it was formerly. Unlike man who, by polluting himself frequently, even during his sleep, benefits from a seed that is always renewed and never remains in his canals long enough to become corrupt.[70]

Venette later returned to the topic: "When the vapors of corrupt seed mix with the blood . . . the result of this mixture is venereal illusions which trouble the imagination. . . . Women are more subject to this than are men, the latter often discharging during their sleep an abundance of the semen which torments them, while women are unable to do this as easily."[71] Venette, or, the praise of pollution: we are in the second half of the seventeenth century.

It was however in this second half of the seventeenth century that, for the first time, physicians began to evince a serious air of consternation on the topic of masturbation.

The German physician Ettmüller, professor at Leipzig, analyzed the causes of gonorrhea in a 1670 treatise. The causes, he explained, are multiple, but the illness can be attributed to "abominable masturbation" (*propter nefariam manstuprationem*).[72] Three decades later, the English physician Baynard, extolling the virtues of cold baths, of which he was a great supporter, emphasized their effectiveness as a treatment for impotence. A target too of the physicians' efforts was that weakness that can be induced "sometimes by that cursed school wickedness of masturbation by which many a young gentleman has been for ever undone, which so weakens the parts, that when they come to manhood renders them (to women ridiculous, because) impotent."[73]

Ettmüller and Baynard are the only examples to be found, no matter how diligent the search, before the beginning of the eighteenth century: two very short passages, little more than allusions. They do not particularly stand out, and they refer not to the overall ravages of masturbation but only to its causal role in the specific cases of gonorrhea and impotence. Nothing in the medical works published before the eighteenth century thus places masturbation in a particularly worrisome light. Society evinced not the slightest hint of worry: there was nothing to suggest that masturbation caused any fear. It is society's indifference to masturbation—except for the moral aspects, as was the case with the theologians—that can be glimpsed in the silences of the texts. The interpretation of silence is always perilous, but here it seems that silence has spoken volumes.

If we turn to the numerous educational manuals published prior to the eighteenth century, what do we find on the topic of masturbation? Not a word. In the beginning of the eighteenth century, the Swiss Ostervald published his *Traité contre l'impureté*, focused primarily on the problem of educating children. Ostervald declared that out of modesty, he would refrain from naming all the vices by their proper names. His description of the immodesty of the child is nonetheless rather explicit.[74] Immodesty is certainly there, but masturbation is neither named nor referred to, even implicitly. Had masturbation been a topic that preoccupied Ostervald, it seems likely that an allusion or two would have found its way into his text.

On the subject of childhood masturbation in English texts, Lawrence Stone observed: "The subject is not even mentioned in post-Reformation English child-rearing handbooks of the sixteenth and seventeenth centuries except in the most guarded terms. Current medical handbooks also largely ignored it."[75]

Beyond the silences, however, there is what was done and what was said. We've seen the advice given by Fallopius on the topic of manipulating the penis: he obviously did not share the fears that would haunt the eighteenth-century mind on the question of touching. Equally extraordinary were the fondlings that the young Louis XIII was permitted to perform himself or that he received at the hand of others. Héroard, the king's physician, left us an invaluable document on this subject.[76] It showed the young Louis as a baby or a toddler playing constantly with his "guillery." Various persons put "their hand up his petticoats." He also showed his "guillery" to others.[77] All this, according to Héroard, was merely in fun. Of course, it is not a question of masturbation, but Héroard seems no more afraid than Fallopius—with his penis extension exercises—that one might possibly be inculcating in the child habits that could lead to masturbation. Later that very idea would hold all the terror of the plague.

During the same period, Charles Sorel's *Histoire comique de Francion* reveals a similarly lighthearted treatment of the topic. Francion recounted the memories of his adolescence:

> At that time, I spent my time . . . in the company of the most generous and the most debauched of schoolboys. Almost all of them indulged a vice for which our school had always been renowned. Urged on by their young passions, they had learned to give themselves sensual satisfaction, for lack of a partner of the opposite sex. For my part I was hardly enamored of that particular passion. . . . I did not wish to make an enemy of the ladies, for they mortally despise those who so deprive them of their own due. But when I think about it, if those boys sinned, they were quite seriously punished,

for no matter how they tried, they never managed to appease their desire which merely grew greater and greater, and which caused them hidden tortures. I find such a martyrdom pitiful, and I curse the fact . . . that so many girls who moreover are pining away in silence for embraces, are not brought together with those tormented souls, so that they might together quench their flames in a liquid more sweet than any other and so that from that time on, they might abstain from sin.[78]

It is a remarkable text, even when the overall audacity of the novel is taken into account. The sin of masturbation is clearly emphasized, but the purely physical disorders to which masturbators are prone, their "hidden tortures," are caused by their inability to satisfy their sexual desires sufficiently. Nothing more. The remedy is simple and would simultaneously eliminate both the "tortures" and the sin: it would be to let young men and young women mate in peace.

Erotic literature, like the novel, must obviously be used with caution, but it too is revealing: it evokes the specters of sin, the physical need to masturbate, the regret of semen wasted instead of used for procreation—but, just as in the *Histoire comique de Francion*, there is no notion, no hint even, of any risks to health.

Saint-Pavin, in the seventeenth century, circulated an epigram on the hand and what it wasted:

Poor devil, you use your hand to screw:
Is this a legitimate pleasure?
If he who formed the greatest of the Romans
Had had nothing more than his hands,
Of what an admirable hero
Would he have deprived the universe;
Think, in these perverse pleasures, that nature
Cries out ceaselessly to you: "Stop, wretch"
Oh! it is a man that has gone to waste.[79]

A sonnet written by—or at least attributed to—Malherbe, evokes the scenario both of the excitement that seizes the author and his "moral dilemma." His member, he wrote, becomes erect, "prepared for combat."

> My pain is proof of its patience
> For whether to masturbate is a moral dilemma:
> Not to masturbate is to die a thousand deaths.
> I do my best to help it contain itself,
> But in mollifying it, I notice not
> That it has spit into my hand both its own fury and my own![80]

Samuel Pepys also encountered a "moral dilemma" when, on December 24, 1667, right in the middle of the Christmas mass in Queen's Chapel, St. James, he did "la cosa" at the mere sight of a pretty girl. "May God forgive me for it, it being in the chapel," he wrote in his journal.[81] The story ends there.

The portrait drawn by several texts and reinforced by the silence of others is that of a society that attributes no more than minor significance to masturbation, and in any event, evinces not the slightest fear of it.

Is it possible that masturbation was less widespread than it would be in later centuries? There is absolutely nothing to suggest that this was the case. Benedicti spoke of it as a very ordinary sin in the late sixteenth century.[82] The Spaniard Toledo, in the same period, described it similarly.[83] A lazarist sermon, in the first half on the seventeenth century, qualified it as "an all too-common sin, alas!"[84] and the Jesuit Philippe d'Oultreman calls it "common and universal."[85] Recalling his own youth—and the testimony is significant—a seventeenth-century English clergyman wrote that masturbation is a sin that "too many young men are guilty of, and look upon it as harmless."[86]

It is thus within these peaceful skies that the storm will burst, in the beginning of the eighteenth century, with the publication of a work entitled *Onania*.

CHAPTER THREE

ONANIA

It was most likely in the last months of 1715 that *Onania* made its first appearance in London. This pamphlet—for it was no more than a pamphlet of several dozen pages—carried an eloquent title: *Onania,* (the story of Onan obviously lay behind this invented word) *or the heinous sin of self-pollution, and all its frightful consequences in both sexes considered, with spiritual and physical advice to those who have already injured themselves by this abominable practice.*

Unfortunately, not a single copy of this first edition seems to have survived.[1] A second expanded edition was announced in the newspapers in February 1716.[2] A third would follow, most likely in the first months of 1717.[3] A fourth edition was eventually published in November 1718.[4]

The earliest copy we have of *Onania* is a copy of this fourth edition. It is an 88-page pamphlet, on sale for the sum of one shilling at three London bookstores, N. Crouch's at the sign of the Bell in the Poxltry, P. Varenne's at Seneca's head in the Strand, and J. Isted's at the Golden Ball in Fleet Street. Let us open it respectfully, since these pages, which now seem both grandiloquent and disordered, were indisputably the starting point for a mental and moral revolution that would bring masturbation into the limelight. It began with this little book.

From one edition to the next, the author would remain anonymous. No contemporary mentioned his name. Who was he? Given the current state of research, the enigma seems insoluble. More than half a century later, Tissot attributed *Onania* to a certain "Doctor Bekkers"—with something less than certainty: "he must be the author," he wrote[5]—but no one has ever been able to connect the name Bekkers to any identifiable Englishman of the period. Putting aside the problem of the name, even the personality of the author is difficult to discern. All that we can be relatively certain about is what he wasn't. In spite of what Tissot said, he was clearly not a physician.[6] Nor, obviously, was he a clergyman, despite some claims to the contrary.[7] Some contemporaries, basing their opinion on his money-making ventures, considered him a quack.[8] He was certainly and in many ways a quack, but he was also a man who had read, who had a certain educational background, who had even a certain flair for declamation. We can perhaps summarize him as a declamatory writer and a quack combined.

Onania is, above all, a flood of curses. The curses in this case—and this is a true novelty—are directed simultaneously toward "the heinous sin," the "abominable practice," and the "frightful consequences." This trinity of ideas that would come to dominate the nineteenth century—sin, vice, and self-destruction—is seen for the first time here.

The author noted, from the very first lines, the extent of the evil: "This practice is so frequent, and so crying an offence, especially among the male youth of this nation, that I have reason to imagine, a great many offenders would never have been guilty of it, if they had been thoroughly acquainted with the heinousness of the crime, and the sad consequences to the body as well as the soul, which may, and often do ensue upon it."[9] What he was about to write was thus indispensable.

The author was uncompromising and unambiguous in his denunciation of the sin of masturbation. There were no extenuating
circumstances for the masturbator. The divine punishment inflicted upon Onan, whose name furnishes the pamphlet's title,
sufficed to demonstrate the seriousness of the crime. Its unpar-
donable nature stemmed notably from its interference with procreation, directly through the loss of sperm and indirectly through
the impotence it frequently causes. "For fornication and adultery
it self, tho' heinous sins, we have frailty and nature to plead; but
self-pollution is a sin, not only against nature, but a sin that perverts and extinguishes nature, and he who is guilty of it, is labour-
ing at the destruction of his kind, and in a manner strikes at the
Creation it self."[10]

The physical consequences of masturbation were no less serious
than the moral consequences. Ettmüller had spoken of gonorrhea,
and Baynard of impotence. The author of *Onania* was familiar
with them and cited their opinions. But he took a broader perspective on the problem. He mentioned other disorders that the
masturbator risked: ulcers, convulsions, epilepsy, consumption.
Above all—and here we are on new terrain from where the future
can be glimpsed—he attributed to masturbation a number of general and dramatic consequences. "It manifestly hinders the
growth, both in boys and girls, and few of either sex, that in their
youth commit this sin to excess for any considerable time, come
ever to that robustness or strength, which they would have arrived
at without it."[11] Adult masturbators appear "with meager jaws,
and pale looks, with feeble hams, and legs without calves, their
generative faculties weaken'd, if not destroy'd in the prime of their
years. A jest to others and a torment to themselves."[12] Death was
at their heels. "Many young men, who were strong and lusty before they gave themselves over to this vice, have been worn out by
it, and by its robbing the body of its balmy and vital moisture,
without cough or spitting, dry and emaciated, sent to their
graves."[13] The masturbator, "who hardly comes to half the age he
might reasonably have expected to arrive at, find . . . his spirits

sunk, his body wasted, and his strength decay'd; in continual danger of being forc'd to resign his impure breath, upon the least
rigour of the season, or any small accident."[14]

Impotence was one of the classic consequences of masturbation. But even if the masturbator managed to procreate, he risked
having sickly children who would not survive to adulthood.
Women who succumbed to the vice ran the risk of sterility or
multiple miscarriages.

Even those who did not experience these physical ailments had
other things to fear in this world: the threat of divine retribution.
Misfortunes, sorrows, business setbacks might befall them. They
had no right to bemoan their fate, for it was God who was exacting his justice upon them.

Remedies for such a dreadful evil were obviously needed. Those
remedies must, first of all, be of a spiritual nature; repentance and
mortification must come first. The physical remedies might include, in part, those already prescribed before *Onania* and cited
with the author's approbation: certain foods were to be avoided
(like beans, peas, and artichokes, which have the effect of swelling
the genitals); exercise and cold baths were to be taken. But the
pamphlet added some new remedies—and here we arrive at what
clearly seems to be its major objective.

On this topic, the author of *Onania* entertains us with a story.
Those who are in need of medical advice are often, he wrote, held
back by the fear of having to admit their sin, and thus they do not
consult a physician. They are in need of remedies. "This made me
communicate what I was about," he wrote, "to a pious as well as
eminent physician" (and this is one clear indication, among others, that he is not a physician himself) "who . . . imparted to me
two medicines of great efficacy, the one in that kind of gonorrhea's spoke of in the preceding chapter, nocturnal effusions,
seminal emissions upon stool or urine . . . and all manner of
gleets and ouzings not occasion'd by any venereal disease. The
other in most cases of infertility and impotence in either sex." He
continued:

I had no other thought at first of all . . . than to insert these prescriptions as I had receiv'd them . . . but seeing the preparations (especially the one) of them, to be somewhat operose, and several of
the ingredients very costly, I found upon second consideration, that
they could be of no use to the patient without employing others;
and that made up for every patient on purpose, they would either
be excessive dear, or else for lucre's sake by many imperfectly
prepar'd. These reflections induced me to have both medicines
made up by *a man of skill and probity*. . . . The person therein em-
ploy'd, has some time since, begg'd of me, in consideration of his
trouble and charge (which he says, and I partly know to have been
considerable) the propriety of these medicines, and that I would
lodge in him the sole power to dispose of them as he should think
fit; which I have complied with, obliging him to print two thousand
of these books at his own expense. . . . I solemnly declare that I neither have, or ever design'd to have, the least interest or share in the
profits that now or here after may accrue from the sale of them.

The one practical conclusion of this little tale was that interested
parties might visit the bookseller P. Varenne, at the sign of
Seneca's Head, where a "Strengthning tincture" was available for
purchase at the price of 10 shillings a bottle, and a "Prolific powder" for 12 shillings a bag. The entire last part of *Onania* was devoted to the use of these two remedies.

The place of *Onania* in the literature of the period is thus clear.
It was one of the many pamphlets that colorfully described a particularly unpleasant and feared malady for the purpose of dissem-
inating therapeutic advice or, better yet, a new medicine.
Newspapers were full of announcements for this type of literature.

Other examples are easy to find. In 1716 we find an ad for a
Practical Scheme of the Secret Disease and Broken Constitutions. In
cases of the "secret disease" and broken constitutions, the pamphlet
extolled the virtues of a "specifick remedy" that had already had
marvelous results, not only in England, but in France, several other
European countries, and even America. A traveler recently returned from a trip to the West Indies declared that it also was a
remedy for yaws. The *Practical Scheme* could be obtained at several

places in London, whose addresses were furnished.[15] In 1718, here was the announcement for the second edition of *A Short account of the Venereal Disease,* by Doctor Joseph Cam. For sixpence (half the price of *Onania*), one could find "observations on the nature, symptoms, and cure" of the disease. Cam included "a short account of old gleets, and other weaknesses" as well, and recommended "specificks" for their cure. Addresses of London bookstores where the pamphlet could be purchased followed.[16] These are merely two of the many examples that are to be found.[17]

Onania, however, stood out from other works of its type. It intertwined the medical, the moral, and the religious. It attacked sin. Herein lay its originality. But what truly distinguished it was its sales success. That success was phenomenal.

As we've already seen, the fourth edition was published at the end of 1718. The fifth edition came out in 1719,[18] the sixth in 1722,[19] the seventh in January 1723.[20] At that time, the editor claimed to have sold nearly 10,000 copies of the earlier editions.

The eighth edition was sold out five months later, having sold 12,000 copies.[21] Before the year was over, it was announced, with the publication of the ninth edition, that 15,000 copies had been sold.[22]

The fifteenth edition came out in 1730,[23] at the same time as the sixth edition of a *Supplement* first published in 1723. We'll discuss the latter below. Afterward, the pace slowed a bit—the sixteenth edition did not appear until 1737[24]—but in 1778, *Onania* was still on the market in its twenty-second edition.[25] Voltaire's claim that there had been "around 80 editions" of *Onania* was certainly exaggerated.[26] Yet the exaggeration itself is telling of *Onania*'s real and considerable sales success. The publication of pamphlets written in response to *Onania* provides additional evidence of *Onania*'s success. At least four appeared between 1717–1718 and 1724.

The first, *Onanism display'd* (of which only the second edition, that of 1719, seems to be extant),[27] is a violent pamphlet denouncing the error of *Onania*. "I shall make it my business," the author said, "to set forth the absurdity, inconsistency, and imposture of this supercilious scribbler."[28]

On two points, however, the two authors were in agreement.
First of all, masturbation remained, for the author of *Onasnism
display'd*, an extremely serious matter. Self-pollution was, he
wrote, "a crime in it self, monstrous and unnatural; its practice
filthy and odious, its guilt crying, and its consequences ruinous: it
destroys conjugal affection, perverts natural inclination, and tends
to extinguish the hopes of posterity."[29]

The second point of agreement lay in masturbation's "pernicious consequences" for the body. The author of *Onanism display'd*
took particular note of impotence, but added an additional complication: the blood may become "so far vitiated and impaired . . .
that it is wholly unable to perform its office of circulation with any
regularity."[30]

Having said that, he directed a volley of criticisms at *Onania*.
The author of *Onania* was mistaken about Onan's crime; it was
not masturbation but *coitus interruptus*. He was completely wrong
about the causes of masturbation. He committed the error of not
putting his readers on their guard against things more serious than
masturbation: debauchery and the frequentation of prostitutes.
His attitude appeared instead to encourage fornication and lewdness. His remedies were no more than snake oil and promoted the
very sin he pretended to attack.

The author of *Onanism display'd* offered his own remedy for all
these errors, "that infallible specifick, in every one's power,
chastity."[31] Chastity was, however, best followed up by an early
marriage, concluded with all possible speed.

The only response that the author of *Onania* would deign to
make to this harsh critique, in later editions of his work, was to
pardon it for its insults and calumnies. *Onanism display'd*, he
would say, is too "silly" too "impertinent" for him to "have vouchsafed an answer."[32]

Around 1720 a second pamphlet appeared. It was an imitation
of *Onania*. Even the title was a pastiche: *Of the crime of Onan . . .*

or the hainous vice of self-defilement, with all its dismal consequences, stated and examined in all those who may ever misfortunately have injured themselves by this abominable practice.[33] The themes were the same as those of *Onania*, with, if possible, even more virulence. We are shown "how this one vice above all others, affects the brain, head, nerves, and eye-sight of the body. . . . For one only moments pleasure, every Onanian incurs an eternity of wailing, torments, misery, and sorrow." He who indulges the vice is blind, and his blindness is not merely moral; since masturbation "drain[s] off those animal spirits which are so the peculiar strength of the optick nerves," it—more than any other vice—has particularly damaging effects on vision and the eyes. The guilty find that their eyes "fail them a deal sooner than otherwise they would." Following the pains of this world are those of the next. "Men are so used to hear talk of Hell, that it very little affects them, whereas if every Onanian was but truly sensible what Hell is, he would tremble at the very thought of committing an action so certainly insures it to him." So that he may well be made aware of hell, its fires and torments were described, in suitably realistic detail.[34] The description of hell aptly captures the tone of the whole work: it is *Onania* intensified.

A second pamphlet targeting *Onania* appeared in 1723. It was entitled: *Onania examined and detected, or the ignorance, error, impertinence and contradiction of a book entitled Onania discovered and exposed.*[35] The author, under the pseudonym of Philo-Castitatis, shared with *Onania*'s author the horror of masturbation, but he argued over biblical interpretation, over marriage, over the fact that he judges masturbation to be more serious than fornication or adultery, over his excessive severity toward women, his anatomical errors, etc., etc. All this was very long, even interminable—over 100 pages—but the boredom emanating from it seems to have had no effect upon the author of *Onania*, who would respond to its critique at great length—over nearly 40 pages—in his *Supplement* to *Onania*.[36]

Eronania, which appeared in 1724, was once again an imitation of *Onania: Eronania, or the misusing of the marriage bed by Er and Onan . . . or the hainous crime of self-defilement, with its nine miserable consequences in both sexes, laid open to all those who may ever have been guilty of its ill action.*[37] This pamphlet, just like *Onania*, but even more blatantly, turned into an advertisement for a whole series of medicines with quite remarkable effects, ranging from a "purging lotion" (price: 7 sh. 6 d.) and a "strengthning lotion for weaknesses" (7 sh. 6 d.) to the "great constitution elixir" (price: one guinea). These remedies were guaranteed to repair the damages caused by the "abominable self-defilement."

Whether works of quackery or of polemics, all this literature was quite repetitive in its approach to masturbation, but revealing, at least, of the echoes to which *Onania* had given rise. What produced these echoes? How can we explain *Onania*'s success? The author himself ingenuously provides at least one of the keys: its novelty.

There are many well wrote books against whoredom and adultery, and a thousand good things have been said to discredit them, which I heartily approve of; but the uncleanness with ones self, which I write against, has never been touch'd upon yet by any able pen, at least not intelligibly, or so much to the purpose, that any good may be expected from it. I made choice of this subject, because the society stood in need of it; and I thought that nothing was actually more wanted.[38]

Translated into modern and less virtuous terms: *Onania*'s author had unearthed a ready market for his ideas.

His observation was entirely correct. Before him, the topic of masturbation had remained largely unexplored, at least in the way it would be in *Onania*. This was doubtless linked, in large part, to a sort of pact of silence dictated by propriety. On this point, we can cite a typical passage from the 1705 *Little Review*. In *The Little Review or an Inquisition of Scandal*, Daniel Defoe published readers' letters, with his answers, on often titillating topics. Masturbation, however, remained a topic unsuitable for public discussion. We read in the August 3, 1705, issue: "the Gentleman that sent a second letter, sign'd A. M. concerning Self-Pollution, may be convinc'd by the word itself, and may as well doubt of the sinfulness of Self-Murther; but his case is not fit to be shown in publick, any more than to be acted in private."[39] "Not fit to be shown in publick": this was the convention that the author of *Onania* violated with an audacity that was to be rewarded. He offered the charms of novelty.

Yet it was not novelty that explained *Onania*'s lengthy success, the number of successive editions over decades. For that, the author discovered a second recipe for success: it was the publication of the letters written by those who sought his professional advice.

The successive editions of *Onania* do not consist of simple reprints. From one edition to the next, the volume increased, the matter expanded. The fourth edition—the first to be preserved, as we pointed out earlier—was 88 pages long, the seventh, in 1723, had increased to 200, and would soon be augmented by a *Supplement*.[40] In 1730, in its fifteenth edition, the *Onania* itself and the *Supplement* together stretched over 344 pages. The whole, moreover, sold for three shillings—that is to say, three times the price of the original work.

What caused the inflation? Editorial additions contributed to a minor extent; we saw, for example, how the author responded to the attack by *Onania examined and detected*. But it was the readers, especially those who wrote for advice, who furnished most of the raw material for the expansion. The author printed their letters along with his responses. From one edition to the next, what thus developed was a sort of serialized novel of masturbation in the guise of an exchange of correspondence.

These letters—or these pseudo-letters, for it is obviously impossible to distinguish the authentic from the fabricated—were of a nature to pique the public's interest and curiosity. They attempted, in fact, to outdo each other in their description of the misfortunes befalling the unfortunate masturbator.

Here, for example, is the letter of a clergyman who reports the case of a pupil in the school he heads. This young man has practiced masturbation since the age of 15. He was also, it must be said, debauched and a drinker. His sexual parts were affected early on. He began to urinate blood and urination became increasingly painful. Eventually, he was afflicted with a bladder ulcer that reduced him to a skeleton and led to his death. During the three months preceding his death, he exuded such a nauseating odor that it was impossible to enter his room without holding something strong-smelling under one's nose. The physicians concluded that the principal cause of his disease was masturbation, far more than debauchery or drink, although they may have aggravated his case.[41]

Here is the case of a young woman whose sensual temperament led her to masturbate from the age of 14. She was aware of the folly of her act but was unable to resist the temptation. At the age of 19, she was seized with a true uterine furor: during her fits, she screamed and called for any man at all to have sex with her. She died during one of these fits, in delirium. An autopsy was performed, and it showed that the gland of her clitoris, which was much larger than normal, was filled with a corroding humor that must have produced an intense itching and that consequently had exacerbated her desire. All of this was the result of her manner of pleasuring herself.[42]

Here is a letter from twins, both masturbators. They were both, they wrote, afflicted with multiple disorders. One of the brothers had so great a weakness in his back that when he bent over, he was nearly incapable of raising himself again; his swollen testicles were painful. The other had groin pain, swollen glands, and a facial irritation. They had both suffered terrible weight loss. Having discovered, thanks to *Onania*, the source of their disorders, they now wrote to its author for his advice on a cure.[43]

These two or three cases were, it must be emphasized, simple cases. Often the letters enumerated illnesses that were more numerous and varied, in horrifying combinations.

Readers in the eighteenth century surely were horrified. Today's reader can only wonder. We've already alluded to the most irritating—because it is practically insoluble—question: that of authenticity. The protests of *Onania*'s author, who swore to heaven that he had printed real letters only, without changing a single word, are less than convincing.[44] A letter signed "The afflicted Onan" (all the letters are either anonymous or signed with pseudonyms) carries as convincing a stamp of authenticity as a letter signed "Brokenhearted" in one of today's advice-to-the-lovelorn columns. What is authentic? What is fabricated? Were there some real letters that were later "improved"? There is no way for us to know.

This problem of authenticity is, however, important, for if a substantial number of letters constitute, fully or even partially, real correspondence actually sent to the author, this would suggest that the publication of *Onania* had provoked what could be called a chain reaction. Pamphlet in hand, people discover the origin of the illnesses that afflict them and that they had been unable to comprehend: it is their unfortunate vice that is the culprit. They write. Others, in turn, are struck and come to understand the origin of their own illnesses. In medicine there are fashions for both remedies and the causes of disease. Did *Onania* truly set the fashion (and sometimes a fashion is truly visible only with hindsight)? The question must be left open.

For the modern reader, in any event, it is quite obvious that, authentic or not, the letters lack any scientific value. None contains a truly serious medical observation. What kind of scientific validity can be given to the mere claim that it was masturbation that was responsible for the death of an individual who was simultaneously a drinker, a debaucher, and a masturbator? Everything in the letters is equally dubious. Yet it is the reaction of *Onania*'s contemporaries that must take precedence over our own. They took the testimony that they read in *Onania* perfectly seriously and, what is essential, they drew from it an increasingly dark picture of the physical consequences of masturbation. With each successive edition of *Onania* and the new letters it contained, the spectrum of illnesses caused by this terrible vice widened.

A typical eighteenth-century attitude, perhaps the most typical, was that of Samuel Tissot, to whom we will return at length later. Tissot, considering *Onania*'s letters as material that he as a physician could and should use, undertook the task of classifying—for as he said, they were in a state of "true chaos" in *Onania*—the "disorders of which patients complain."[45]

This page from Tissot is a bit long, but it is worth quoting in entirety, because it is absolutely essential to our argument. It shows how what initially resembled (at least on the formal level) letters from the lovelorn was transformed into a scientific treatise.

Tissot wrote:

I will categorize the illnesses of which the English patients complain under six headings . . .

1. All the intellectual faculties weaken, they lose their memory, their thought becomes confused, they even sometimes fall into a state of slight dementia; they are constantly harassed by a kind of internal anxiety, a continual anguish, by pangs of conscience so strong that they are often brought to tears. They are prone to dizzy spells; all their senses, but especially sight and hearing, weaken; their sleep, if they are able to sleep at all, is disturbed by troubling dreams.

2. The body loses all of its strength; the growth of those who indulge in these abominable practices before they reach their full height is significantly stunted. Some do not sleep at all, others are almost continually drowsy. Almost all become hypochondriacs or hysterics, and are afflicted by all the troubles that accompany these unfortunate diseases; sadness, sighs, tears, palpitations, choking fits, fainting spells. Some have been seen to spit up calcareous matter. For others, coughing fits, slow fevers, consumption are the wages of their sin.

3. Patients also complain of sharp pains; some of headaches, others of chest, stomach or intestinal pain, external rheumatic pain, and sometimes of a painful numbness throughout the body resulting from the application of even the slightest pressure.

4. We see not only pimples, one of the most common symptoms, but true suppurating pustules on the face, the nose, the chest, the thighs . . .

5. The organs of generation are also subject to their share of miseries, of which they are the primary cause. Some patients become incapable of erection; for others, the seminal liquid pours out at the slightest pruritis and the weakest erection, or in their attempts to move their bowels. A great number are afflicted with chronic gonorrhea, which saps all of their strength, and which produces a discharge that resembles a fetid pus or a dirty mucus. Others are tormented by painful priapisms. Dysuria, strangury, burning upon urination, the weakening of the stream cause some patients to suffer cruelly. Some have very painful tumors on the testicles, the penis, the bladder or the sperm ducts. Finally, either the impossibility of coitus or the degeneration of the seminal liquid, rendering sterile nearly all those who have indulged in this crime for a long time.

6. The functioning of the intestines is sometimes completely disrupted, and some patients complain of persistent constipation, others of hemorrhoids or of a flow of fetid matter from the fundament.

That was what Tissot called "The Portrait taken from *Onania*." There is no reason to doubt that it was what readers—perhaps with even bleaker interpretations—retained from *Onania* and its correspondence. Their terror is easily imaginable.

One person, in any case, profited from this terror: it was the author of *Onania*. This was his livelihood. His pamphlet sold well, just like the "Strengthning tincture" and the "Prolifick powder," but he charged, too, for his consultations. Beginning in 1723, in fact, he announced that he may be contacted by letter at the address of the bookseller Thomas Crouch. He would either respond or set up an appointment with his correspondents.[46] "But then," he added, "he expects his fee." The fees take up quite a bit of space in succeeding editions of *Onania*.

We come back here again to the problem of the author's personality and of the interpretation of his launching of *Onania*. We have said it earlier; he had the bright idea to choose a new topic, but doubtless, without the slightest doubt even, he did it in the hopes of profit. That wish was fulfilled. One of his critics specifically reproached him for that.[47]

The bright idea of a charlatan, a quack who was looking to make a profit: if our analysis is correct, this is what lay at the root of what would become a great and powerful social phenomenon.

CHAPTER FOUR

ONANIA'S INFLUENCE

*O*nania created a stir: a 1723 pamphlet described it as "a book which had so long made so much noise in the world."[1] It was a commercial success, as we've already seen. Yet looking beyond its popular and commercial success, we come to the question of its influence. Was *Onania* also influential, and did that influence last? That is the real question.

Part of the answer is to be found in the language of the day. *Onania* gave rise to *onanism*. *Onanism* is a term that seems to have been unknown in either English or French before the beginning of the eighteenth century. Curiously, even the author of *Onania* never used it himself. His work, as its title indicates, was centered on "Onan's crime," but he referred to that crime as "self-pollution." The word *onanism* did not appear until 1719, in a short pamphlet directed against *Onania* entitled *Onania display'd*. We mentioned it briefly in the preceding chapter. Both the pamphlet and its title were obviously the byproducts of *Onania*.

Several years later, both the product and the by-product would make it into the dictionaries. We read in 1728: "*Onania,* and *Onanism:* Terms some late Emperics have framed to denote the crime of self-pollution, mentioned in Scripture to have been practised by Onan, and punished in him with death."[2]

Under the entry *Pollution*, or *Self-Pollution*, we read similarly that "the crime has been denominated by some Emperics *Onania*—see *Onania*."[3]

Thus, according to the *Chambers Cyclopaedia*, it was the quacks (the "Emperics") who coined the terms *onania* and *onanism*. It must be noted here that if it is true that the author of *Onania* did indeed coin the term that serves as his title, it is a word that he never used, no more than he did *onanism*, in referring to the crime. Who used it first? To be truthful, the substantive *onania*, used in precisely that sense, has never been found in any work. Until something more is discovered, all we have are the claims of the dictionaries.

The *Chambers*, in any event, stuck to its definition. The definition of *Onania* and *onanism* in the 1728 edition was repeated in the following editions of 1738, 1741, 1752, 1781, and 1788. Since one of the characteristics of dictionaries is that they copy each other, other dictionaries followed suit. The entries *onania* and *onanism*, with definitions similar to that of the *Chambers*, appear in the *Dictionarium Britannicum* of 1730, the *New General Dictionary* of 1768 and the *Encyclopaedia Britannica* in 1771.[4]

Onania, however, was quickly knocked out of the running. *Onanism*, on the other hand, appeared once again in the title of a 1767 booklet, *A short treatise on onanism, or the detestable vice of self-pollution*.[5] It reappeared during the same period in the title of an English translation of Tissot, *Onanism*.[6] Beginning in the late eighteenth century, English dictionaries dropped the entry *onania*, retaining only *onanism*.

Onanisme also entered the French language in the last decades of the eighteenth century, thanks, it seems, to Tissot.[7] But Tissot, greatly influenced by the English *Onania*, had simply adapted the word from its title. In 1758, in a treatise published in Latin, the *Tentamen de morbis ex manustupratione*, he spoke of the "Onaniae aegri," the "patients who suffer from onania" (*onania* is thus used here to refer to the illness, but in Latin). Two years later, the work that was to make him famous appeared: *L'Onanisme, ou Dissertation physique sur les maladies produites par la masturbation.* Immediately afterward, Dutoit-Membrini followed his lead with a work entitled *De l'onanisme ou Discours Philosophique et moral sur la luxure artificielle et sur tous les crimes relatifs* (Lausannne, 1760).[8] Dutoit-Membrini would have no followers.[9] Tissot's success, on the other hand, would be enormous, spreading the use of the word *onanism.* It appeared in 1774 in Voltaire's *Questions sur l'Encyclopédie,* and passed from there into the *Dictionnaire philosophique.*[10] *Onanisme* and *masturbation* thereafter function synonymously.

That entire episode in the history of language was the result, let us repeat, of *Onania.* Let us look more specifically at *Onania's* influence on contemporary thought.

A striking case in which *Onania's* influence is clear is that of Bernard de Mandeville, a diplomaed physician from Leyden who had set himself up in England at the beginning of the eighteenth century.[11] In 1711, Mandeville published a weighty treatise on the *Hypochondriack and Hysterick passions, vulgarly called the Hypo in men and Vapours in women.* Here he discussed the consequences of sexual excesses, which may be fatal, emphasized that even excesses committed within marriage can have dire results—but said not a word about masturbation.[12] In 1724, he returned to the topic, that is to say, to the manner in which "lewd young men" might destroy their health, in a new book entitled *A Modest Defence of Publick Stews. Onania's* influence is visible; masturbation had now become the principal culprit.[13]

Mandeville's solution to the problem of preventing youthful indulgence in harmful excesses—be it masturbation or other dissipations—was, to say the least, original: he recommended the establishment of public brothels or "stews." Better the brothel than masturbation.[14] This is the first time we encounter a proposal like this, but later it will be implicitly evoked more than once, especially in the nineteenth century.

The country in which *Onania* and its ideas had the greatest impact, however, was not England but Germany. A German translation of *Onania* was published in Leipzig in 1736.[15] In 1740, the theologian Sarganeck published a voluminous "Warning against all the Sins of Uncleanness and Secret Lewdness," *Warnung vor allen Sünden der Unreinigkeit und heimlichen Unzucht.*[16] The German translation of *Onania* was used, quoted, analyzed at length.

In 1743, in volume 36 of the *Grosses vollständiges Universal Lexicon,* edited by Zedler, we find a detailed article on *Selbst-Befleckung* or *Crimen Onaniticum.*[17] It paraded before the reader the story of Onan's crime, a merciless moral and religious condemnation, a description of the "dreadful consequences" for the guilty, with an enumeration of the ills that await them. A single reference throughout: the German translation of *Onania. Onania*'s ideas had now gone so far as to be popularized in a major encyclopedia.

Direct references to *Onania* are one thing. But we need, too, to take into account other evidence of influence that, albeit sometimes more subtle, is equally significant. In this respect, two works, one by the English physician Robert James and the other by Jean-Jacques Rousseau, are particularly important.

James left to posterity his weighty medical dictionary, *A Medicinal Dictionary,* published in London in 1743–1745 and in French translation in 1746–1748. One of the translators was none other than Diderot.[18] It is "a vice not decent to name, but productive of the most deplorable and generally incurable disorders."[19] Here the double nature of the condemnation is clearly visible. First of all, the moral aspect. The dictionary repeatedly insisted that it was "a crime not to be mentioned, much less to be practis'd, in a country where virtue, decency or politeness have the least regard paid to them," a "vile and unmanly practice."[20] But there was also the medical aspect: this "abominable and unmanly practice" was "productive of the most deplorable and generally incurable disorders."[21] The disorders included "incurable impotence, lowness of spirits, hypochondriacal disorders and almost all sorts of chronical distempers."[22]

And if we ask: what is the source of this panoply of ills, arrayed before the eyes of James's readers? There is but one possible response: *Onania*.[23]

In another passage from the *Medicinal Dictionary*—which curiously was not included in the French translation—under the entry for *Gonorrhea*, James again denounced the "preposterous method of venery" which masturbation constituted. It is an "enormous vice" and "there is perhaps no sin productive of so many hideous consequences."[24]

The case of Jean-Jacques Rousseau is doubly interesting. First, there was his personal experience with masturbation, which he recounted in his *Confessions*. He was initiated into the vice, he said bluntly, by a Moorish bandit he met in Turin,[25] and succumbed:

> I learned this dangerous supplement which deceives nature and leads young men of my disposition to many excesses at the expense of their health, their vigor and sometimes even of their lives. This vice which shame and timidity find so convenient, is, moreover particulary attractive to active imaginations: it allows them to dispose at will, so to say, of the entire female sex, and to make a tempting beauty serve their pleasures without needing to obtain her consent. Seduced by this deplorable advantage, I worked to destroy the good constitution with which nature had endowed me. . . .[26]

Beyond this, the *Confessions* contain little more than fleeting allusions to masturbation.[27] Yet, despite its somewhat discreet nature, the confession remains unambiguous: Rousseau indulged in the practice for years.

He did so, if the *Confessions* are to be believed, in full knowledge of its dangers. Yet the Rousseau who is the most interesting, in this respect, is the Rousseau who teaches, the Jean-Jacques Rousseau of *Emile*.

The text of *Emile* is equally allusive, yet how vigorously it denounces the evil and enjoins educators:

> Watch over the young man with care; he will be able to protect himself from everything else, but it is up to you to protect him

from himself. Never leave him alone night or day, at least sleep
in his room; he is not to go to bed until he is overcome with
sleep and is to leave his bed the moment that he awakes. Beware
of instinct. . . . It would be dangerous if your student were to
learn from instinct how to deceive his senses and to multiply the
opportunities for satisfying them; if he once comes to know this
dangerous supplement, he is lost. From then on his body and his
heart will be enervated; he will carry to his grave the sad effects
of this habit, the most deadly habit to which a young man can
be subject. Doubtless, it would be better yet . . . if the furors of
an ardent temperament become invincible, my dear Emile, I pity
you; but I will not hesitate for an instant, I will not allow nature's purposes to be eluded. If you must be subjugated by some
tyrant, I prefer to surrender you to one from whom I will be able
to deliver you; no matter what, it will be easier for me to tear you
away from women than from yourself.

Until the age of twenty, the body is growing and needs all of its
strength: continence during this period is part of the natural
order . . . After the age of twenty, continence becomes a moral
duty; it teaches us in an important way how to reign over ourselves,
how to remain master of our appetites. But moral duties have their
modifications, their exceptions, their rules. When human weakness makes a choice between two alternatives inevitable, let us
choose the lesser evil; in any event, it is better to commit a misdeed
than to contract a vice.[28]

Clearly, the basic modern arsenal of anti-masturbatory terror is
already in place here: the terrifying nature of the evil (the young
man is "lost," he is heading for the "tomb"), the necessity of strict
surveillance at every moment ("never leave him alone night or
day"), the remedy of sleep-inducing fatigue. Bernard de Mandeville said earlier: better the bordello than masturbation. Rousseau
said: better a misdeed than a vice, better women (he doesn't spec-
ify what women, but we can assume it is not the most virtuous
that he has in mind) than the most dangerous of habits.

Emile is from 1762. Tissot's book on onanism had appeared
two years earlier. Rousseau might thus seem to be one of the Swiss
doctor's disciples. The chronology, however, is misleading: at the

moment of *Emile*'s publication, Rousseau knew nothing whatsoever about Tissot's work. He would not become aware of it until July 1762, just after *Emile*'s publication, when Tissot himself sent him a copy of his book.[29] Rousseau would discover it fully corroborated his ideas. He was, he wrote Tissot, "sorry not to have known about *Onanisme* earlier, for its reasoning and its authority would have reinforced and proven what I had to say myself on this point. . . . I feel that you and I were naturally bound to agree and be friends; those who think like us are our friends and brothers, and it is as such that I conclude in brotherly simplicity, Sir, with my most heartfelt wishes."[30]

If Tissot was not the source, where then did Rousseau's ideas come from? It is certainly imaginable that they were at least partially his own creations, built upon his own experience and observations. Yet is it not also entirely plausible that *Onania*'s wrath, along pathways now impossible to retrace—perhaps James's *Dictionary*—might have found its way to Rousseau?

The regrettably few texts that we have collected do seem to permit us, however, to draw one conclusion: it is that *Onania*'s ideas had indeed penetrated. Zedler's *Lexicon* and James's *Medicinal Dictionary* furnish the clearest proof. Yet it could not be said that *Onania* had succeeded in creating an atmosphere, at least not of the type we later find in the nineteenth-century, when an atmosphere of horror surrounded the topic of masturbation.

There is evidence, moreover, that the atmosphere of horror had not yet spread. Procope-Couteaux, for example, in the mid-eighteenth century, noted the continued existence of what he called a "mistaken notion"—the target of his own combat—which "allows solitary pleasures to be regarded as a trifle."[31] *Trifle* was precisely the word that will later be totally condemned.

For *trifle* to disappear, for the idea that it represented to be defeated, *Onania*'s assault, which had been partially successful, would have to be supported by a second offensive, this time decisive. It would be led by Tissot.

Chapter Five

Tissot

With Tissot, we enter the circle of European celebrities.[1]

Samuel-August Tissot was born in Vaud, Switzerland, in 1728. He attended high school in Geneva, then studied medicine at the University of Montpellier, where he received his doctorate in 1749, at the age of 21. He set up a medical practice in Lausanne, where, except for several trips and a stay in Italy from 1780 to 1783, he would live for the rest of his life, until his death in 1797.

Tissot's early career in Lausanne was distinguished by his successes in the treatment of smallpox. Tissot was a proponent of inoculation, which was the topic of his first publication, *L'inoculation justifiée, ou Dissertation pratique et apologétique sur cette méthode,* published in Lausanne in 1754, and well received.[2]

Fame was quick to follow, based in part on his books, several of which created a great stir, in part on his reputation as a practitioner, which earned him a huge clientele.

Among his published works were several on the topic of onanism (in Latin in 1758 and in French in 1760), which we will discuss at length below; *Avis au peuple sur sa santé,* published in

1761; *Avis aux gens de lettres sur leur santé* in 1767; *Essai sur les maladies des gens du monde* in 1770; *Traité de l'épilepsie* and *Traité des nerfs et de leur maladies.* The complete collection of his works, compiled at the end of his life, fills 14 volumes.

Among these works, the *Avis au peuple sur sa santé,* a popular medical and hygiene manual, was the most famous in its day. It saw a huge number of editions and was translated into practically all the European languages. "This work has been amazingly popular," the *Correspondance littéraire* noted in 1767. It added this note of praise: "It is the work of such a great and decent man, a book that is so truly useful to mankind, and of which its author must so justly be proud that, if I were to have to decide between the glory of being the author of *la Henriade* or the satisfaction of having written this *Avis au peuple,* you would pardon me, I think, for not being able to make my decision on the spot."[3] It is a book, wrote Masson de Pezay in 1771, "that should be taught immediately after the catechism, and perhaps even at the same time."[4] Alexandre Vinet would still point out in 1839, certainly not without a touch of Swiss chauvinism, that "perhaps no other book has ever become so popular and so European as the *Avis au peuple sur sa santé.*"[5]

The man whom a contemporary called "the famous Hippocrates of the banks of Lake Geneva" was a practitioner known throughout all of Europe. People from everywhere consulted him by correspondence and patients from everywhere flooded into Lausanne for his treatments.[6] "The beauty of our country, our Academy and M. Tissot attract foreigners from every country," we read in a "Lettre écrite de Lausanne."[7] Vinet explained it well: "Tissot attracted a host of ill nobility, princes, gentlemen, scholars whose gathering lent our city an activity and a renown that were all the more surprising given that Lausanne was, in all other respects, but one of our country's second-rank cities."[8] In 1773, for example, a city notable wrote in a personal letter: "We will be swamped this summer with the French ladies that our Aesculpius brings in."[9] And later: "Most of our ill ladies arrive in succession. . . . We see nothing but Countesses (the list follows) and [a]

Marchioness, all from Paris."[10] Some patients remained under treatment in the city for long periods.[11]

Of course, there were those who sought to lure Tissot from Lausanne. The king of Poland offered him the position of principal court physician in 1765. But he resisted all the offers. The only offer he did accept, temporarily, was that of Joseph II; at his request Tissot occupied a chair of medicine at the University of Pavia from 1780 to 1783.

Lausanne was anxious to keep him, not only because he was the city's biggest celebrity, but also because he served as a significant source of city revenues. The author of *Lettres sur la Suisse* noted in 1781, on the subject of the "famous Mr. Tissot, who has become doubly famous through his writings and his treatments," that the foreigners who came to consult him "spread a considerable affluence throughout the country."[12] The notable whose personal letter of 1773 is cited above jubilantly added up the thousands of francs that the ladies who had come to consult the "Aesculpius," and their retinue, would bring in. In a letter of thanks to Tissot, a member of the cantonal government wrote: "There is no doubt, Sir, that you are the principal cause of the increased prosperity . . . of Vaud, and above all of Lausanne: and, were you to be authorized to tithe the sums that you have brought in, you would be the richest man in the canton."[13]

Tissot's fame placed him, in his day, among the ranks of the great. In 1781, as the tutor of a young Russian aristocrat prepared himself for his pedagogical task, studying "physics, morals, teaching," it was "from the reading of Tissot, Rousseau and Locke," that he drew his principle inspiration.[14]

Tissot's work on onanism dates, as we have said, from the early years of his career. He published it first in Latin, in 1758, as an appendix moreover to a treatise on bilious fevers. The title was *Dissertio de febribus biliosis . . . Acedit tentamen de morbis ex manustupratione* (Lausanne, 1758).[15] Two years later, in 1760, again in Lausanne, Tissot published a French version of his treatise, now considerably expanded, entitled: *L'Onanisme, ou Dissertation physique sur les maladies produites par la masturbation.* A third edition, once again expanded, was to appear in 1764. This third edition, like the two preceding editions, indicated it was edited in Lausanne, but it was actually published in Paris.[16] After this, the editions multiplied.[17]

At the time of the first two publications—that of the Latin edition in 1758 and the French version in 1760—Tissot's fame had yet to be established. Yet in the wake of his personal fame, the work would take on new weight. Bearing a famous name, *L'Onanisme* would impress the public all the more.

Where did Tissot's interest in the problem come from? Doubtless from two sources: on the one hand from his lectures, and on the other from his observations of his patients (it is only a question, at this stage, of his local and regional clientele, and not of the international clientele to come).

Tissot had read Baynard and Ettmüller, whom we mentioned earlier.[18] He also possessed a copy of the observations of the great German doctor Friedrich Hoffmann. In case 104 of his *Consultationes et responsia medicinalia* of 1734, Hoffmann recounted his observation of a 25-year-old man who had begun to masturbate at the age of 15, and who had indulged his vice almost daily for eight years. When Hoffmann met him, he had been free of the vice for some time but continued to suffer from assorted ills: intense pain in the testicles, eye pain and abnormal dilation of the pupils, dreadful emaciation. Hoffmann analyzed the case, paying particular interest to the relationship between overfrequent ejaculation (for it is not specifically masturbation but the general problem of "the immoderate exercise of pleasure" that he targets) and vision problems. He described the regimen that allowed him to cure the patient.[19] Tissot would cite this case.[20]

He also cited cases that he observed himself. He noted, among certain patients given to masturbation, the presence of symptoms that were worrisome, and even highly so.[21] Those who consulted him by letter described those symptoms as well. "I certainly feel that this evil action has diminished the strength of my faculties, especially that of my memory," one wrote in September 1755.[22] "If religion did not restrain me, I would already have put an end to my life, cruelly ravaged as it is through my own fault," said another patient in 1756.[23]

All that certainly struck Tissot. Yet, in the way of readings and observations, there is no doubt that the two great shocks that most affected Tissot, and that truly unleashed the emotions that were to evolve into an obsession with onanism, were on the one hand the reading of *Onania* and on the other his meeting with a young watchmaker-masturbator.

> L. D***, watchmaker, had been good, and had enjoyed good health, up until the age of seventeen; at this period, he began to masturbate, an act which he reiterated daily, and often as many as three times a day . . . Before a year had passed, he began to notice a great weakness after each act; this warning was not sufficient to pull him from the mire; his soul, already given over to this filth was no longer capable of other ideas, and the repetitions of his crime became daily more frequent, until he found himself in a state where he feared death was imminent.

The young L. D*** then decides to be "good" again, but it is too late. His illnesses have become incurable. He is afflicted by spasms in the genitals which produce "not cries, but screams": "He lost all of his strength; obliged to give up his profession, incapable of all activity, sunk in wretchedness, he languished with almost no help for several months; all the more pitiful in that a glimmer of memory, which would not be long in extinguishing itself, served only to remind him incessantly of the causes of his misfortune."

It is at this point that Tissot intervened.

> I learned of his state, I went to his home; what I found was less a living being than a cadaver lying on straw, thin, pale, exuding a loathsome stench, almost incapable of movement. A pale and watery blood often dripped from his nose, he drooled continually; subject to attacks of diarrhea, he defecated in his bed without noticing it; there was a constant flow of semen; his eyes, sticky,

blurry, dull, had lost all power of movement; his pulse was extremely weak and racing; labored respiration, extreme emaciation, except for the feet, which were showing signs of edema. Mental disorder was equally evident; without ideas, without memory, incapable of linking two sentences, without reflection, without fear for his fate, lacking all feeling except that of pain, which returned at least every three days with each new attack. Thus sunk below the level of the beast, a spectacle of unimaginable horror, it was difficult to believe that he had once belonged to the human race. . . . He died after several weeks, in June 1757, his entire body covered in edemas.[24]

This ghastly story had its counterparts in the equally ghastly stories Tissot read in *Onania*. He possessed a copy of the seventeenth edition, from 1752.[25] This nearly 300-page volume made a profound impression upon him: he found that the numerous letters addressed to the author of *Onania* contained what he called *pulcherrimae observationes*—"magnificent observations."[26]

Onania and the young watchmaker: these were what set Tissot in motion. "I felt then," wrote Tissot of the unfortunate young man who died in June 1757, "the need to show young people all the horrors of the abyss into which they voluntarily leap."[27]

There is certainly a somewhat cynical commentary that can be made on these triggers for Tissot's work. He met his young watchmaker only at the time when the latter, although having stopped masturbating, was in a state of total physical decay. That is to say that Tissot knew the origin of his patient's malady only through the patient's tale: it was not a medical observation, but a reconstruction through hearsay. This reconstruction was based, moreover, on the words of a man who, as Tissot tells us himself, had almost entirely lost his memory. So much for the watchmaker. As for *Onania*'s *pulcherrimae observationes*, the picture is clear: they were, entirely or in part, mere forgeries.

So at times goes the course of history. *Onania* had made its mark, had had an effect, but this effect might have weakened over time. Tissot struck the blow that would irreversibly lead to the great anti-masturbatory fear. And Tissot entered the scene because of a case that had horrified him but that was not based on serious medical observation, and because he had read what was perhaps a work of quackery.

Not a trace of irony, in any event, is to be found in the commentaries of his contemporaries. The *Tentamen* and *L'Onanisme* were warmly received. The *Journal des Savants,* in 1758, devoted four pages of analysis to the *Tentamen.* This book by M. Tissot, the article read, "merits careful reading" and "serves to confirm the favourable impression we already have of his zeal and his talents."[28] The *Journal de Médecine* wrote two years later on *L'Onanisme:* "This work is filled with good moral and physical principles, with interesting commentaries, useful observations and curious investigations, which display not only the erudition and the talents of the author, but also his zeal and his love for humanity."[29]

The work seemed—and herein lay its novelty and its force—a strictly scientific work. In *Onania,* as we've seen, moral and religious imprecations were mixed with medical considerations. Tissot, for his part, did not hide his feelings on the moral level—he spoke of "infamy," of "crime," of "odious and criminal habits," of a "horrible act," an "infamous practice," an "odious action"—but vocabulary aside, he remained exclusively on medical grounds. He took pains to clarify: "I took it as my task to write about the illnesses produced by masturbation, and not of the crime of masturbation; is the demonstration that it is an act of suicide not, in any event, sufficient proof that it is a crime?"[30]

Tissot was respected as a man of science. His name alone would soon command respect and serve to validate his work. The book itself, however, intrinsically possessed all the necessary qualities for impressing the public. It was simultaneously dramatic, preemptory, and—seemingly—learned. Its drama lay in the pages that brought shivers to the spine. Its preemptory effect came from its forceful, self-assured style. It was, moreover, built upon a considerable base of references, upon an entire scholarly apparatus.

The explanation of the ravages of masturbation imparts an impression of considerable scholarship.

The book is filled with quotes from authorities and passages "drawn from the best authors." Tissot called upon both the venerables of antiquity—Hippocrates, Celsus, Aretius, Galen—and an impressive series of modern authors—Sanctorius, Lommius, Gaubius, Boerhave, Hoffmann, Van Swieten, to name only the most famous. The reader is convinced that his views on masturbation are merely the successors of those of the most recognized authorities.

It is, however, only a sham. When one examines the texts and the authors mentioned by Tissot, each time going back to the original source—and we have done this carefully, taking them one by one—one notes that it is almost never a question of masturbation in the original texts. There are one or two exceptions, such as Hoffmann's case 104, which we've already mentioned.[31] Everywhere else however, the theme of both the ancient and modern authors is that of disorders produced by venereal excesses in general or by involuntary nocturnal emissions. Masturbation is not cited.

The citations are thus improper, but that matters little, for the reader is thunderstruck by this arsenal.

Tissot also offered a learned theory. What was involved, Tissot revealed, is the "functioning of our machine," and, within this "functioning," the specific role of the "humors."[32]

The "humors" were the principal elements of the functioning of the human body, but they were arranged in a hierarchy. They were, in fact, more or less "perfected." Milk, for example, was less "perfected" than blood. "A robust nurse, who would be killed if we took several pounds of blood from her in twenty-four hours, is able to furnish the same quantity of milk to her child, four or five hundred days in a row, without being noticeably indisposed, because of all the humors, milk is the least perfected; it is a humor which is nearly foreign, while blood is an essential humor." At the summit of the hierarchy we find sperm: "the seminal liquid, which has such a strong influence on all the forces of body, and on the perfection of the digestions which repair them, that physicians of all centuries have unanimously believed that the loss of one ounce of this humor was more debilitating than that of forty ounces of blood."

Sperm dominated all. It was "the essential oil of the animal liquids, or perhaps, more precisely, the *directing spirit*, the dissipation of which rendered the other humors weak, and in a way, stale." Its importance lay in that it was an "active liquid," which was absolutely indispensable to the "play of the organs."

"Let me explain," wrote Tissot.

> There are humors, such as sweat and perspiration, which abandon the body at the moment they are separated from the other humors, and are expelled from the circulatory vessels. There are others, such as urine, which, following this separation and expulsion, are retained for a certain period within reservoirs designed for this purpose, and which they exit only when they are of sufficient quantity to excite, upon these reservoirs, an irritation which forces them mechanically to empty themselves. There is a third type, which are separated and retained, like the second type, in reservoirs, not for the purpose of being evacuated, at least not entirely, but in order to acquire within these reservoirs, a perfection which renders them suitable for new functions, when they return to the mass of the humors.
>
> Such is, among others, the genital liquid. Separated within the testicles, it passes from there along a rather long canal into the seminal vesicles and is constantly repumped by the absorbing vessels and, from one to the next, returned to the total mass of the humors.

It passed similarly into the blood. Tissot cited Haller on this point: "The greatest quantity of semen, the most volatile, the most odorous, that which has the greatest force, is repumped into the blood, and produces there, upon its entry, quite astonishing changes: beard, body hair, horns; it alters the voice and the behavior; for it is not age that produces such changes in animals, those changes are produced by semen alone."

Its influence on the various functions—which need to be stimulated by the precious liquid—could thus be explained.

This liquid is a *stimulus,* a thorn which irritates the parts it touches. . . . It is understood that these acrid particles, continually repumped and remixed with the humors, gently yet continually stimulate the vessels which, as a result, contract more strongly; they act more effectively upon the fluids; circulation is more lively; nutrition more precise; all the other functions are accomplished in a more perfect manner. When this aid is lacking, several functions never develop at all, . . . all work poorly.

When the semen is of insufficient quantity to function as a stimulus, in fact,

digestion, coction, perspiration, and other evacuations do not work normally; as a result of which there is a perceptible reduction of strength, of memory and even of reason; blurred vision, all the nervous disorders, all types of gout and rheumatism, weakening of the organs of generation, blood in the urine, disturbance of the appetite, headaches, and a great number of other disorders which we need not detail here.

Seminal losses are thus a true catastrophe for the overall functioning of the human body. The entire "machine" seizes when such losses deprive the organism of its "essential oil."

Mutatis mutandis, a similar phenomenon, is produced in women who, when they masturbate, lose not sperm but their own humor. "The troubles experienced by women are just as explicable as those experienced by men. The humor they lose being less precious, less perfected than male sperm, its loss does not perhaps weaken them as quickly; but when they indulge excessively, their nervous system being weaker and naturally more inclined to spasm, the troubles are more violent."

Tissot, however, encountered two difficulties—one significant, the other less so—in his logic. The minor difficulty was the case of eunuchs: "Why aren't eunuchs, who have no semen, at risk of the same illnesses which we've just described?" The major difficulty was to explain why, if seminal losses have such serious consequences, those consequences were not produced through simple copulation.

The case of eunuchs was dispatched rather quickly. The reason for their immunity

> is that if they do not reap the benefits of this liquid, when it has been prepared and repumped, on the other hand, they do not lose that precious part of the blood destined to become semen. . . . One could, to borrow the language of the metaphysicians, distinguish *semen to be made, semen in potentia*—that is the precious part of the humors that is separated in the testicles—and *formed semen, semen in actu.* If the former is not separated, the machine lacks the benefits it draws from the prepared semen, and does not experience the changes which are dependent upon it, but it does not deteriorate; it neither gains nor loses; the individual remains in a state of childhood.

To deal with the principal difficulty—why the effects of masturbation were infinitely more pernicious than those of coition, and even of "excesses with women"—Tissot needed an entire chapter. Yet he achieved what must have been, in his own eyes, one of his greatest successes: he discovered no less than eight "sources of danger" that were "peculiar to masturbation." We will analyze them briefly.

First source: coition was generally "solicited by nature" while solitary pleasures were "solicited by the imagination." When nature directed the act, there was little danger. "Nature, in a state of health, only inspires desires when the seminal vesicles are filled with a quantity of liquid that has thickened to such a degree that its reabsorption is rendered more difficult; and that indicates that its evacuation will not noticeably weaken the body." In the case of masturbators, on the other hand, "it is imagination, and not nature" which leads to the act. In this way, they "take away from nature that which is necessary to it, and that which nature was careful not to eliminate."

Second source: "the influence that this odious practice has over the senses." Masturbators have "a continual tension of the mind, always occupied by the same project." This tension attacked the brain. The "part of the brain that is thus active, makes an effort that can be compared to that of a muscle that is stretched too long and too hard." As a result, "worn out by continual fatigue, these patients are afflicted by all the maladies of the brain, melancholy, catalepsy, imbecility, loss of reason, weakening of the nervous system, and a host of similar ills."

Third source: "the very frequency of the acts," resulting in the moral as well as physical "mire" of the "habit." On the moral level, "the habit of having only one thought renders the individual incapable of having others; it takes over, and reigns despotically." On the physical level, "the organs, incessantly irritated, acquire a morbific disposition which becomes an ever-present stimulus . . . There are maladies of the urinary parts, which create a constant desire to urinate; the repeated irritation of the organs of generation produces in them a similar illness." The moral and the physical combined, the effect is horrendous. Even if the soul "is momentarily distracted by other ideas," if it attempts to escape, "the acrid humors which irritate the organs of generation will soon drag it back into the mire."

Fourth source: "besides the emissions of semen, the frequency of the erections, even partial, from which they [masturbators] suffer, fatigues them considerably." In fact, "every part which is in a state of tension, produces an expenditure of energy; the spirits flow there more abundantly, they dissipate, which causes a weakening; they are lacking for the other functions which, because of their lack, work imperfectly" (as in the case of the seminal liquid, the "spirits," we can see, appear here as a capital that is wasted).

Fifth source: the position in which the masturbator indulges in his practice. In coition, one is "lying down and stretched out," which incurs hardly any expenditure of energy. The masturbator, on the other hand, is seated or standing. "A person who is standing or seated, needs, in order to maintain himself in these positions, particularly in the first, the action of a great number of muscles, and this action dissipates the animal spirits" (the precious capital which we pointed out just a moment ago). It is thus a weakening factor.

Sixth source: the question of perspiration. Perspiration, in the case of a healthy person, "has a nourishing and fortifying element to it." The fortifying element, "inspired" by a partner, "helps to give him vigor." "These are observations which explain why the girl who slept with David gave him strength; why this same attempt succeeded with other old men, to whom it had been recommended." In the process of coition, there is an exchange of perspiration: "one inhales what the other exhales." "Each, in this case, compensates for the other's loss." In the case of masturbation, on the other hand, "the masturbator loses and recovers nothing."

Seventh source: the "joy that stems from the soul," which is found in the "pleasures of love," but not, of course, in masturbation. This joy "aids in digestion, animates circulation, furthers the other functions, restores energy." In the case of the pleasures of love, it "aids in restoring the strength that they can take away." Tissot cited Sanctorius on this point, who remarks that even "after excessive coition with a woman whom one loved and desired, one does not feel the weariness which would normally be the result of this excess, because the joy that the soul feels increases the strength of the heart, favors the functions and repairs what has been lost."

Eighth and last source: the regret and the shame which overwhelmed masturbators. "The shame that follows them infinitely increases their misery." This shame produces a constant sadness which in turn brings about "the loosening of the fibers, the slowing of circulation, imperfect digestions, nutritional lack, obstructions . . . spasms, convulsions, paralyses, pains, an infinite increase in anguish."

All of this is merely the summary of a very detailed account that took up a full chapter in the book.

Tissot's scientific accounts obviously included borrowings—we've met Haller, Sanctorius, and the "animal spirits" along the way. But, we must emphasize, the system that he constructed was his and his alone. In this respect he was an innovator.

This system can only really be appreciated when placed in comparison with other physiological systems from the same period. To be brutally frank, it was representative of eighteenth-century physiology. Except for several very partial advancements in experimental physiology, it is speculative physiology that, worthy of its name, continued to dominate the field of science. Instead of listing all its various schools, let us quote instead the criticism which Emile Guyénot leveled at the theories of the period in his book *Les sciences de la vie aux XVIIe et XVIIIe siècles:* "infantile theories," "crude and gratuitous representations of life phenomena," "elusive and unprovable principles," "jumble of confused ramblings and inconsistent hypotheses which fill so many weighty volumes."[33] One has to keep in mind the general setting of this period and the fact that the light of modern physiology had yet to appear in order to understand Tissot's reception by the public; practicing the same genre as his contemporaries, he too was welcomed as a man of science.

But Tissot was also a physician. He therefore needed to propose remedies for the illnesses he described. His therapeutic indications were: pure air; a good diet that excludes "hard and indigestible" meats and fruits; a lot of milk; neither tea, nor coffee; sleep that should not be excessively long; a lot of exercise; tonics, principally quinquina; cold baths; and iron-rich waters, among which the most highly recommended are the waters of Spa, "one of the most powerful tonics known."[34] But the most effective course of action in tearing the unfortunate masturbator from his deplorable habits remained the drawing of a "portrait of danger."[35] One should—one must—bring him face to face with the "terrifying image, one that will make him shrink back in horror" at the future that inescapably awaited him. Tissot again took up his litany: "a general wasting of the machine; the weakening of all the corporeal senses and all the faculties of the soul; the loss of imagination and memory; imbecility; contempt; shame; the resulting ignominy; the functions that are disturbed, halted, painful; the long, deplorable, bizarre and disgusting illnesses; the sharp and always renewed pains," etc., etc.[36] It was cure by terror.

At this point, it would be premature to attempt to fully assess the corpus of Tissot's work; it is his influence that merits our attention. Yet we can make at least one or two observations.

Tissot has been forgotten as a man of science. He is known for no discovery, no medical innovation. As early as 1870, Daremberg's acknowledgment of Tissot, in his *Histoire des sciences médicales*, was harsh: "Of Tissot's numerous productions," he wrote, "and just as in the case of Berquin, nothing, nothing more than a vague memory of respect, remains. Tissot is the Berquin of medicine."[37] *L'Onanisme*, once so admired, had become nothing more than an archaeological object, simultaneously illustrating the vanity of "speculative" theories and the consequences of an absence of rigor in the examination of concrete cases. Christian noted in 1881: "If the good faith and the excellent intentions of the author are admirable, one yet remains stupefied at the naive candor with which he approaches the most disparate facts. In his zeal to combat onanism, he lost all critical discernment."[38]

Yet even if what he did was not science, didn't Tissot at least do some good? Didn't he help, cure? His contemporaries turned to him as one of their best sources of help. A patient who wrote to ask his advice, because he had masturbated and was experiencing great weakness, said in 1774: "Sir, you are the benefactor of mankind; please be mine as well."[39] Tissot wanted to be, surely believed himself to be, humanity's benefactor. However, on the subject of masturbation, the number of those he perhaps aided is obscured by the infinitely greater mass of all those who, generation after generation, were frightened or more properly terrified by his work and for whom it caused suffering and sometimes anguish. The great anti-masturbatory fear, for which he was in the main responsible, was a painful page in the history of youth. This profoundly estimable man was also a scourge.

Left Four-pointed
urethral ring

Right
Preventative
Undergarments

Appareils contre l'onanisme.

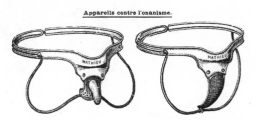

circuit at this point. With the ring and bolt are connected two
insulated wires (B, B), which convey the current to two binding
screws (C1, C2). Of these C1 is in communication with one of

"An electrical alarum for arresting
nocturnal emissions."

Toothed urethral ring.

Images courtesy of The Wellcome Library, London.

General appearance of the features through Onanism.

The meagre appearance of the features through Onanism.

Spermatorrhœal Opthalmia consequent through Onanism.

"Effects of Masturbation." Courtesy of the National Library of Medicine.

Right "Device to discourage masturbation." Courtesy of the National Library of Medicine.

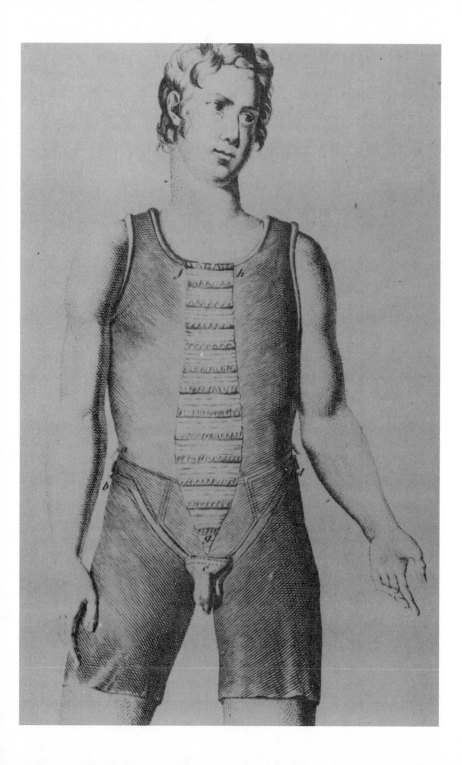

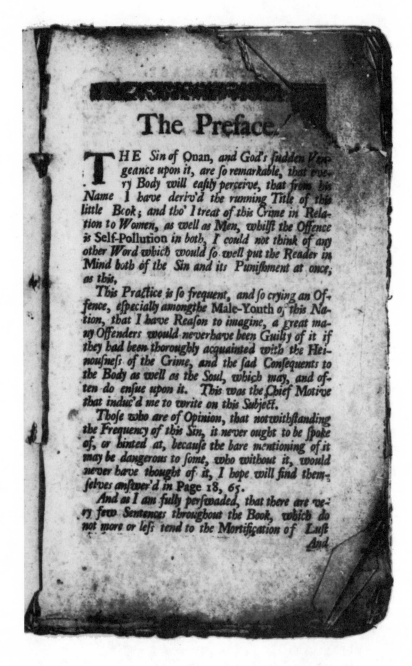

The Preface.

THE *Sin of* Onan, *and God's sudden Vengeance upon it, are so remarkable, that every Body will easily perceive, that from his Name I have deriv'd the running Title of this little Book; and tho' I treat of this Crime in Relation to* Women, *as well as* Men, *whilst the Offence is Self-Pollution in both, I could not think of any other Word which would so well put the Reader in Mind both of the Sin and its Punishment at once, as this,*

This Practice is so frequent, and so crying an Offence, especially among the Male-Youth of this Nation, that I have Reason to imagine, a great many Offenders would never have been Guilty of it if they had been thoroughly acquainted with the Heinousness of the Crime, and the sad Consequents to the Body as well as the Soul, which may, and often do ensue upon it. This was the Chief Motive that induc'd me to write on this Subject.

Those who are of Opinion, that notwithstanding the Frequency of this Sin, it never ought to be spoke of, or hinted at, because the bare mentioning of it may be dangerous to some, who without it, would never have thought of it, I hope will find themselves answer'd in Page 18, 65.

And as I am fully perswaded, that there are very few Sentences throughout the Book, which do not more or less tend to the Mortification of Lust

And

Preface pages from 1718 edition of *Onania*. Courtesy the New York Public Library

The PREFACE.

... one that can give Offence to the chastest
... this in the Opinion of Others, as well
... self, and in Particular of a very Learned
and Pious Divine, (as by his Letter sent me, which
follows) I dare recommend the serious Perusal of it
to both Sexes.

SIR,

I Received the Favour of your little Book
  against *Self-Pollution,* and have given it, as it
  well deserv'd, a second Reading. I am much
  pleas'd with your Arguments and Admoniti-
  ons, which are both cogent and swasive, and
  I hope in God, will answer your Design by it,
  in doing a great deal of good in the World,
  both to the Soul and Body, by awakening the
  Guilty, (who are *Daily,* and oftentimes *Dan-*
  gerously wounded by that foul Practice) and
  deterring the Innocent and Unwary from falling into it. Would all Masters of Schools have
  but a strict Eye over their Scholars, (amongst
  whom nothing is more common, than the
  Commission of this vile Sin, the Elder Boys
  teaching it the Younger) and give suitable
  Correction to the Offenders therein, and shame
  them before their School-fellows for it, I am
  perswaded it would deter them from the Practice, and by that means save them from Ruin;
  Thousands of the Youth of this Kingdom learning it there, who probably might never have
  known any Thing of it elsewhere.

  I am, Yours, &c.

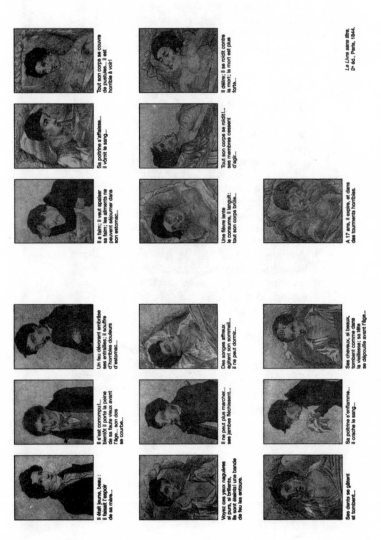

"Successive stages of a masturbator." From *Le livre sans titre* (Paris: 1830), 2nd edition (Paris:1844)

CHAPTER SIX

TISSOT'S TRIUMPH

Tissot enjoyed a triumphal success.

Following 1764, when he added the last touches to *L'O-nanisme,* new editions and translations multiplied. From 1765 to 1782, the work was reedited almost yearly.[1] During these years it was translated into English, German, Italian, and Dutch. The German translation was widely distributed and appeared in several editions.[2]

Yet beyond the sales success, it was the reception of the author's ideas that was striking. His portrait of onanism was quick to become a classic.

As early as 1763, we find Le Bègue de Presle, who devoted long pages to masturbation in his work *Le Conservateur de la santé ou Avis sur les dangers qu'il importe à chacun d'éviter, pour se conserver en bonne amitié et prolonger sa vie.* The tale of the young watchmaker occupied a privileged position. "L. D***, watchmaker, had been good and had enjoyed good health, up until the age of 18. . . ." The argument, with its catalog of horrors, the "infinite and inevitable illnesses" caused by masturbation, was Tissot intensified.[3] Right off the bat, Tissot had found a follower who would even be able to outdistance him.

Tissot quickly became the figure of reference. The secretary of the Academy of Berlin, Formey, who contributed his *Emile chrétien,* an adaptation of Rousseau's *Emile,* in 1764, emphasized that on the subject of the "dangerous supplement," the "risks have been revealed by M. Tissot."[4]

We could certainly draw up a list of all the texts in which Tissot is cited, used, or plagiarized. We'll limit ourselves, however, to two remarkable testimonies to his triumph: the *Encyclopédie* and the writings of Voltaire.

The article from the *Encyclopédie* on *Manstupration,* or *Manustupration,* appeared in 1765. Its author was Ménuret de Chambaud, a physician from the Montpellier medical school and one of the principal medical collaborators of the *Encyclopédie.*[5] From the outset, Tissot was hailed as the author "of an excellent study from which this article has drawn considerably."

Ménuret de Chambaud in fact was a faithful follower of Tissot. Certainly he expressed a certain slight reserve. Masturbation "which is not frequent," he wrote, "which is not excited by a seething and voluptuous imagination, and which is determined merely by need, is followed by no physical troubles, and is not a bad thing (medically)." However, Ménuret added—and here his reserve shows its limit—"one rarely avoids excess." That reserve, in any event, is almost imperceptible, drowned amid the descriptions of the "infinite number of very serious, and most often mortal illnesses" that befall the masturbator, victim of his deadly passion. On the subject of illnesses, he borrowed heavily from Tissot. The young watchmaker, of course, made an appearance (his story takes up an entire column). Ménuret added his personal grain of salt:

No one who has ever lived among young people has failed to see someone who has not incurred the most serious of illnesses through his abandonment to masturbation; I was the pained witness as several of my school fellows, carried away by this criminal passion, began to visibly waste away, loose weight, become weak and languishing, and eventually fall into an incurable phthisis; it is a memory that I still recall with horror.

It was not only his description of the consequences of masturbation, which was as horrific as can be; it was the underlying mindset that drew its inspiration from Tissot. "Leaving it up to the theologians to decide upon and to make known the enormity of the crime," he emphasized, "we believe that, by presenting the horrible portrait of the calamities which will befall them, we will be able to dissuade them all the more effectively."

In a later volume of the *Encyclopédie,* the article *Nutrition* explained that it was "an excessive evacuation of seminal liquid" that was "one of the most frequent and most common causes of nutritional insufficiency and resulting exhaustion."[6]

The *Encyclopédie*'s stamp of approval on Tissot's ideas was obviously crucial. Voltaire's contribution followed a bit later.

In 1774, in his *Questions sur l'Encyclopédie,* Voltaire devoted an article to *Onan* and *Onanisme.* The story of Onan gave him the opportunity to poke fun at the Bible. On the topic of onanism, he mentioned the English *Onania,* then noted:

Mr. Tissot, a famous physician from Lausanne, also wrote an *Onanisme* that is more thorough and methodical than the English work. These two works reveal the dire consequences of this unfortunate habit, loss of strength, impotence, degeneration of the stomach and the viscera, tremblings, vertigo, the stupor, and often premature death. There are examples that will make you tremble with fear.

M. Tissot discovered through experience that quinquina was the best remedy against these illnesses, provided that one completely ceased to practice this shameful and harmful habit, which is so common among schoolchildren, pages and young monks. But he noticed that it was easier to take quinquina than it was to triumph over what had become second nature.

Combine the effects of onanism with the pox, and you will see just how ridiculous and wretched the human race is.[7]

Here the jokes and the irony are gone: the "dire consequences," the "examples that will make you tremble with fear" appear truly to be dreadful calamities. Tissot had been fully adopted. The text of the *Questions sur l'Encyclopédie* would later appear in the *Dictionnaire philosophique*.

Another text bearing a famous name and revealing, at least indirectly, the influence of Tissot's ideas was Diderot's *Rêve de d'Alembert*. Written in 1769, it would not be published for the first time until the beginning of the nineteenth century.

In the *Rêve*, Diderot's conceptions are frequently unorthodox. So are his ideas on "solitary actions." His spokesman in the dialog, Doctor Bourdeu, treats them with smiling indulgence. "It is a need, and even when it is not done from need, it is still is a pleasant thing." He continues his reflection: "I blame all excesses, but in a society such as our own, if there is one, there are a hundred reasonable considerations that must be taken into account, . . . lack of family fortune, a man's fear of bitter regrets and a woman's of dishonor, which reduce a wretched creature dying of languor and boredom, a poor devil who doesn't know to whom he may turn, to dealing with himself in the manner of the cynic (that is to say the manner of Diogenes)." Should the temptation be resisted? "What! Because circumstances deprive me of the greatest happiness imaginable, that of mingling my senses with the senses, my intoxication with the intoxication, my soul with the soul of a companion chosen by my heart, . . . I should deprive myself of a necessary and delightful moment!" It is nature, moreover, that urges and incites us. "Nature tolerates nothing that is useless; and in what way, in helping it, would I be guilty, when nature has requested my assistance with the least equivocal of signs? We must never provoke it; but let us lend it a hand when the occasion calls."

One could hardly—especially given the final play of words on "a hand"—imagine a more provocative proposal, one that could more surely go against the grain of the ideas of the time. Yet, and this is what is significant, Diderot was fully aware of this. Doctor Bourdeu, in fact, hastens to add that he would not for an instant dream of expressing his theories in public. "To divulge these principles would be to trample on decency, to arouse the most odious suspicions concerning myself, and to commit an outrage against society." Not only would he be silent; he would repudiate any who adopted his attitude: "I would not raise my hat in the street to a man suspected of practicing my doctrine; it would suffice for me that others called him infamous."[8]

To say anything in favor of masturbation had thus become "an outrage against society": a perfect illustration of Tissot's triumph.

There was the secret Diderot we've just met. There is also the Diderot who signed his texts and expressed generally accepted ideas in them. The contrast between the two is clear. In the memoirs he wrote for Catherine II during his stay in Russia, his ideas appeared to be completely orthodox. His advice to the cadet school: "I've heard that there are even young children who are familiar with the vice. That is unfortunate. Where does this come from? From the servants, undoubtedly; one should keep an eye on the domestics."[9] His advice for schoolchildren in general: "Assiduous monitors are needed, especially in the places designated for nature's call: for this is where they pollute themselves."[10]

In just a few years, Tissot's ideas on masturbation had thus become a sort of shared treasure trove: they were "the ideas shared by all physicians," the physician Contencin wrote in 1772.[11]

The profound impression made by the author of *L'Onanisme* would have numerous repercussions. We'll look at several of the more striking ones. They began as early as the eighteenth century.

In medicine, Tissot's influence radiated in multiple directions: specialists in different illnesses began to implicate masturbation and its deleterious effects in the maladies specific to their fields. To take just one example, Chopart, a well-known surgeon and specialist in renal disorders, wrote in 1791: "Masturbation is a complicating factor in renal disorders. I have known schoolboys who, through overindulgence in this act, have become hunchbacks, developed curvature of the spine with vertebral caries, and died."[12]

Faced with mortal danger, extra precautions were taken and every imaginable way of avoiding contagion was dreamt up. There was, for example, Dr. Duplanil, who, in his *Médecine domestique,* was particularly interested in the case of female masturbators. The "fair sex" who "indulge in this destructive vice" were in fact to be found in "large cities, convents, [religious] communities, boarding houses, private schools, etc." A major precaution to be taken: we "cannot more strongly recommend that mothers, superiors, schoolmistresses, etc. take care to ensure that their children, their pupils . . . are never alone; that they never become familiar with chambermaids, hairdressers, dressmakers, etc., all females for the most part."[13] One must stay away from the "dangerous classes."

Mechanical preventive devices began to appear in the form of special articles of clothing. The first mention we have of one of these devices appeared just before 1875 in a letter written to the *Journal de Littérature* by a Parisian doctor named Le Clerc.[14] Le Clerc was a great fan of the "famous Tissot," but noted that Tissot's "excellent work, which has become, so to say, a classic," occasionally had the curious effect of stimulating the senses of certain young people instead of dulling them. These "untamable temperaments" required something else. Le Clerc thought he'd found it. It was "an external method which is a simple as it is effective, . . . a particular kind of garment which the intelligent worker, who seconds my views, will fashion to look like a regular article of clothing." Le Clerc gave no additional details but assured the reader that his procedure was tried and true. In this way, he wrote, "I have returned to the maternal breast dear children who, without my zeal, would have been cut down in the springtime of their youth."

Beyond medical literature, even erotic literature would be influenced by Tissot's ideas. In his 1793 *Erotika Biblion,* Mirabeau emphasized that "continual erections, frequent pollutions . . . are tremendously exhausting." He added:

> It must also be noted that the attitude of onanists contributes in no small way to the weakening caused by their solitary operations . . .

Nature never cedes her rights or allows her laws to be violated with impunity. She more readily tolerates shared pleasures, even when excessive, than she does a sterile ruse designed to coerce her. The satisfactions of mind and heart contribute to a prompt repair of the losses which the transports of the imagination cause and can never repair.[15]

As the physical fear of masturbation increased, so too did the moral horror it inspired. The evolution of morality seems to have been clearly dependent—and this is of great significance—on that of medicine; morality followed medicine.

The trial of Marie-Antoinette offers a striking milestone in the evolution of the moral code. The revolutionaries who sought the downfall of Marie-Antoinette wanted to pad the list of charges against her. They were particularly on the lookout for immoral activities. To this end, they questioned the young Louis XVII, then in solitary confinement in the Temple, and the child signed—under conditions that will forever remain a mystery—a damning declaration.[16]

The public prosecutor for the Paris Commune, Chaumette, who had led the interrogation, made his report to the Council General on October 10, 1793:

> The prosecutor of the Commune cannot find words to describe for the council the horrors of which he must speak. Simon [Simon the shoemaker, Louis XVII's guard] has often caught the child in the most indecent acts which the child says he learned from his mother and his aunt, who often put him to bed between them; it appears, from this child's statements, that he was frequently both witness to and actor within the most scandalous, the most libertine of scenes.[17]

In his indictment, Fouquier-Tinville would evoke this charge with grandiloquence: "In short, the widow Capet, immoral in every sense and a new Agrippina, is so perverse and so familiar with every sort of crime that, forgetting the role of mother and the limits prescribed by the laws of nature, she did not fear to engage in—

with Louis-Charles Capet, her son, and according to the latter's testimony—indecent activities the idea and even the mere name of which are enough to produce shudders of horror."[18]

Before the revolutionary tribunal, Hébert, substitute for the commune's prosecutor, was more specific. He testified:

> Simon caught the young Capet, whose physical constitution was growing weaker every day, in pollutions that were both indecent and harmful for his temperament; to the question of who had taught him this criminal behavior?, the latter responded that he was indebted to his mother and aunt for his knowledge of this dreadful habit. According to the declaration that the young Capet has made in the presence of the mayor of Paris and the prosecutor for the Commune, these two women often put him to bed between them; there the most unbridled debaucheries were committed; and there is even no doubt, according to what the young Capet has said, that an incestuous act occurred between mother and son."[19]

It was upon being questioned about Hébert's declaration, to which she had not responded, that Marie-Antoinette would make her famous exclamation: "If I did not answer, it is because nature recoils from responding to such a charge made against a mother. I appeal to all those mothers who might be here today."[20]

Marie-Antoinette's appeal to all mothers represented an intensely emotional moment, and that emotion, even today, has not died. But from the perspective that we have taken, the interesting aspect is the manner in which the queen's "crimes" were depicted: the "criminal behavior" into which she had supposedly initiated her son, the "most unbridled debaucheries," and even an "incestuous act," were all on equal footing. The "indecent pollutions" in which the young Capet was caught and for which Marie-Antoinette was held responsible had certainly taken on, in moral terms, the dimensions of an abominable act.

The moral judgment is, we repeat, patterned, in this case, on the medical verdict. This verdict, stemming from Tissot, was clear and final. It was pronounced by a French doctor in 1801: "Of all the destructive vices of the human species, the worst is unquestionably masturbation."[21]

What we've just said holds generally for France and French-speaking Europe. Turning to England, we find the same scenario. We can cite English physicians who were followers of Tissot.[22] Of particular note was the sanction Tissot received upon his admission to the national monument that is the *Encyclopaedia Brittannica*. Beginning with the second edition in 1781, the *Encyclopaedia* extended him a royal welcome: the article on masturbation, that "very great crime," was essentially a summary of his views. This summary would be reproduced successively in the third, fourth, fifth, and sixth editions, in 1797, 1810, 1817, and 1823.[23] Here again, Tissot reigned as the established authority.

The same was true for Germany. In Germany, Tissot would have two types of disciples and admirers: physicians on the one hand, but also, and perhaps more importantly, pedagogy experts.[24] For, in the last third of the eighteenth century, German pedagogy would be characterized by the rise of a famous school, known as the "philanthropists," who paid keen attention to sexual problems, and in this school, Tissot and masturbation would be the topic of the day.

Let us start with the German physicians, in particular Börner in 1769, Vogel in 1786, and Peschek in 1789.

Börner, a physician from Leipzig, published an anonymous work in 1769, *Der ratende Artz,* "The physician adviser," which he would rework in 1776, this time publishing under his own name and under the more explicit title of *Werk von der Onanie.* The treatment of masturbation was one of his primary concerns. He attached particular importance to diet—he provided standard diets for children ranging in age from 4 to 15 years—but also to baths and physical exercise. Generally, for Börner, the grand danger lay in what was hot or heat-producing. Feather beds, for example, were forbidden. "Under and between the feather mattresses, the emanations gather together and spread around the periphery of the body; the oil contained in the feathers evaporates due to the heat and enervates the body."

Vogel, in 1786, recommended more sophisticated methods. He suggested a "fine linen undergarment that will prevent the touching of the genital organs," or better yet, the wearing of an undergarment that is completely closed in the front, the back of which is fitted with a small lock for which the child is obliged to request the key. Vogel also described a system of straps going across the shoulders and back and wound around the arms to prevent the child from touching anything below his navel.

As for Peschek, he thought that when marriage was impossible, bordellos, although intrinsically bad, were yet preferable to "insane masturbations."

Yet it is primarily the cohort of pedagogy experts, all haunted by the peril of onanism, that is particularly impressive. Zimmermann took up the banner in 1772. Then came Basedow, the most famous figure in the philanthropic school, who denounced the "crime against nature" as "fatal to health," and Huffnagel, who thought that catechism lessons must take up the question of masturbation. In 1785, Salzmann devoted an entire book to the "secret sins of youth," *Ueber die heimlichen Sünden der Jugend,* in which the plural in the title is misleading; masturbation was the only of the "sins" under study. He was followed by Campe, another famous name in German pedagogy, and then by Oest and Villaume in 1787. It took these different authors a mere 15 years or so to develop a complete and detailed anti-masturbatory pedagogical system.

Rather than analyzing the various aspects of this system—which involved not only education in the strict sense, but also clothing, food, physical exercise, living arrangements, children's beds, etc.—let us take a brief look at Salzmann's book, for it is the most striking.

Salzmann, who began his career as a pastor, left his pastoral duties to join the *Philanthropinum,* the famous model school founded by Basedow. Then in 1784, he opened his own educational institution, which became quite famous. His work, *Ueber die heimlichen Sünden der Jugend,* was based on an original methodology. Before publication, Salzmann made a public appeal for testimony and advice on the subject he was planning to treat.

The appeal was successful. The work, like the English *Onania*, is thus full of letters addressed to the author, with one significant difference. Given Salzmann's moral standards, one cannot, in his case, question the authenticity of the letters.

Salzmann's correspondents lamented the horrendous moral and physical consequences of their vice which was, as one described it, a form of suicide.[25] Salzmann himself threw in a purple passage or two along the way. He described masturbators as the "many old men of twenty years ("die vielen zwanzigjährigen Greise") who can be seen everywhere, their eyes empty, their cheeks pale and sagging, dragging their trembling limbs and their empty marrow-less bones."[26] If a schoolmaster were to organize a reunion of all the students he had had 20 years earlier, he would find them decimated, as decimated as a general would find his soldiers had their regiment been subject to a barrage of canon fire. And what enemy was responsible for these ravages? There were several, but the most dangerous of all, without question, was the vice that Salzmann denounced and that cost the greatest number of human lives.[27]

As would any good pedagogy expert, Salzmann made an inventory of all that could lead youth onto the paths of sin, or facilitate the sin itself. It is an extremely detailed inventory. The danger of bad books is particularly noted. These books might even be schoolbooks. There were pernicious Latin authors. Certain pages from Ovid were particularly dangerous. The Bible, with its tales of Lot, David, and Solomon, could be dangerous. Even dictionaries could have serious drawbacks, for their detailed explanations of certain impurities could stimulate the students' imagination.[28]

Physical exercise in itself was good, but it ceased to be good when it caused frictions, as involuntary frictions led to voluntary frictions. One must not allow children to climb trees by tightly embracing the trunk. There are several known examples, Salzmann said, of children who have begun to climb a tree with light heart, but who have come back down in such a state of giddiness that they fell into the clutches of the enemy under the very same tree. Salzmann indicated methods for teaching children how to climb without causing friction to their private parts.[29]

Horseback riding, for the same reason, could also be perilous, particularly in the case of the gallop. It was preferable to allow horseback riding only when the child's character was sufficiently formed, and to recommend the trot rather than the gallop.[30]

In schools, according to Salzmann, the long coats that students were made to wear particularly facilitated the vice. It was under these coats that they masturbated, sometimes right under the schoolmaster's nose.[31] This type of coat was to be avoided and classroom furniture and setup were to be changed. His solution: Long tables that hide the lower part of the students' bodies from the professor are to be prohibited. Still, the peril is particularly great when the professor, his back to the class, is not in a position to read the muscular contractions that reveal the moment of ejaculation on his students' faces.[32]

It was toilets, however, that represented the height of danger for Salzmann. He denounced them as dens of iniquity, as "tombs of innocence." In the course of the book he delivered three violent diatribes against toilets, places where vice is not only learned but taught.[33] What is thus required: toilets are to be laid out so that the child's position can be observed; one must watch the period of time the child spends in the toilet; two or more children should never be allowed to go to the toilet together.

"Watch": the term we've just quoted is at the heart of Salzmann's pedagogy. What he recommended to parents and educators was constant vigilance. If the downfall was to be prevented, the child must never be left to his own devices.

Beyond the description of this arsenal of precautionary measures, the main interest of Salzmann's text, like that of some of the letters he published, lies in the sense it imparts of a marked evolution in thought that followed Tissot (and Tissot is, of course, cited several times).[34] The awareness of danger that Tissot spread was changing, under its own impetus, into a driving psychological force.

Salzmann cited the case of masturbators who attributed all their physical disorders, all their illnesses, all their troubles to masturbation alone: in their minds masturbation had come to dominate everything.[35] The author of a letter explained how, after reading Tissot, he lost all joy in life. All hope seemed henceforth precluded; he was in despair. He dared not confide in anyone, not even his doctor.[36] In a case such as this, it seems evident that the origin of the problem lay less in masturbation than in Tissot himself: the torture came from Tissot.

Salzmann's work was particularly effective in sounding the alarm and in shaping German opinion. Like Tissot's book, it served as a reference work for all those who would continue to treat the problem of onanism. In the preface to the third edition, published in 1799, Salzmann declared proudly that he had reached his goal: "Germany has been awakened from its sleep; the German people have been warned of an evil which was gnawing at the roots of humanity. Thousands of young Germans, who ran the risk of ending their abject lives in a hospital, have been saved, and today devote their restored energies to the good of humanity, and above all to German humanity. Thousands of other children have been snatched from the jaws of the venomous serpent before he was able to bite."[37] Salzmann's fight against masturbation was conducted as a battle for the nation.

Germany was, in any event, poised for battle at the end of the eighteenth century. At this time, it was in Germany, and only in Germany, that the supreme and radical solution for the defeat of onanism in boys—infibulation—gained the approval of some. Infibulation was performed by pulling the foreskin as far as possible over the glans, piercing two holes in it and, once the scarring was healed, passing an iron ring through the holes. Campe and Vogel recommended this procedure for the most serious cases.[38] Campe expressed regret that no similarly radical method existed for the treatment of girls.

It should not be thought, however, that this unrelenting and nearly barbaric approach set the tone for all of Germany. The dominant tone, much more measured but nonetheless strict, can be seen in Kant's writings. Kant noted in his *Traité de pédagogie*, published in 1803:

> Nothing so weakens the mind as well as the body of man as does the type of pleasure one indulges on one's own body; it is entirely contrary to human nature. Yet nor should it be hidden [no more than any of the other aspects of sexuality of which Kant has just spoken] from the adolescent. It must be shown to him in all its horror [*in ihren ganzen Abscheuligkeit*], he must be told that he is rendering himself incapable of propagating the species, that he is ruining his physical force, that an early death awaits him, and that his mind is also being consumed, etc.
>
> The method of avoiding this sort of temptation is to remain constantly occupied and to not devote more time to bed and sleep than is necessary. By this means, one will be able to chase the evil thoughts from one's mind, for even when the object exists only in the imagination, it still consumes the vital force. When the desire is directed towards the opposite sex, it always encounters some resistance at least; but when it is directed towards the self, it can be satisfied at any moment. The physical effects are absolutely disastrous; but the consequences, from the moral perspective, are even more regrettable. One transgresses the limits of nature, and the desire rages without end, for it never finds any real satisfaction.

Kant raised the problem of the choice, for a young man, between masturbation and a "liaison with a person of the opposite sex." "If a choice must be made between the two, the latter is assuredly the better."[39]

It hardly needs saying that Kant's name carried particular weight; it shows that Tissot commanded recognition even upon the loftiest philosophical heights.

We've just glimpsed Tissot's success, which could be termed a triumph, through texts and testimony. Yet what is still missing, albeit essential, is an explanation of the phenomenon. Why did Tissot triumph?

No body of authority whatsoever, it must be noted from the outset, contributed to it. The civil authorities, the academies, the Church—nothing that could be said to represent authority played the slightest role in the process. The Church in particular, although it did condemn the sin that preoccupied Tissot, remained uninvolved in the popularization of his ideas. The movement, moreover, had not used religion, as it could have, to influence the public. The reference to Onan's crime was not what terrified. If religion entered the picture at all, it was primarily in the form of a polemic between Protestants and Catholics. Salzmann denounced monasteries and toilets with the same virulence. The chastity regulations, he declared, combined with the idleness of monastic life have turned cloisters into dens of iniquity whose horrors can only inspire disgust. According to Salzmann, monasteries, supposedly places of education, were instead one of the main sources of youthful corruption.[40]

To return to our initial remark: Tissot's views spread—among physicians, educators, and the general public—spontaneously, without any institutional mechanism of support. Society was receptive at this time. It is tempting to think that an explanation might thus eventually be found within society itself; within its expectations, even if unconscious; and within the reactions of different social classes.

Any discussion of social classes leads almost inevitably to finger-pointing at the bourgeoisie, an eminently useful class for this type of explanation. Some scholars think they've found the key in what could be viewed as an essentially bourgeois reaction. They paint a picture of a bourgeoisie anxious on the one hand to confirm its specificity and its superiority through strict moral codes, and on the other hand to protect its health—and especially genetic—capital, just as it protected its capital in the stricter sense.

"In the fervor for Tissot," write Aron and Kempf, "the physicians address the bourgeoisie, their brothers, whose rise they sense, whose authentic power they define, well before the latter is legally founded: it is a power that, beyond the possession of riches and the exercise of government, is expressed through symbols. Faced with a dissolute nobility, what could be more edifying than purity, more exalting than dissuasion from libertinism?"[41]

Or here again:

The repression of deviant sexuality (thus particularly of masturbation) . . . has a very precise goal: to legitimize the bourgeoisie. At the beginning, as the bourgeoisie takes over the reins of power, it acknowledges only political and economic legitimacy. Yet it has yet to have any symbolic power. On the contrary, it is haunted by the aristocratic models of birth and honor. . . . Its own honor will reside in morals, in virtue. Since the nobility, whose place it wants to take, had been debauched—read Sade—the bourgeoisie will be prudish. Since the nobility had been spendthrift, the bourgeoisie will be thrifty.[42]

Thrift is the second element.

The bourgeoisie knows that its prosperity comes from savings, from industrious accumulation; it hates all forms of waste, of loss of energy. Sexuality is something that threatens, at every moment, to elude the wise ordering of the genetic instinct, and descend into frenzies of waste. That is what frightens the bourgeoisie. . . . Its obsession with onanism and its "disastrous consequences" surely has its origins here, for it is as scandalous to spill one's sperm as it is to throw money from the window.[43]

Philippe Lejeune writes:

The crusade against masturbation targets, in fact, sexuality as a whole: it is supported by a theory of "sexual excess," of exaggerated *expenditure* which leads to weakness, exhaustion, and death. These medical concepts become meaningful when translated into economic language. A free and uncontrolled activity, governed by pleasure, is incompatible with an economy based on savings, self-control and forethought. This fear of the expenditure and the exhaustion of the life-force becomes the phantasm of Balzac's *Peau de Chagrin;* it is the foundation of bourgeois ethics up until the beginning of the 20th century.[44]

Jos Van Ussel, the finest specialist in the study of the anti-masturbatory battle of the eighteenth century, also sees it as a bourgeois phenomenon: "The battle against autosatisfaction may be considered as an attempt to get the individual's house in order, all in the service of productivity."[45]

These views are not lacking in appeal or intellectual panache. Yet can they stand up to criticism—even if that criticism, compared to their brilliance, might appear just a bit flat?

We have three comments, which are limited to the problem of masturbation (for the studies of Aron and Kempf or Lejeune, as we've seen, sometimes deal with a more broadly defined realm of sexuality).

1. On the question of the repression of sexuality, no class-based attitude is apparent anywhere in the texts, not even if the reading is forced in that direction. It is society as a whole—or more accurately, at the beginning, the upper strata of society—that seems to be swept up in the movement, and the search for a tone that could be qualified as "bourgeois" is futile. No one would think of referring to the medical battle against masturbation as "bourgeois medicine." It is unclear why the ethics linked to this medicine would have been bourgeois in nature.

2. Not everything, however, is in the texts. Might it not be plausible that the bourgeoisie had subtly created a mindset? Supposing that this had been the case—and we are in the realm of pure hypothesis here—it is still unclear how in this way the bourgeoisie might have lent moral weight to its public image or asserted its own particular form of "honor." The peculiarity of masturbation, like that of its repression, is that it occurs in secret. Given this, the bourgeoisie could hardly flaunt anything at all in this realm. A public image is, in essence, the product of display. Moreover, we need to take the other side of the coin into consideration. In order to save a wretched young man from masturbation, the authoritative sources—we've already heard Rousseau and Kant on this point—allow him to have a liaison, or even to frequent brothels. From the publicity angle, the bourgeoisie runs a

serious risk of tarnishing its public image. It runs the risk of playing a losing game.

3. The notion that throwing away sperm is as scandalous as
throwing away money is viable only if one is convinced from the
outset that the loss of sperm does clearly have "disastrous consequences." Above all, it means that one has been convinced by Tissot or his followers. The fact that they were convincing remains to
be explained.

The nobility—of both sexes—along with the wealthy bourgeoisie made up the bulk of Tissot's clients in Lausanne. The
treatments they sought were generally for things quite other than
masturbation. The clients, if we can call them so, for *L'Onanisme*
seem to have been recruited in the same way; no class-based logic
was apparent there.

Yet if Tissot's success cannot be attributed to a certain social
logic, could it be attributed to developments in medical thought,
developments that would have supported Tissot's ideas?

There is, however, on this point no medical coherence to be
found. What is evident, on the contrary, is a remarkable incoherence.

Tissot sounded the alarm on the loss of semen, which he declared was the loss of a particularly precious "humor." At the moment he sounded the alarm, one of the principal medical practices
was the merry pumping of another bodily humor, undoubtedly
less precious than semen, but indispensable nonetheless—blood.
On the topic of "humors," we find ourselves right in the middle of
a paradox. That paradox merits a closer examination.

To better understand it, we need to go back to Tissot himself
and his *Avis au peuple sur sa santé*. In the case of "inflammation
of the chest" or "pneumonia," what is to be done? "The principal remedy," according to Tissot, "is bloodletting." "Twelve
ounces of blood are to be drawn at one sitting, and even four-
teen or fifteen if the patient is young and robust." In the case of
pleurisy, "one of the most frequent and most deadly" illnesses,
the patient must also be bled. "The first bleeding, especially if it
is considerable, almost always reduces the pain and often dissi-

pates it entirely. . . . When the pain fails to diminish, or only diminishes slightly . . . the bleeding is to be repeated." Among the colics, the "inflammatory colic" is the "most violent and most dangerous type." The only method of cure is to let a great quantity of blood from the arm. . . . Often it must be repeated two hours later." Bleeding is necessary in general "when there is inflammation." It is also necessary "when the body has experienced or is going to experience some occurrence that is likely to shortly result in inflammation or some other accident, if the vessels were not relaxed by the bleeding. It is for this reason that bleeding is performed following wounds and contusions, in the case of a pregnant woman with a violent cough, and as a precautionary measure in other instances."[46]

On the topic of bloodletting, Tissot had nothing original to contribute. He was simply a man of his times. Bloodletting as a therapeutic—and also preventative—measure was certainly an ancient practice, but it did not reach its peak until the seventeenth and particularly eighteenth centuries.[47] In his article *Saignée* in the *Encyclopédie*, Louis described it as "one of the greatest and most rapid methods of cure known to medicine."[48] "There are few remedies," he continues, "so widely used."[49] It is valued as a preventive measure as well. "There is not a more excellent, instantaneous, and efficacious remedy for removing various diseases, both of the acute and chronical kind, than venesection, prudently and cautiously used," wrote James's *Medicinal Dictionary*.[50] On the topic of bloodletting, medical theory was extraordinarily refined and detailed. It distinguished among bleeding for the purposes of "evacuation," "revulsion," and "derivation." It specified the part of the body and the optimal time and conditions under which the bleeding was to be performed.

Bleeding was an almost mechanical gesture in the eighteenth century. "The majority of those who practice medicine," wrote Louis, "would consider themselves to be flouting the most respectable laws, if they refrained from opening the vein, when called to the aid of a patient with a fever."[51]

This does not mean that there were no differences among physicians. There were, but they were mainly a question of degree. There were relentless bleeders, others who set limits, and still others who displayed more moderation. Louis cited cases that seemed excessive to him: "One cannot but be shocked at the case of a 76-year-old man who, broken and weakened by physical and mental labors as much as by a long and pious abstinence, having been subject to dizzy spells—a result, it seems to us, of his weakness— was bled four times during a one-month illness and notably four hours prior to his death."[52] But James held: "Venesection is not only often useful to old persons; but, also, powerfully contributes to longevity, or the protraction of their lives. . . . And that venesection is not unfriendly to old-age, is sufficiently obvious from this, that almost all the Swiss, even when eighty or ninety years of age, use venesection every year."[53] Tissot, it should be noted, was more of a moderate. He enumerated numerous cases in which bleeding was counterindicated, and he was against repeated bleedings: "Repeated bleedings lead to weakening, enervation, aging, a diminution of circulatory force, . . . and by destroying digestion, eventually lead to dropsy."[54]

Beginning with the early nineteenth century, leeches would take up where bleeding let off.[55] Broussais, with his imperious— and absurd—theory of "irritation," would cover France with leeches.[56] For a malady such as gastroenteritis, he applied as may as 100, and sometimes even 200 leeches. He and his disciples would spill literally torrents of blood. The phenomenon, of course, was European. An English physician wrote in 1836: "Generally speaking . . . as long as bloodletting is required, it can be borne; and as long as it can be borne, it is required."[57]

A British writer more recently made the humorous commentary: "doctors are the people who told Victorian children that masturbation would cause their brain to leak away, and who tried to save Byron's life by applying huge quantities of leeches to his forehead."[58]

That was the paradox of Tissot's time, one that he, in a sense, incarnates: for the sake of health, one essential "humor" was abundantly let while, and still for the sake of health, the wasting of another "humor" was considered an irremediable harm. Even if the illogicality of the notion did not apparently do him any harm (for it goes without saying that the "scientific" explanations differed in the cases of blood and sperm), one could hardly suggest that Tissot was helped by medical logic.

What then, did help him? Doubtless the psychological preparation due to the English *Onania* and the echoes it provoked were significant. Beyond that, however, the only properly social factor that could be singled out and that could have served Tissot is, it seems to me, a certain climate of rationalism and an increasing interest, within cultured circles, in medical problems. There was a need for rational explanations of the origins of numerous and still-mysterious illnesses. Tissot's demonstration of the harmful effects of masturbation seemed to provide answers to many questions: he was applauded.

This might appear simplistic and it is, in fact, quite simplistic. Yet given the society of Tissot's day and its receptivity, it is the only plausible factor that can be singled out. Tissot, at least in this respect, satisfied expectations. Thanks to him, many things that were obscure become clear: masturbation furnished the explanation. In September 1800, Heinrich von Kleist visited a Würtzburg hospital where he observed a case of horrendous insanity; an 18-year-old adolescent who had fallen into a state of total physical and moral decrepitude, and who was even too weak to speak. Understanding such a case required no great mental effort, for the explanation was simple: the insanity was brought about by the "unnatural vice"—*durch eines unnatürliches Laster.*[59] In a case such as this, and in a host of others, Tissot offered an easy key.

The fact that his contemporaries grabbed onto the key is doubtless, up to a certain point, a phenomenon of a societal nature. But the essential, one gets the feeling, lay not in the receptivity of Tissot's audience. It lay in his own talent, in his ability to persuade. His great asset, his strength, as we've already shown, was the combination of a moving, dramatic presentation of the problem and an analysis that had the look of serious science. This was a learned man—and a well-known, even famous one at that—who knew how to impress his readers with his scientific arsenal and how to move their hearts. In this case, the man, the individual played the significant role.

Once public attention had been drawn to masturbation and its consequences (and let us not forget, attention had already been drawn by the English *Onania*), Tissot would benefit from a snowball effect.

The snowball effect was created by other doctors who, inspired by his work, would soon add their "observations" and their cases to his, broadening and supporting his notions. As early as 1768, in the *Journal de Médecine, Chirurgie, Pharmacie, etc.,* Dr. Le Nicolais du Saulsay, physician in the general hospital in Fougères, published a *Tableau d'onanisme* in which he noted several horrifying cases.[60] In his *Tableau des variétés de la vie humaine,* in 1786, Dr. Daignan, one of Tissot's disciples, declared that solitary pleasures were "the most subtle and destructive poison of the human species and a source of "irreparable disorders." He presented no less than eight detailed "observations" of masturbators.[61] Two of the masturbators died following horrible suffering, one "in a state of marasmus at the age of twenty-seven," the other "imbecile and emaciated." In the last four cases, the malady had proven incurable: a young 19-year-old "remains weak and invalid," another had contracted a "hypochondriacal ailment which deprives him of the pleasures of life," a third had fallen into a state of "imbecility," the fourth had become "deformed and obliged to spend three quarters of his life in bed, in a wheelchair or a sedan-chair." These cases served as impressive new "proof" added to the already existing evidence.

Another aspect of the snowball effect, which increased the public fascination with Tissot's views, came from the sequence of prohibition-disobedience-punishment. From the very moment that, in Tissot's wake, masturbation began to be pursued and repressed, this very repression would, in certain cases, function as an incitement to taste the forbidden fruit, resulting in an even harsher repression. Casanova commented on this in a passage on Germany (where, as we've seen, on the question of masturbation, pedagogical discipline reached particular heights of refinement) in his *Memoirs*. "Communities of boys in Germany, where the directors make a point of prohibiting masturbation," he wrote, "are where masturbation reigns." The young student reacts. "The prohibition excites him." Even if he does not experience the physical need for the act, "he does it for the pleasure of disobeying, a natural human pleasure since the time of Adam and Eve, and one that is embraced at every opportunity."[62] We will certainly not take Casanova as an infallible authority on the subject, yet, as we listen to the German pedagogues bemoaning the empire of the evil they claim to witness, his observations, at least in part, are not unworthy of attention.[63]

It would not be exaggerating to say that Tissot left his mark on the eighteenth century. The most remarkable fact, however—one that was glimpsed in our first chapter and to which we will now return—was that Tissot influenced not only his own day but an entire epoch in Western civilization.

Chapter Seven

An Obsession of the Western World

In our first chapter we mentioned the great anti-masturbatory fear in France and French-speaking Europe in the nineteenth century. Our analysis focused on the period from approximately 1815 to 1875.

Dr. Clément's 1875 introduction to a new edition of Tissot's *Onanisme* can help us recapture the ambiance of the time:

Today, in the midst of our modern societies, there exists a widespread and universal vice which penetrates the whole of society with a perpetual source of corruption and destruction.

The tragic habit of onanism impoverishes and extenuates the organism. Source of precocious destruction, onanism is a slow and sure poison which, before destroying life, strips it by degrees of all that activates it, and fatally drags its victim to degradation and death.

Like the individual organism, all of society is subject to its debilitating effects. It is an intrinsic evil which leads to the destruction not only of the individual, but of the species as well, by rendering the seeds of life improlific. There is no calamity on earth

which should be of so much concern to men, no matter what their
rank in society.[1]

This text, obviously at the leading edge of the discussion, came
from France. Yet the horror of masturbation—a horror that was
both medical and moral—represented a phenomenon that, in the
nineteenth century, spread throughout European society and even
across the ocean. In its company, we can take a trip that goes from
Russia and the Scandinavian countries to the United States.

In Russia, we find Tolstoy's "The Kreutzer Sonata," whose hero
tells the story of how, in high school, at the age of sixteen and despite his lack of experience with women, he had already ceased to
be "an innocent young boy." "My solitary moments were impure. I
was obsessed, just as are ninety-nine percent of our young boys. I
was horrified, I suffered, I prayed . . . I lost my way all alone." Then
a friend took him to prostitutes. Was that wrong? No one, he emphasized, had told him it was. It was, for him, a striking observation: "Among grownups, those whose opinions inspired respect in
me, none had told me it was wrong. On the contrary, I had often
heard men I admired say it was good. I heard that my struggles and
my suffering would subside afterwards; I heard it and I read it; I
heard grownups say that it was good for the health."[2]

This is a valuable testimony, for it is revealing of a milieu that
was simultaneously that of the novel's hero—who belonged to
the world of landowners—and of Tolstoy himself. Young people
were warned of the dangers of the solitary vice, and when they
succumbed to temptation, they were afraid and trembled. Yet
their amorous escapades were regarded with an indulgent eye.
They were even considered useful, for they could serve to divert
young people from dangerous habits. Even doctors themselves,
the hero of the novel added, said "that it is necessary for the sake
of health."[3]

After Russia we move to Sweden, where we find Strindberg
and his short story "The Reward of Virtue," published in 1884 in
the collection *Getting Married*.

Theodore, whose story is the subject of the tale, is a schoolboy in Stockholm enrolled in a religion course taught by a young Lutheran curate. Here he is in the company of children from the lower classes:

> One evening they were given their instruction in the chancel of the church, for the curate employed every means in his power to produce an effect on their hardened young minds. It was well on in January. Two gas-jets in the chancel shed a faint light which distorted the proportions of the marble statues of the altar-piece in a horrifying way.... The curate had been giving an exposition of the sixth commandment. He had been talking about adultery, both in marriage and outside it. He had not been able to explain exactly how adultery was practised by married couples, even though he himself was married, but he knew all about it outside matrimony. Then he turned to the subject of self-abuse. A kind of sigh came from the gathering of young boys when he uttered the words and, with pale cheeks and hollow eyes, they stared at him as if they had seen a ghost. So long as he talked about the torments of hell they remained comparatively calm, but when he took up a book and read them the story of a young man who had died in the arms of God at twenty-five, with his spinal-cord rotted away, they shrank down in their pews and felt the floor rock beneath them. Finally he told them about a boy who had been shut up in a madhouse when he was twelve, and had died at fourteen, believing in his Redeemer. They felt as if they were looking at a hundred corpses, washed clean and hung up on iron bars. And the remedy for this evil? There was but one, Jesus' sacred wounds. He gave them no detailed instructions on how these could be used to cure precocious puberty. But he did tell them to refrain from dancing, from visiting the theatre, from spending their time at recreation halls and, above all, from having anything to do with women.... [4]

Theodore, thus informed, would begin a furious battle against temptation. He would succeed in vanquishing it. He would be pure. But this purity, as the years went on, would end up costing him his health: that was "the reward of virtue."

We've already seen the rather sensational debut of the antimasturbatory movement in Germany. At the turn of the century, we encounter the famed Christophe-Guillaume Hufeland, professor at the University of Iena, then at the University of Berlin, physician to Wieland, Herder, Goethe, Schiller and the king of Prussia. In his *Macrobiotique,* or *L'Art de prolonger la vie humaine,* an immensely successful work that would remain popular throughout much of the nineteenth century,[5] Hufeland denounced all that was likely to shorten life. At the top of his list were amorous excesses (which brought about "the dissipation of the fluid in which the primitive life spark is contained"), and heading them, masturbation. Because the latter was unnatural and because of nature's tendency to wreak terrible vengeance upon those who offend her, the consequences of masturbation were all the more dire. "How awful is the seal with which nature stamps those who outrage her in this way! It is a dying rose, a dried out tree in bloom, a walking cadaver. This abominable crime suffocates all principles of fire and of life, leaving nothing but weakness, inaction, mortal pallor, a wasting of the body and a degradation of the soul."[6] It is not hard to guess that this was the prelude to the lengthy classical description of all the misfortunes and maladies that await the masturbator.

On the subject of prevention, Hufeland combined the recommendations of the physicians and pedagogical specialists who preceded him: diet, clothing, mattresses, bed linens appropriate for children, the careful observation necessary to ensure that they would be kept away from anything that might enflame their imagination, and above all exercise, lots of exercise, which would produce a healthy fatigue (a child was not to be put to bed until he was "well tired"). Having taken these multiple precautions, one might hope to prevent an evil that was "one of the most sure and most horrifying ways to shorten life and to fill that life with bitterness."[7]

Nineteenth-century Germany would witness a series of equally vigorous denunciations of masturbation written by doctors. They would be joined by numerous popular manuals which, with tragic overtones, sounded the alarm again and again. In the second half of the nineteenth century, a pamphlet by Dr. Retau on the "preservation of the self," in which onanism was of major concern, would see no fewer than 80 successive editions, with a total publication of more than 300,000 copies.[8]

Moving on to England and the texts of British physicians we find an equally scathing condemnation of masturbation. The denunciations of a Dr. Ryan, who believed masturbation "leads to the most formidable and incurable disorders,"[9] or a Dr. Acton, who believed that the obstinate masturbator risked sinking into imbecility or precocious senility,[10] were no less virulent than those of their continental colleagues. Yet one of the characteristics of Victorian England, it must be remembered, was a modesty that prevented certain turpitudes from being discussed openly. Thus, the work that is undoubtedly the most representative of its period is a novel in which masturbation is never named, although it is present, and present in a terrifying way. *Eric, or Little by Little,* by Frederic William Farrar, is the story of a young, handsome, and vigorous boy—Eric—who, upon being sent to school, will succumb "little by little" to sin. At the beginning, little misdeeds, apparently insignificant, lead to others. The sins become more and more serious, until we get to the one that is the worst of all, and which Farrar simply refers to as "it." If Eric succumbs to "it," it is not for lack of solemn warnings from his schoolmasters. The headmaster preaches against "it" in an awful sermon on Kibroth-Hathaavah—the "graves of lust" that are the burial place for the children of Israel who were struck down as punishment for their craving (Numbers 11, 33–35):

> Kibroth-Hathaavah! Many and many a young Englishman has perished there! Many and many a happy English boy, the jewel of his mother's heart—brave and beautiful and strong—lies buried there. Very pale their shadows rise before us—the shadows of our young brothers who have sinned and suffered. From the sea and the sod, from foreign graves and English churchyards, they start up and throng around us in the paleness of their fall. May every schoolboy who reads this page be warned by the waving of their wasted hands, from that burning marle of passion where they

found nothing but shame and ruin, polluted affections, and an early grave.

Masturbation meant death. Poor Eric would not escape it. Despite his repentance, he would come to know the destiny of those who were guilty of doing "it."[11]

When he wrote these lines in 1858, Farrar was a schoolmaster at Harrow. He was, moreover, quite typical. He would later become headmaster of a large school, then, within the Anglican Church, archdeacon at Westminster and dean of Canterbury.[12] At his death in 1903, *Eric, or Little by Little*, which had never ceased being read and admired, was in its thirty-sixth edition. It had taught a lesson to several generations of English children.

Crossing the Atlantic to the United States, we encounter the anti-masturbatory obsession of the older Europe with perhaps even more pronounced and systematic features. The declarations of war against masturbation would reach heights of eloquence in nineteenth-century America.

"No words," we read in a work from 1870, "can describe the miseries it inflicts throughout your whole life down to death. . . . They follow and prey on you forever. . . . You may almost as well die outright as to thus pollute yourself."[13]

"The sin of self-pollution," said another author in 1888, "is one of the vilest, the basest, and the most degrading that a human being can commit. It is worse than beastly. Those who commit it place themselves far below the meanest brute that breathes. . . . A boy who is thus guilty, ought to be ashamed to look into the eyes of an honest dog."[14]

Yet far more significant than these impassioned texts was the attitude of the medical profession: in the fight against masturbation, the profession would adopt, in the nineteenth century, an intransigent position.[15]

The greatest names of American medicine would rub shoulders in this respect with the most humble practitioners. Abraham Jacobi, the father of pediatrics in the United States, the first to hold a chair in diseases of children, tracked down cases of masturbation in children as young as three.[16]

Tissot had fully conquered the United States, just as he had conquered Europe. The United States provides, in fact, some of the most extraordinary texts.

In 1812, Benjamin Rush, who was considered the greatest American physician of his day, listed the multiple consequences of onanism in his *Medical Inquiries:* "seminal weakness, impotence, dysury, tabes dorsalis, pulmonary consumption, dyspepsia, dimness of sight, vertigo, epilepsy, hypochondriasis, loss of memory, manalgia, fatuity, and death."[17]

We reach a peak, however, with the fire and brimstone of Fowler, a popular lecturer who ran about the United States, enflaming audiences with his impassioned speeches. This "Professor" O. S. Fowler (an apparently unearned title he yet managed to wear with impunity) left some of his diatribes to posterity in his 1875 book: *Creative and Sexual Science, or Manhood, Womanhood and their Mutual Interrelations . . . as Taught by Phrenology and Physiology* (for not only did Fowler claim to have expertise in physiology, he was a confirmed phrenologist). The pages on "self-pollution," "the worst of sexual vices," are particularly eloquent.

Self-pollution is, Fowler declared, "man's sin of sins, and vice of vices." It

> has caused incomparably more sexual dilapidation, paralysis, and disease, as well as demoralization, than all the other sexual depravities combined. Neither Christendom nor heathendom suffers any evil at all to compare with this. . . . Pile all other evils together—drunkenness upon all cheateries, swindlings, robberies, and murders; and tobacco upon both, for it is the greater scourge; and all sickness, diseases and pestilence upon all; and war as the cap sheaf of them all—and all combined cause not a tithe as much human deterioration and misery as does this secret sin.

One can almost hear Fowler inveighing from the pulpit, like the great American Evangelists—but claiming to have a "scientific warrant" for his assertions.[18]

The Kellogg brothers provide an odd example of the indirect consequences of the attention paid to masturbation in the United States. John and Will Kellogg, basically men of piety and morals, set out to design diets that would avoid excitation. The result was cornflakes—and fortune.

The image that we've just painted, admittedly with a few rather impressionistic brushstrokes, is visibly coherent. This does not, however, rule out shifts in emphasis from one school of thought to another.

In the Anglo-Saxon countries, far more than elsewhere, much emphasis was placed on masturbatory insanity, on mental illness due to masturbation.[19] Ellis, a well-known psychiatrist, held that "by far the most frequent cause of fatuity is debility of the brain and nervous system . . . in consequence of the pernicious habit of masturbation."[20] Henry Maudsley, whose work was taken as authoritative, gave a detailed description of masturbatory insanity in 1868. It is, he said, "a miserable picture of human degradation."[21] We find the same claims in the United States. Continental specialists, however, were more reserved. In Germany, Griesinger admitted that "onanism is often a cause of insanity, as it is of all types of physical and moral degradation," but considered that, in more than one instance, masturbation constituted not the cause but rather a symptom of mental illness.[22] Accents, we repeat, shifted from country to country. The overall unity remains striking nonetheless.

In any event, on the question of the relation between masturbation and illness, no medical school offered a new and valid scientific explanation. Medical science, in the nineteenth century, continued to live off of its eighteenth-century inheritance. Its contribution was limited to the addition of new examples, to a host of new "cases."

Even if the vocabulary had changed, Tissot remained, from one generation to the next, the great inspiration. His arguments were repeated. In 1801, it was Tissot who served as a model when a physician wanted to show why "coition is far less harmful than masturbation," explaining that "in coition, the loss is compensated by a true pleasure which recreates the soul and soothes the body by facilitating its functions and also by the absorption of an invisible dew which escapes abundantly from the pores of the beloved object."[23] A century later in 1902, this time in different packaging—the dew has disappeared—we still get a serving of Tissot from another doctor when he writes, in his comparison of coition and masturbation:

> A fact which is worth taking into account is that, during normal coition, a magnetic compensation occurs between the man and the woman. This magnetic contact, which culminates, at the height of the voluptuous sensation, in a shock of the entire body similar to that of an electric discharge, increases the vital force of the two partners in the sexual act. The conditions are quite different in the case of the solitary onanist who, lacking the magnetic compensation afforded by a sexual partner, weakens his vital force with each repetition of the act.[24]

From 1801 to 1902, we've simply gone from "dew" to magnetism.

In his vision of treatable disorders, the nineteenth-century physician—at least throughout a large part of the century—had no doubt about masturbation's damaging effects. Why should he have? An abundant medical literature was there to confirm them. Multiple "cases" were known, proving them. The cause of an ailment or state of ill health was easy to pinpoint.

Take for example the procedure of Dr. Sabatier, who was one of the great names in French surgery at the beginning of the nineteenth century: "I have seen a fair number of young people of both sexes in whom intellectual faculties seemed to be completely lacking. When this sort of self-complacency is combined with pallor and overall thinness, and when the subjects who display these symptoms are prone to sleep and idleness, I have not hesitated to conclude that these symptoms are the result of onanism."[25]

Or take the logic of a British psychiatrist in 1861:

> When insanity is suspected in young men under twenty-five years of age, particularly those who have been carefully brought up . . .

and have lived apparently in the most exemplary and becoming manner . . . and if the symptoms are chiefly of a negative character . . . such as secluding themselves from society, avoiding conversation; if they are at the same time pale and out of health, generally morose and apathetic, occasionally impulsive, violent, and irritable; if they . . . have a . . . dull expression, damp, clammy hand, . . . there is every reason to fear that these symptoms are due to habits of a most pernicious nature.[26]

How could they fail to be attached to an item in the medical arsenal that appeared to produce such diagnoses, when medicine was still largely incapable of any other sure and convincing explanation of the origin of certain ailments?

Tissot had been taken for a man of science because physiology was still in its infancy in his day. His influence continued because medicine was unable, in numerous cases, to come up with any better-founded diagnoses to replace those that derived from his works.

On the matter of physicians, let us add a last element, doubtless subtle, but perhaps not without importance. When their diagnoses privileged, as they unquestionably did, the role of masturbation, there was perhaps another element—perhaps even an unconscious one—at play, at least for some. It was that they found themselves in those cases relieved of their obligation to heal. Masturbation was a form of suicide; no one could require that a physician save a person who was committing an act of suicide.[27] In a subtle fashion, this too may have had a role.

Up until now, we have spent much time on the physicians themselves. Children and young people, however, deserve attention as well. For them, the anti-masturbatory obsession represented, above all, suffering, and sometimes a great deal of suffering at that. On the topic of suffering, what stands out are the operations and the instruments that were inflicted upon the young. A surgical operation was the supreme weapon against inveterate masturbation, in the case of girls as well as of boys. To the modern sensibility, it often appears—incorrectly—as if surgeons approached the topic with a certain sadism.

Take, for example, a debate that took place on January 13, 1864 in the Surgical Society in Paris. Broca—the great Broca—introduced it while sharing one of his own recent experiences. "I recently had the opportunity," he said, "to perform an operation that was rather unusual, particularly in light of the therapeutic indication. . . . It was a case of nymphomania for which I performed an infibulation.

My patient was a little five year-old girl, quite intelligent before her deplorable habit began; she had been masturbating repeatedly for some time and thwarted all attempts to curb her habit. Neither the constant surveillance of her mother, nor the use of a chastity belt fabricated by M. Charrière had the slightest effect. We know, in any event, that this device is much more effective in the case of little boys, by imprisoning their penis in a metal case, than it is for girls. Our little girl, thin, wasted and extremely flexible, managed to insert her toe between the belt's metal plate and her soft parts, and thus succeeded in masturbating.

Her memory, her intellect were weakening; momentary mental blanks were becoming increasingly frequent. My colleague M. Moreau, of the Salpêtrière hospital, had been consulted and had considered amputation of the clitoris. Questioned in turn, I indicated that I found the section of the clitoral nerves, a procedure employed by some surgeons, to be of doubtful efficacy, leaving the door open to recidivism; that the amputation of the clitoris was the destruction, the irreparable ruin of the organ of pleasure and an excessive thing in the case of a young girl whom one is seeking to cure, and I thus came to the idea which I then put into practice.

I operated on the child on December 31 . . . I joined the top two superior or anterior thirds of the major labia at their thickest point with the aid of a metal suture, leaving in the inferior section an orifice barely large enough to accommodate the small finger, to permit the flow of urine and later, of menstrual blood. Today the union is perfect, and the clitoris is placed out of all reach underneath a thick cushion of soft parts.

I propose to continue the use of all the other mechanisms; active surveillance, chastity belt, etc., considering infibulation only as an important adjuvant.

Dr. Morel-Lavallée remained unconvinced. He said: "I fear the operation will not produce the desired result. The child will perform a mediate masturbation through the covering of the joined major labia."

From Dr. Deguise:

I must admit I share the concerns of M. Morel. In one way or another, the child will continue her vicious behavior. . . . At such an advanced stage, the vice is incurable.

I did, however, once succeed in curing a young boy of masturbation and I ask M. Broca why he did not try the method which I successfully used, cauterization. For an entire year, with a persistency that was almost cruel, and despite the pleas of the young patient, I maintained a constant irritation in the urethra by means of repeated cauterizations, that irritation being sufficiently painful to render any touch impossible. Today the young boy is a young man who thanks me for my tenacity.

Dr. Richet:

It seems to be generally believed that it is in the external genitalia and more precisely in the clitoris that the masturbatory impulse is located. Along with M. Stolz and other observers, I believe that these excitations can be produced along the entire length of the genital organs. A fact which I observed in my practice appears to confirm this opinion.

A 27-year-old girl from a good family, came to the Saint-Louis hospital in order to be delivered, by operation, of the irresistible impulse to masturbate repeatedly. Her general health had been severely compromised and the patient was extremely thin. I performed a total amputation of the clitoris. . . . For several months, it seemed that a full cure had been effected. . . . The patient left the hospital and returned home.

A year later, she asked to be admitted to my unit at the Pitié hospital. What had arisen were . . . very frequent excitations (that is the word the patient used) of the vagina and the neck of the womb, excitations which led her to fondle the neck of the uterus. During eight months, . . . all possible treatments of these excitations which, in the absence of the clitoris were now produced in the deep parts of the genital organs, failed. This failure seems to support the opinion that I expressed earlier.

And Dr. Guersant: "My attempts to cure masturbation have generally failed; however, I did manage to put an end to this baneful habit in three cases by performing a sort of incomplete operation on the phimosis [Guersant means he narrowed the opening of the prepuce], including the prolongation of the bandages for six to eight weeks, or, in the case of little girls, by resecting the preputial fold of the clitoris." It is easy to see that these operations had, above all, a moral effectiveness, by inspiring a salutary terror in the children.

The possible effectiveness of certain medications, like potassium bromide, was also discussed. Dr. Guérin commented: "All these medications can stop an erection or render it impossible, but none can cure the desire. Once, in the case of a patient from the city, I totally destroyed the clitoris without managing to extinguish the desire to masturbate."

Broca closed the debate with the response that, despite the criticisms of his operation, he "has not given up hope of success." He thought that the infibulation he had performed would produce results: "I cannot share the opinion of my colleagues who consider the barrier I established on top of the clitoris as ineffective. It is a covering more than one half a centimeter thick which perhaps, at rare intervals and in the absence of all surveillance, might allow some contact to occur, but which will thwart that incessant fondling which constitutes the real danger of masturbation."

Broca concluded:

I will not draw a parallel here between the amputation of the clitoris and infibulation. Infibulation is a palliative operation which preserves the future, while amputation of the clitoris represents a definitive and total abolition of sensual pleasure. Moreover, no method is successful in all cases, but each may be successful or at least partially successful, depending on the case and the indications;

thus I think that M. Richet rendered a true service to his patient by amputating her clitoris.[28]

There, spread before our eyes, is the range of surgical operations to which some had recourse: infibulation, which Broca performed on a little girl, but which is known to have been performed on boys (in Great Britain in 1876, Dr. Yellowlees declared that he performed it successfully and that he was struck by "the conscious-stricken way in which they [his patients] submitted to the operation upon their penises";[29] this operation can, he was still explaining in 1892, be performed by passing metal safety pins through the foreskin);[30] a variation on infibulation that consisted in narrowing the opening of the prepuce in order to prevent erection; ablation of the clitoris, the particularly radical method of clitoridectomy, a number of cases of which are known[31] (Yellowlees indicated in 1892 that the procedure had its partisans, but that in Great Britain, at least, it was generally deemed ineffectual and unsatisfactory[32]); cauterization of the urethra, certainly painful but, according to some, effective.[33]

Added to the operations were the instruments inflicted upon children. Some, aiming to eliminate nocturnal emissions as well as masturbation, were highly sophisticated. Dr. Milton recommended, in 1887, various types of rings armed with sharp points that were placed on the penis and caused sharp pain in the event of an erection. He also furnished the sketch of a ring connected to an electric alarm bell; the erection set off the alarm. This instrument was less painful than those with teeth or points, but its drawback, unfortunately, was its price: it cost five pounds sterling.[34]

Complicated instruments and various operations: all this paints a tragi-comic picture—comic when we forget about what those suffering children endured—that, however, should not obscure the underlying reality. Recourse to those sorts of procedures was quite rare, if only because of their cost. What formed the backdrop, in those nineteenth-century circles haunted by the specters of masturbation or nocturnal emissions, were procedures that were much more simple, elementary even, and also much less painful for the child. Dr. Acton in 1851 spoke of the "ordinary mode of muffling the hands, or applying a sort of strait-waistcoat."[35] "Ordinary mode": the expression is revealing. It obviously still remains to be seen to which social classes it applied, but at least we know, thanks to Acton, what, in Great Britain in any event, was the most frequent practice.

Pain was sometimes the lot of nineteenth-century children who were subjected to physical treatments. Yet, within the history of their suffering, that physical pain was comparatively minor when compared to the mental suffering inflicted upon them. Nineteenth-century children suffered, more than anything else, from the pain of mental anguish.

An excellent observation was made on this subject in France by Dr. Hallé in 1787:

> The timid man, when suffering and weak, is prone to exaggerate his ills in his mind; and if you offer an excessively terrifying portrait of an exhausted patient to one who is beginning to lose his forces, he will soon see himself as withered and on the verge of death. It has been seen more than once that M. Tissot's excellent work *L'Onanisme*, placed in the hands of young persons in that state, has thrown them into a state of profound melancholy which has finally taken them, by a hideous route, to the very precipice from which it had been hoped to lead them away.[36]

Hallé repeated his observation and his warning in 1812, in his commentary on a reedition of *L'Onanisme:*

> Among the useful effects produced by the publication of this study, there is one quite regrettable one, which has occurred more than once, and for which any reasonably experienced practitioner can provide several examples: it is the profound melancholy which develops in the soul of some young people following their reading; some of them, filled with self-loathing and believing themselves already destined for all the deplorable effects of the unfortunate vice to which they have succumbed, have even preferred to end

their days by their own hands, instead of continuing their progress, beset with remorse, towards an ignominious death.[37]

Anguish, for the young man, combined with shame. Anguish, for he believed himself condemned to the worst physical and moral decline. Let us give one of its victims a name: that of young Amiel. Amiel was a chaste young man who would not know a woman for the first time until the age of 39. As he neared the age of 20, however, his nocturnal emissions filled him with dread. Let us read his *Journal intime* for the years 1840 to1841. March 5, 1840: "I spent a miserable night: I had forgotten to wash my abdomen with vinegar, the bed's heat reacted upon my senses, and I had an emission . . . Terrified, I repeat to myself the doctor's warning: Each pollution is a knife thrust to the eyes!" October 9, 1840: "The deadly discharge has already had its effect on me. . . . May God protect me: my career is wrecked, I feel myself weaken, my spiritual reflections are cruelly blunted, my pride is gone as well." October 16, 1840: "Again last night, a deadly emission. To put an end to them, I resolve for six months (until Easter) to eat nothing in the evening except my soup, and raw or cooked fruits when I have them. That is the price of my health." October 23, 1840: "Curse it! Last night's tea caused me another of those deadly nights . . . I must double my precautions and above all take more exercise. What a tragedy if I become ill this winter. Besides the lost time, my health and perhaps my life could be at risk as well. Once in bed, I would be dead, since it is in bed that all my relapses occur. . . . I bought ice. I ate some, crushed, before I went to bed, to cool my rest." November 1, 1840: "Sight, spirits, memory, youthful energy, overall ability and zeal, that is what is gone, that is what my repeated emissions have taken from me." June 7, 1841: "My continual illness has rendered me effeminate, stupid, fearful, mistrustful, mysterious." June 12, 1841: "Nothing is more horrible than to see one's life fatally dissipated, several nights have cost me several years of life . . . I see that I am dying." June 13,

1841: "Above all, I must live, that is to say I must stop these losses; a single emission, according to Tissot, is equivalent to four ounces of blood. My vein is open; to cease trying, to let myself go, would be a suicide, for the end is certain."[38]

The young man experienced shame, self-hatred, and a sense of guilt, for he was convinced that his vice was dreadful and he often felt himself incapable, despite his own efforts, of ridding himself of it. Among the victims of guilt we can cite young Gladstone, a student in Oxford in 1831. Deeply religious, his nocturnal emissions filled him with a sense of his sinfulness: "As to general progress I would hope there is some against my besetting sins, except for one which returns upon me again and again like a flood. God help me for Christ's sake."[39]

Doubtless, the nineteenth century did, in certain instances, heed the type of warnings proffered by Hallé, but on the whole, the impression is—and how, alas, can we go beyond mere impression in this realm?—that it most often sought, faithful to Tissot's lessons, to frighten children deliberately. Dr. Debreyne explained in 1844 how masturbators were to be treated: "They must be threatened with dishonor, with infamy, with ignominy, with all the horrors of the most painful, the most degrading and the most shameful maladies, and finally with an early death to be followed by eternal punishment."[40] What must be used, according to Debreyne, was an "apparatus of terror." Dr. Descuret similarly recommended "warnings delivered in a severe tone": "the child's imagination will be struck by the fear of the most serious illnesses, of a painful operation, of death even, should he fail to renounce his deplorable penchant."[41] Dr. Devay, in his *Hygiene des familles,* emphasized as well the "feeling of terror" (the term was always the same) that "it is good to inspire in some cases." "We have sometimes seen," he wrote, "young subjects who have given up their sad habits after they have been given to understand that their parts would become gangrenous as a result of the fondling. This threat, which in the end is nothing but a fabrication, ordinarily makes the strongest and the most salutary of impressions on the mind."[42]

What is quite striking is that warnings and observations similar to those of Hallé are not to be found again in the works of either physicians or psychologists until the beginning of the twentieth century.

Auguste Forel, speaking moreover of adults and not of children, wrote in 1906:

> Certain onanists accuse themselves, moaning and profoundly distressed, of having ruined and destroyed their existence by their bad habit. They seem, at first glance, to be quite numerous. They wear themselves out from whining before the doctor and their acquaintances, they wring their arms in despair, and plead with everyone to come to their aid. They see themselves as miserable sinners whose life has been ruined ... They've read Dr. La'Mert's *Self-Preservation* or other sensational and quackish works designed to terrify ... These poor devils believe themselves lost, and have a truly pitiful air.[43]

Stekel, one of the best psychoanalysts of the Vienna school, observed somewhat later:

> Onanists bind themselves by a thousand oaths, by prayers and promises. They have decided not to relapse. This time is the last—and despite all the oaths and the promises, they always come back to their instinct. The moral uneasiness created by the failure automatically leads to severe depression. To this is added the effect of intimidating books and charitable advice freely dispensed by teachers, parents, and the family doctor. . . . These warnings have unfortunately had more ill effects than onanism itself. The inhibitions they create in the onanist produce a severe psychological conflict. . . . After the orgasm, the inhibitions are transformed into reproaches and cause that depression which, even in the eyes of the experienced practitioner, simulates neurasthenia.[44]

Another psychoanalyst from Vienna even declared in 1901 that he was convinced that "almost all suicide attempts during puberty are linked to the incapacity to overcome masturbation, to put an end to it by giving it an expiration date."[45] Much later, in the

United States, Kinsey noted that there were suicide attempts that were interpretable in this fashion.[46]

Between Hallé on the one hand and the authors of the beginning of the twentieth century on the other there was, on the subject of the anguish and moral suffering of the masturbators, a long period of silence, during which the subject received hardly any systematic treatment at all (of course, we do find an allusion from time to time). If it was of little concern that the child or the young man feared and was ashamed, and that he suffered from his fear and his shame, was it not quite simply that this shame and this fear were considered to be extremely useful for him? Psychologically, this was the dominant climate of the period. Here resided in the nineteenth century, far more than in the effect of the physical treatments, the real, the principal suffering for the child.

Yet there was still a third aspect of his tribulations that must be mentioned: they were the potentially devastating effects of suggestion and, in this case particularly, of autosuggestion.

Stekel wrote on this subject, with an obviously improper tendency to overgeneralize: "If the onanist believes he has done himself harm, if he has read a book on the harmful effects of onanism or if he has received flawed teaching from doctors or educators, the feeling of guilt will, after each masturbation, provoke the various symptoms that have been attributed to onanism." There could thus be a true harm that "results from anxious autosuggestive representations."[47]

There is no need to emphasize the power of autosuggestion in some cases. It can cure illnesses; it can also provoke disorders. There have been many reliable medical observations in this realm. We can use them to construct several highly plausible reinterpretations of past history. Autosuggestion doubtless provides one of the keys to understanding the great period of witchcraft. The bewitchings and spells of that time did, in all probability, have real victims: those who, through autosuggestion, came to suffer the ills to which they believed themselves condemned. There is a certain degree of kinship between witchcraft and the antimasturbatory obsession of the nineteenth century.[48] The unfortunate masturbator, knowing the ills to which his vice condemned him, yet often incapable of ridding himself of it, also seems to be a victim of autosuggestion.

To what extent was this a factor in the nineteenth century, what harm did it really cause? It is an enigma—among many others—that is now insoluble.

The entire history of masturbation is marked by similar enigmas; we have glimmers of knowledge, but we run into enormous areas of shadow that remain impenetrable and that will undoubtedly always remain so. Amiel trembled for his health, Gladstone for the salvation of his soul. But alongside them and all those who suffered, how many young people were there who masturbated joyously, without fears or scruples? We have no idea.

On the other hand, what we read are the indictments of masturbation, which educators are asked to share with young people. But in a nineteenth century often marked by Victorian modesty and sexual taboos, how many families might not have preferred to keep a chaste silence on the subject in the upbringing of their children?

Those are only some of our questions. To what social classes do our observations apply? To what social strata did the phenomena we've described penetrate? We asked these troublesome questions earlier, at the end of our first chapter. All we can do now is repeat them, and then listen to the silence that is their only answer.

We can, however, quote a brief text, which has remained unnoticed until now, and which breaks this silence. In 1821, a young physician from a little town in the Flemish province of Limbourg submitted his doctoral thesis in medicine to the University of Liege. The subject of Georges Claes's thesis was *De Onania* and its treatment was entirely classical, for Claes was a faithful follower of Tissot. Claes made a distinction between large cities, where the vice was common (*per magnas urbes quasi commune quoddam vitium grassatur*), and the countryside, where it was practically unknown (*inter ruris incolas propemodum ignota est onania*).

Claes despaired of the situation in the cities, where the illegitimate practice now inspires hardly any shame at all, he wrote.[49] The interpretation of Claes's distinction, however, is less than certain: it could mean that masturbation was a phenomenon to which urban dwellers devoted much attention, while it remained of little concern to those in rural areas.

Another, far more recent, remark is found in the text of a Belgian writer, René Hénoumont, who was born in 1922. "I recall," he wrote, "that in my Ardennes countryside, group masturbation was a kind of exercise in which one had to prove one's virility." These were "harmless contests full of merry life." Hénoumont added: "The 'great fear' seems to me to have been a phenomenon of the cities."[50]

In the realm of the history of ideas and mentalities, more than in any other field of history, one must become resigned to great gaps in knowledge.

Chapter Eight

The Faith Starts to be Shaken

Up until the last half of the nineteenth century, the notion of masturbation as a destroyer reigned practically unchallenged. Authors differed, of course, in their judgment of masturbation's harmful effects. Yet those differences were only differences in emphasis; on the notion of the evil, on the harm caused by masturbation, the authors were unanimous. There was not a heretic to be found.

From time to time, a particular passage seemed to suggest that a heretic might actually have been just around the corner. Yet we are quickly brought back onto the straight and narrow of popular belief. In 1826, in a medical dictionary, we find Dr. Georget's entry *Onanisme:* "Most of the authors who have written on onanism, and Tissot in particular, have generally exaggerated its unfortunate effects, by presenting the most serious disorders, which are only observed in the smallest minority of cases, as its ordinary effects." Here we have a promising start. Yet the rest of the passage takes us back into the realm of common belief. The danger of such exaggerations, according to Georget, is that masturbators, failing to experience from the start the terrible disorders of which they've been warned, are reassured and "continue their destructive practice." At the same time, parents have "a false sense of security, as long as no serious illnesses threaten the health of their children" and leave their children "unsupervised just when surveillance is the most necessary."

Georget set up a scale of masturbation's effects. In the first stage of masturbation: overall thinness, sluggishness of mind, unfitness for work, suffocations, cephalalgias, gastralgia. If masturbation continued, second stage, more acute, with overall languor, weakened intellect, blackouts, etc., etc. Finally, continued excesses result in the most serious stage, which led to death. Georget, it is clear, was not a heretic.[1]

The first heretics did not appear until the period from 1875 to 1881. At that moment, three men: Sir James Paget, Charles Mauriac, and Jules Christian appeared, one right after the other. They were the first doctors to shake the faith.

Sir James Paget was one of the great figures of English medicine during the second half of the nineteenth century. Physician and surgeon, his reputation was based on his equally notable talents as a practitioner, professor, and man of learning. He was the first to describe *osteitis deformans,* which was named Paget's disease after him. In England, he reached the summit of honors; vice-chancellor at Oxford University, he was also honorary doctor at Oxford, Cambridge and Edinburgh, and Queen Victoria's physician.[2]

In 1875, Paget published a lecture on sexual hypochondria in a collection of essays and addresses.[3] It was not a dry scientific work, but rather friendly advice. In a tone that was simple and familiar, Paget managed, however, to drop a bombshell or two.

You will encounter among your patients, he told his audience of physicians, many who attribute their chief distresses to the practice of masturbation. "Now, I believe you may teach positively that masturbation does neither more nor less harm than sexual intercourse practised with the same frequency in the same conditions of general health and age and circumstance."[4] Doubtless, "practised frequently by the very young . . . masturbation is very likely to produce exhaustion." Yet equally frequent copulation would probably produce the same effects. "The mischiefs are due to the quantity, not to the method of the excesses."[5] "I have seen," Paget said, "as numerous and as great evils consequent on excessive sexual intercourse as on excessive masturbation: but I have not seen or heard anything to make me believe that occasional masturbation has any other effects on one who practises it than has occasional sexual intercourse."

And Paget, who was an extremely moral and pious man—otherwise he would not have been Queen Victoria's physician—added: "I wish that I could say something worse of so nasty a practice; an uncleanliness, a filthiness forbidden by God, an unmanliness despised by man."[6]

As for the moral aspect, Paget was moreover quite strict on illicit sexual relations, on "fornication." He provides a valuable glimpse into the psychology of his time. Some of your patients, he told the physicians he was addressing, "will expect you to prescribe fornication."[7] Paget remarked that he would just as soon prescribe lying or stealing. Yet we must emphasize just how valuable this glimpse is: we see patients simultaneously bemoaning the disorders that they attribute to masturbation and thinking that their physician might just agree that a bit of fornication would be good for them. There were certainly physicians who were of this opinion. Just recall what Tolstoy wrote.[8]

Later in his lecture Paget came back to masturbation, now considering it in its relation to insanity. Asylums, he emphasized, were full of men whose state had been diagnosed as the result of masturbation or sexual excess. This explanation seemed to him less than plausible. Doubtless, in many instances, the men have masturbated because they were demented; they did not become demented because they masturbated.[9]

In all that Paget tells us, there were no great scientific demonstrations, no reliance on theory or new medical discoveries: there were only the words of a good observer, a freethinker, who calmly and simply declared—and this is a first—"the emperor has no clothes."

Dr. Mauriac was not, in his own time, a man of Paget's stature. His name, however, was also attached to a medical discovery, that of *syphilitic erythema nodosum,* which he was the first to describe in 1880. He was in fact a specialist in venereal diseases, noted for his work on syphilis, and a physician in the Paris hospitals. His publications in the field were significant.[10]

In 1877, Mauriac was drafting his article *Onanisme et excès vénériens* for Jaccoud's *Nouveau Dictionnaire de médecine et de chirurgie pratiques.* He did not count this 45-page article among his original scientific works (four years later, when he published a list of *Titres and travaux scientifiques du Docteur Charles Mauriac,* he provided an often detailed analysis of his scientific contributions but merely mentioned the title of *Onanisme et excès vénériens);*[11] but for what it was, a personal judgment, it marked an epoch.

In more than one respect, Mauriac remained a prisoner of tradition. Like his predecessors, he described masturbation's unfortunate consequences. He managed, however, to vigorously shake off tradition at several points. He proposed three new and daring innovations.

First, he denounced the exaggerations and lack of critical thinking that dominated the field. "Sexual abuses have been made responsible," he wrote,

> for almost all nosological disorders. Without taking the effort to analyse the causes which governed this or that simple or complex morbid state of the organism, it was easier to attribute all disorders, of immediate or remote cause, to masturbation or unnatural acts. Surely, it was not hard to discover such an etiological basis for all illnesses; since onanism is an inherent human vice, there are but few subjects in whom it could fail to be manifest at that period when it occurs most frequently, that is to say childhood. Yet to see it as an inexhaustible source of all sorts of diseases is obviously going beyond the boundaries of legitimate logical induction.[12]

It was thus necessary "to constantly warn the reader of the exaggeration that mars all writings on onanism." The latter reported extraordinary cases which sometimes, Mauriac said, "are impossible not to laugh at." Even if we don't laugh, "what trust can we have in them?"[13]

Mauriac even targeted Tissot himself. "The venerable Tissot, in the presence of each of the cases he recounts, invariably *quakes* or is *stricken with dread, horror, compassion,* etc.: with such a mindset, the science one does is untrustworthy and one falls into pathos."[14]

Second, in a number of cases, according to Mauriac, the real causal relation between onanism and illness had been inverted. "Quite often, onanism, far from being a *cause,* is an *effect.*" "It has to be seen as the manifestation of certain innate or acquired morbid states, . . . the manifestation of an anterior and superior morbid state." The examples Mauriac gave were those of insanity, which was possibly most often a cause rather than an effect of onanism; epilepsy ("Here, as in the case of insanity and all other neuroses, I believe that onanism is more often an effect than a cause"); hysteria, and hypochondria; idiocy "which, far from being the consequence of masturbation, can more likely be said to be its cause."[15]

Finally, Mauriac made a clean sweep of those illnesses and disorders that had been attributed, erroneously in his opinion, to masturbation. "Convulsions, contractions, paralyses that have too quickly been attributed to onanism"? They are nearly always the result, in fact, of hysteria. Serious vision problems and blindness? The problem has not yet been resolved, but onanism unquestionably is not implicated. Hearing problems? "Loss of hearing, like many other disorders, could not fail to be attributed to onanism. It is one more etiological banality that can be added to all the others." Disorders of the urinary system? "Dysuria, frequent need to urinate, urinary or seminal incontinence, discharge and inflammations of the urethra, the bladder and the kidneys, are all part of the countless trail of disorders for which unfortunate masturbators are held to blame. Here, as in other cases which I do not tire of pointing out, the exaggeration has been flagrant."[16]

Mauriac, like Paget, whom he apparently didn't know, displayed a free and independent frame of mind.

It is the same frame of mind we find in the case of Jules Christian. Christian, who had begun his career in his home region of Alsace, had been practicing in the Charenton hospital since 1879. He was a noted psychiatrist.[17] The article *Onanisme*, in Dechambre's *Dictionnaire encyclopédique des sciences médicales* in 1881, bears his name.

This time, the attack on Tissot and his work was direct:

> We can hardly comprehend the prodigious influence that this work has had, not only upon the public, but upon the physicians of his time.... Written in a declamatory style, ... the treatise *Onanisme* is marked by a laughable tendency to exaggerate. If the good faith and the excellent intentions of the author are admirable [this is a passage we've already quoted, but which is worth citing again here], one yet remains stupefied at the naive candor with which he approaches the most disparate facts. In his zeal to combat onanism, he lost all critical discernment.[18]

And again, elsewhere, Christian called Tissot a "friend of the marvelous."[19]

"It is, moreover," he continued, "a general and curious fact. Whoever has written on the subject has been led, almost fatally, to overdo things, to darken the picture, to over-generalize troubles which were neither as serious nor as frequent, as they were made out to be."[20]

In fact, Christian said forcefully on the subject of the consequences of onanism, "imagination was given free rein, and one can hardly believe one's ears when confronted with the outrageous commentaries proffered by the most serious of authors."[21]

Christian summed up the classic picture, drawn by Tissot, of masturbation's harmful effects:

> This picture has been reproduced so often, even by the most serious authors, that it has come to be taken as accurate.
>
> And yet, I'm not afraid of saying it, over the more than twenty years that I have been treating patients, never, not in the hospitals, nor in the psychiatric wards, nor among my private clientele nor

that of my colleagues, nor in the city, nor in the country, have I ever observed anything similar.

There, Christian had said it, as did Paget, as Mauriac nearly did : I observed; I saw nothing.

"Does this mean to say," he continued,

> that I consider onanism to be harmless? No, in truth. From the moral perspective, onanism is a vice against nature, a crime against the species, and it cannot be condemned energetically enough. Yet, as a doctor I am obliged to recognize that it does not present the dangers that have been attributed to it. We must not be afraid to admit it and I think that it is best to tell the truth, onanism is a practice that is so widespread, that very few individuals can boast of having escaped it completely; it is consequently an absolutely commonplace cause that can always easily be advanced. But like many other problems of an etiological nature, this one disappears completely under close examination.

"Disappears completely under close examination": the formula admirably expressed the adoption of a critical stance. Christian himself performed a close examination, reasoning as follows:

> It is noteworthy that it is the nervous illnesses (hysteria, hypochondria, epilepsy, mental illness) and those that are characterized by exhaustion and consumption, . . . that have been blamed on onanism and sexual excesses. But these are nearly always assertions that lack sufficient proof. . . . There is always room for doubt. A young man has masturbated; he goes insane. Before deciding if the insanity is due to masturbation, one must wonder if masturbation were not the result of the pre-existing cerebral excitation . . . Here is an epileptic: each time he indulges in coitus or onanism his attacks are stronger and more frequent. Is one to conclude that the epilepsy is caused by these excesses? Is it not also legitimate to allow that they were merely a secondary, incidental cause, that they merely aggravated an already existing problem? . . . I cited earlier the case of the young man in my employ who only masturbates during his fits. The sexual excitation which marks the beginning of general paralysis is merely one of the symptoms of the illness, not

its cause. . . . It is clear that a rigorous examination can serve to distinguish cause and effect.[22]

Christian felt, however, that onanism could present real danger in certain cases: it was dangerous in the case of very young children, it could entail serious risks for the adolescent, it was dangerous for adults when practiced excessively. Christian gave tradition a hearty shake but stopped short of toppling it.

Let us repeat, in the case of Christian, what we earlier said of Paget. What we find here was neither the fruit of any medical discovery nor the application of any new scientific theory. Paget was simply a good observer—his observations stretched over more than twenty years—who was free of prejudices and who knew how to reason.

In Germany, the disruption of old ways of thinking about masturbation is visible in the text of a famous and classic dictionary, the *Meyers Konversations-Lexicon*.

In the second edition of the *Meyers* in 1866, the article *Onanie* was very harsh.[23] While it recognized that the physical consequences of masturbation had sometimes been greatly exaggerated, it pointed out the worrisome signs of masturbation that were generally present in children who practiced the vice: thinness, paleness, sluggishness of mind, tendency towards melancholy, et al. Moreover, it added, it could not be denied that in certain cases masturbation could be the cause of profound physical decay as well as of mental illnesses.

The text remained unchanged in the third edition in 1877.[24] The fourth edition, however, in 1896, showed significant changes.[25] The worrisome signs, in the case of children, were no longer usual, but possible (*pflegen* was replaced by *können*). The serious consequences that were undeniable in 1866 and 1877 simply disappeared. Contrary to the earlier editions, the fourth emphasized that in the case of mental illness, masturbation was to be considered as one of its symptoms, and not as its cause. *Onanie* shows that something new was obviously in the air.[26]

An evolution in thinking was not limited to reference works and studies of general interest. It was also visible in studies devoted to particular illnesses. In a study published in 1884, one year after his death, Charles Lasègue discussed the problem of spermatorrhea, one of the disorders generally attributed to masturbation. He said (the text reflects his spoken style):

> The story is always the same. A man who is still youthful—he is forty—comes to see you; he is humiliated, blushing, tormented. He tells you that he leaks semen once, twice, or three times a week, a month or a year. He has a dream at night, he feels wet and the next day he wakes up exhausted, faint. Light hurts his eyes. Then he blushes again—he is an emotional man—he blames school habits.
>
> Well, masturbation, leaks of semen, fatigue . . . all this doesn't make sense. What is true is that his health is poor and the leaks are secondary to his state of health. Do not practice a medicine of reflection, a photographic medicine [in other words don't simply repeat what has always been said]. Onanists are a dime a dozen. Spermatorrhea is much rarer. There is no cause and effect relation.[27]

In another study also published in 1884, Lasègue, speaking of insanity, declared on the basis of "long experience"—it was in fact one of his favorite fields of investigation: "Onanism is the symptom of a morbid state, of a cerebral neurosis: there is no such thing as insanity resulting from onanism."[28]

Psychiatrists at the end of the nineteenth century had, on the whole, evolved in the same direction as Lasègue; we see them abandoning the notion of masturbatory insanity. For some, it meant a straight-out retraction of what they said before. The great Maudsley was, in the sixties and seventies, one of England's staunchest proponents of masturbatory insanity. In 1895, in the new edition of his *Pathology of Mind*, he made a complete about-face. In the case of insanity, he wrote, we can never be sure that it is not more of a symptom than a cause.[29]

It has been rightly noted that this change in Maudsley's way of thinking, like that of others, including most specialists (the comment we made earlier on Paget, Mauriac, and Christian applies in this case as well), was not the result of any discoveries or any new scientific ideas. The facts had not changed, but the system of reasoning had. Once someone remarked that the emperor had no clothes—that is to say, that the old ideas had no real basis—his nakedness became visible.

If we stop at the century's close, we can take our bearing on the new ideas and tendencies from a man who belonged himself to a new species, that of the "sexologists." That man was Havelock Ellis.[30]

Havelock Ellis's *Studies in the Psychology of Sex* provoked a scandal in its day. Ellis, who relied upon broad documentation in his approach to sexual problems, for he was above all a compiler, aimed for the greatest possible objectivity in his description of the phenomena he studied, and he did not shy away from the most delicate of problems. What was shocking was his apparent lack of modesty joined to a lack of moral sense, for he refused to moralize.

The first volume in the series, devoted to sexual inversion, was published in England in 1897. Here Ellis described homosexuality without condemning it; he discussed it with understanding even, for what he wanted above all, was to understand nature. It was shortly after the trial of Oscar Wilde. Legal action was, curiously, not taken against the author but against a distributor; the work, in the eyes of the courts, was obscene.

With understandable prudence, Ellis did not publish the succeeding volumes in England. Volume II was published in the United States, in Philadelphia, in 1899. It is of direct interest for our study, as it deals with what Havelock Ellis called "auto-erotism."

Ellis devoted many pages, from the outset, to demonstrating the widespread nature of masturbation. He did so with the aid of a great many citations, drawn from a variety of different sources. This method, somewhat ethnographic in nature, was considerably novel in the field.

His treatment of Tissot was unsparing. Tissot and his followers were:

certainly responsible for much. The mistaken notions of many medical authorities, carried on by tradition, even down to our own time; the powerful lever which has been put into the hand of un-scrupulous quacks; the suffering, dread, and remorse experienced in silence by many thousands of ignorant and often innocent young people. . . . During the past forty years the efforts of many distinguished physicians . . . have gradually dragged the bogy down from its pedestal, and now . . . there is even a tendency to-day to regard masturbation as normal.[31]

Ellis recalled the impressive and endless list of illnesses attributed to masturbation.

That many of these manifestations do occur in connection with masturbation is unquestionable; there is also good reason to believe that some of them may be the results of masturbation acting on an imperfectly healthy organism. But in all such cases we must speak with great caution, for there appears to be little reliable evidence to show that simple masturbation, in a well-born and healthy indi-vidual, can produce any evil results beyond slight functional dis-turbances, and these only when it is practiced in excess.[32]

Ellis goes over the list of some of the most serious disorders for which masturbation was held responsible, citing in each case the physicians who, at the turn of the century, undermined the old medical conceptions. In the case of insanity, for example, he cited Kellogg who wrote in 1897: "if it [masturbation] caused insanity, the whole race would long since have passed into masturbatic de-generacy of mind."[33]

Ellis said: "We may reach the conclusion that in the case of moderate masturbation in healthy, well-born individuals, no seri-ously pernicious results necessarily follow."[34]

Excesses, he admitted however, could be dangerous. They could be particularly so when the organism was unhealthy. "Excesses may act, according to the familiar old-fashioned adage, like the lighted match. But we must always remember the obvious truth, that it makes a considerable difference whether you threw your lighted match into a powder magazine or into the sea."

On the topic of excesses, Ellis's tone was serious:

> Any excess in solitary self-excitement may still produce results which, though slight, are yet harmful. The skin, digestion, and circulation may all be disordered; headache and neuralgia may occur; and, as in normal sexual excess or in undue frequency of sexual excitement during sleep, there is a general lowering of nervous tone. Probably the most important of the comparatively frequent results—though this also arises usually on a somewhat morbid soil—is neurasthenia with its manifold symptoms. There can be little doubt that the ancient belief, dating from the time of Hippocrates, that sexual excesses produce spinal disease, as well as the belief that masturbation causes insanity, are largely due to the failure to diagnose neurasthenia.[35]

Havelock Ellis, it is clear, aligned himself with a school of psychiatrists who had eliminated insanity as a result of masturbation, but who had replaced it by a sort of neurosis that could, they thought, be caused by excessive masturbation.[36]

For Ellis, the only real risks lay in excess. But the sexologist went even further, and it is here that the scandal he provoked becomes understandable. He delighted in citing the cases of famous or illustrious men who masturbated—Moritz, Lenau, Jean-Jacques Rousseau, Goethe (with a question mark), Gogol—without apparently harming their work. These examples provided evidence that "a notable proportion of those in which excessive masturbation is admitted, are of persons of eminent and recognized ability."[37]

Masturbation, he emphasized, could relieve, have a sedative effect. "My own observations," said Ellis, agree with those of a physician who asserted that "both masturbation and sexual intercourse should be classed as typical sedatives." This sedative effect was important in understanding the penchant for onanism. "Judging from my own observations," he wrote, "I should say that in normal persons, well past the age of puberty, and otherwise leading a chaste life, masturbation would be little practiced except for the physical and mental relief it brings."[38]

Finally, and undoubtedly above all in the eyes of many of his contemporaries, Ellis had the audacity not to reject masturbation as a vice. He classified it as one of the "inevitable" phenomena. "It is our wisest course to recognize this inevitableness of sexual and transmuted sexual manifestations under the perpetual restraints of civilized life."[39] It is not only civilized life but, at the level of the human organism, the sexual drive itself that is involved. "In the phenomena of auto-erotism, when we take a broad view of those phenomena, we are concerned, not with a form of insanity, not necessarily with a form of depravity, but with the inevitable by-products of that mighty process on which the animal creation rests."[40]

It is clear to what extent these views represented a reversal of traditional notions. Havelock Ellis would live long enough—until 1939—to see many of his ideas accepted and even become commonplace. At the turning point of the century however, he was a forerunner, a representative only of the avant-garde. If we follow the bulk of the troops, we see that traditional notions remain strongly entrenched. We need, therefore, to take a look in their direction.

CHAPTER NINE

TRADITION HOLDS ON

In 1899, the same year that Havelock Ellis's "Auto-Erotism" was published, a German physician, Hermann Rohleder, published a work entitled *Die Masturbation. Eine Monographie für Aerzte und Pädagogen.*[1] Rohleder considered masturbation a vice—*ein Laster*—but to examine it, he took a scientific rather than a moral stance.[2] For him the harmful effects of masturbation had often been exaggerated, but such effects, particularly in the case of prolonged masturbation, were really to be feared. Rohleder believed they could be particularly damaging to the nervous system. Ultimately, he declared, some of Tissot's descriptions could be verified. Since, moreover, the moral consequences of masturbation were disastrous, it was to be energetically combated. Rohleder continued to advise, for example, tying the hands of children at night when it proved necessary.

We won't continue our analysis of this quite detailed work—it is 337 pages long—but will limit ourselves to the following conclusion: in 1899, we can still find a specialist writing with scientific authority who denounces masturbation as a real danger. When we speak of a tradition that held on, let us not imagine that there were simply a few followers who remained attached to old ways of thinking. There were also men of learning who, to a great extent, continued to defend traditional notions.

Let us, at the beginning of the twentieth century, retake our tour of Europe and the United States and meet a series of learned men who remained largely faithful to tradition. In Sweden, there was Anton Nyström, one of the best-known scientific personalities in his country, who stated as an obvious fact that "the habit of masturbation presents grave danger and often ruins the body and the mind of the person who acquires it."[3] In Switzerland, there was Auguste Forel, a particularly respected scientist, for whom the "detestable habit" of onanism "renders the child lazy, weak and ashamed, . . . disturbs his nutrition and digestion, and disposes him to sexual perversion and impotence."[4] In Great Britain, there was Henry Morris, a respected physician at the turn of the century who would later reach the summit of his profession. In his *Injuries and Diseases of the Genital and Urinary Organs,* Morris gave the generally traditional prognosis for the masturbating child; he would become, in particular, "prematurely old."[5] In the United States, there was Stanley Hall who, at the beginning of the twentieth century, was the undisputed authority in child psychology. For him, too, masturbation caused "early physical signs of decrepitude and senescence."[6]

It is of course true that during this period a scientist rarely picked up his pen without aiming a few barbs at the exaggerations committed by his predecessors. All the same, in the case of Rohleder, Nyström, Forel, Morris, and Hall, it is clear that old ways of thinking, for the most part, remained firmly entrenched.

Our little tour of masturbation did not include Austria. We could, however, have passed by Vienna and added a name to our list: that of Sigmund Freud. Little notice has been taken of the fact that on the topic of masturbation, Freud was, rather curiously, in the camp of the conservatives.

The members of the Psychoanalytic Society of Vienna, grouped around Freud, had a lively interest in masturbation. It was for them an important object of study. During their famous Wednesday evening meetings, the Viennese psychoanalysts devoted two special discussion series to the topic of masturbation. The first series involved two meetings, in May and June of 1910. The second spread over nine sessions, from November 1911 to April 1912.[7]

The reports of these meetings are quite illuminating. They reveal the extent to which the participants were divided. The analysts disagreed, firstly, on the very significance, on the psychoanalytic level, that should be attributed to the phenomenon of masturbation. The interpretations they proposed were widely divergent. This controversy extended to succeeding generations, and continues to exist. To look at that controversy thoroughly would entail a lengthy discussion that would take us too far afield. But the Viennese psychoanalysts disagreed as well in their evaluation of the effects of masturbation and whether it was harmful in nature or not. Many—seemingly the majority—perceived masturbation as harmless, or nearly so.[8] However, Freud, for his part, took a far less indulgent stance. Masturbation, in his eyes, could be truly harmful. He offered three reasons:

First, masturbation could lead, according to Freud, to neurotic disorders, especially neurasthenia. What was involved for Freud was not the anxiety or the anguish of the masturbator seized by a sense of horror at his act, but a physical, "somatic" mechanism leading to neurosis.[9] He admitted that the link was not always clear (he spoke of an "unknown mechanism" in which "considerations of excess and of inadequate satisfaction" must be taken into account),[10] but was convinced of the masturbation-neurosis connection.[11]

Second, on the physical level, masturbation could result in a "reduction in potency." Freud invoked his own personal medical experience which, he said, did not allow him to exclude, among the consequences of onanism, "eine daurende Abschwächung der Potenz," or "a permanent reduction in potency."[12]

Third, there was the "greater harm of masturbation" that occurred in the psychic sphere.[13] The harmful effects here were "more extensive and transparent" than those in the physical realm.[14] Freud listed them:

- the "character change that is brought about through this short-circuiting between desire and satisfaction, by a by-passing of the external world";[15]
- a "loosening of the individual's interconnections with his fellow men; masturbatory gratification is an antisocial act that brings the individual concerned into opposition to society";
- a "preponderance of fantasy life over reality, a situation that forms a pattern for a number of other functions";
- "the excessive demands that the individual concerned, as a result of being spoiled by fantasy, makes upon reality, which can never satisfy him";
- the "individual's inability to tolerate sexual restrictions, which life—especially married life—makes unavoidable";
- the "fact that masturbatory activity" is "identical with the preservation of the infantile condition in every respect." "Therein lies," Freud continued, "the main psychic harmful-ness of masturbation, because with it there has been created the basis for a psychoneurosis, which sets in when conflict and rejection are added";
- finally, "the general debasement of sexual life, which results from the cheapness and easy availability of the sexual act and the social disdain attached to it. Masturbators of this type are thereafter unable to have intercourse with persons whom they love and esteem, but only with those whom they disdain."[16]

Clearly this feuled the indictment of masturbation.[17]

He conceded, however, that despite its harmful effects, mastur-bation could have several benefits. It could "represent a sexual gratification that discharges the sexual tension that otherwise would often have a pathogenic effect." In addition, there was "the avoidance of infection."[18] Freud took particular note, in masturbation's favor, of what he termed "the virtues of its failings." The reduction in potency that it caused could at first glance seem nothing other than a drawback. But this reduction and the accompanying diminution of the aggressivity linked to the sexual drive were also useful to social life. They furthered the sexual moderation that civilization demanded. Freud emphasized that he said this not cynically but realistically: "Virtue accompanied by full potency is usually felt as a hard task": "Tugend bei voller Potenz wird meist als eine schwierige Aufgabe erfunden."[19]

In spite of the positive effects he mentioned, the dominant term in Freud's discussion of masturbation remained *Schaden:* "damage," or "injury." It would thus be difficult to include the Viennese authority among those who, in this realm, helped to point the way to a new liberation in thought.[20]

In psychoanalytic circles, however, we must emphasize that the future would belong far more to a man like Stekel—Freud's principal adversary in the Vienna discussions and the principal proponent of the thesis of masturbation's innocuousness—than to Freud himself.

If we leave the confines of science, our domain up until now, for the realm of popular literature, we can obviously find defenders of tradition with even more simplified formulas.

In France, from 1890 to 1914, we see a succession of physicians and popular scientists who remain violent, terrifying on the subject of masturbation. To cite several representative figures from this gallery; Dr. Rengrade, writing in 1881:

> Livid, gasping for breath, the miserable wretch wears himself out in the search for those sensual spasms which now do no more than fatigue him, and quickly, his lifeless eyes sink into their sockets, ringed with dark circles, his lips hang, his nose becomes pointed, his gaunt face is reminiscent of the physiognomy of the monkey, his head hangs in shame, his back curves into a stoop, his limbs grow thin, and these first phenomena of profound exhaustion are fatally followed, soon after, by such serious disorders as phtisia, epilepsy, hysteria, imbecility, insanity and spinal consumption;[21]

Alexis Clerc, 1885 ("shameful habit," "insanity whose ravages extend further day by day"; when required, approved of infibulation or clitoridectomy);[22] Dr. Garnier, whose *Onanisme* saw nine successive editions, from 1883 to 1886 ("the yawning abyss of suffering, infirmities, and remorse which threatens to engulf anyone who succumbs to the deplorable habit of masturbation");[23] Dr. Monin, 1890 ("Nervous exhaustion, cardiac neurasthenia, medullary irritation, and eventual ataxia are the results of all varieties of onanism");[24] Dr. Surbled and his *Vice solitaire* in 1905 (whose originality lay in the fact that he considered that the results of onanism were more serious for women than they were for men);[25] Dr. Galtier-Boissière's *Larousse médical illustré*, in 1912 ("a great physical weakening, a diminution in memory and intelligence, a state of intense degradation").[26]

The entry in the *Larousse médical illustré* is illustrative of tradition's tenacity. The advice was that of old: "Continual surveillance, so as to prevent the repetition of the act, surveillance of servants, surveillance of reading materials." The text was accompanied by the drawing of an anti-masturbatory belt. "The instrument," it was noted, "can be useful."[27] This was, let us not forget, 1912.

Among the names we've just cited are those of Catholic doctors—Dr. Surbled in particular was obviously a man with a cause. Yet what we have is far from a confessional gallery: Alexis Clerc, for example, belonged to the left, even to the extreme left, and the *Larousse médical* had no apparent stake in Catholic causes. Just as in earlier centuries, as we emphasized in our first chapter, rightwing and left-wing authorities in France continued to work hand in hand.

In Germany at the turn of the century, one could doubtless draw up an equally impressive anthology of popular medical texts on the topic of masturbation. In England, on the other hand, the task would be more difficult. Here the popularizer was more discreet, for he ran up against Victorian modesty. In 1901, a publication as serious as the *Lancet*, when reviewing Havelock Ellis's *Studies in the Psychology of Sex*, emphasized that such a book must be strictly reserved for physicians and jurists. It must not be sold to the public: "The reading and discussion of such topics are dangerous."[28] This type of attitude obviously paralyzed publication. But what was "not discussed" in England should not be taken as an indication of any greater indulgence.

Moreover, beyond what was written, it is far more important to know what was done; what was practiced in the case of children and what the attitude of physicians, educators, and parents was. It is here that we must attempt to gain a sense of the truth.

In the case of the ordinary physician, a great conservatism is evident throughout the first two or three decades of the twentieth century. An American specialist made a striking observation about the United States in 1916, writing that "most physicians" still entertained old notions about masturbation.[29] Hardly a month goes by, he specified, without his seeing at least one patient whose nervous or mental condition had been attributed by the family doctor to onanism.[30] In the first decade of the century, a large Philadelphia hospital continued to organize a weekly masturbatory clinic, where patients with a variety of often strange and undefined afflictions, all attributed to masturbation, were exhibited for the students.[31]

Certain physicians used threats to wrest the child from the grip of vice. The classical method—the German physician I. Bloch described it in 1908 as a rather traditional one—consisted in appearing before the child with a large knife or scissors and threatening him with a painful operation, or even, if he persisted in abusing his genital organs, with "cutting them off."[32] That was the psychological treatment inflicted by the family doctor on the young André Gide in 1878, when he was eight. As a student Gide was expelled from school when his "bad habits" were discovered. Dr. Bouardel lectured him and showed him "the instruments to which we must have recourse, those with which we operate on little boys like you." "And continuing to gaze at me with a scowl," Gide recounted, "he pointed, at arm's length behind his armchair, to a panoply of red Touareg spear heads."[33] Dr. Brémond, in 1893, boasted of the success of his own method, which he had practiced: "In front of children given to masturbation, I spoke of taking my sharpest bistoury, in order to make them renounce those practices which, if continued, would have necessitated a supposedly indispensable operation."[34]

There were also, of course, a variety of prescriptions, including that of tying the child's hands. The young Julian Blanc, while a boarder with some "petits bourgeois" in the south of France just after World War I, in 1920, was suspected of "touching himself." The doctor's prescription was to tie his hands to the bedposts at night. The procedure would be inflicted on the young boy for several weeks.[35]

It was doubtless an exaggeration to claim that tied hands were commonplace at the beginning of the twentieth century, but the recommendations to this effect and the examples that were cited were numerous. A Scottish woman recalled that, as a child during this period, her hands had sometimes been so tightly tied that her piano teacher questioned her about her striped wrists.[36]

Educators felt a particular responsibility. Jules Payot, who was one of the leading figures of lay education in France, propounded gravely on the topic in his *Education de la volonté*, published in 1893 and republished in innumerable reeditions until after 1914. Masturbation, for him, was a "shameful vice," a "taint," which procured nothing but "ignoble pleasures," and whose "ravages," even though they might occasionally be better hidden than those of other forms of debauchery, "are no less terrifying."[37] The remedy, following traditional advice, was fatigue, healthy fatigue—and not staying too long in bed. It was primarily the young student whom Jules Payot addressed: "One must rigorously regulate one's sleep, never go to bed unless tired, and always rise immediately upon awakening. Overly soft beds, which encourage lying about in bed in the morning, are to be avoided. If our will is too weak to propel us from the bed upon awakening, we must have recourse to a person who will be appointed for this task and who will force us to get up in spite of our protests." The best fatigue was that produced by a good walk. The young man "should go out nightly, meditating on the next day's work and continue his walk until he is tired; he should then go to bed."[38]

Teachers had their attention drawn to their serious duties in this realm. Let us take two teaching manuals from Belgium as examples. The first, which dates from 1916 and was reedited in 1922, was by a teacher at the Ecole Normale de Charleroi and a solid layman, Dr. Langelez. For Langelez, "masturbation is followed by a procession of troubles of all sorts (melancholia, loss of attention, impotence, etc.)," thus "one will take particular care to prevent these "lamentable habits."[39] The second manual is from 1928, reedited in 1936. It contains lectures given for teachers in the province of Luxembourg. The advice was the same: "You can never watch too closely." The author, Dr. Lomry, was still writing in 1936 of the "intellectual, moral and physical ravages of masturbation" that were "numerous and disastrous": "I know of a school where these unnatural acts were particularly widespread. Out of a good thirty students, twelve were afflicted with tuberculosis during their adolescence; five died and the others came down with serious cases of pleurisy."[40] In this rural province a bit off the beaten track, the bogey was still around in 1936.

It is without a doubt that the advice on masturbation retained its harsh tone for the longest in boarding schools. A former boarder in a Catholic home, in Wallonia in 1943–1944, recalled that on sexual matters, his schoolmasters "only became explicit when it was a question of castigating masturbation." "For that, there was no indulgence and no remission."[41]

Another realm, which was also, in its way, an educational realm, and in which masturbation was apparently also taken particularly seriously for a long time, was scouting. Baden-Powell, who left his mark on scouting, expounded, on this topic, ideas that were as energetic as they were easy to understand. In his basic work, *Scouting for Boys*, we find, in the 1914 edition, under the heading "Continence":

Smoking and drinking are things that tempt some fellows and not others, but there is one temptation that is pretty sure to come to you at one time or another, and I want just to warn you against it. . . .

It is called in our schools "beastliness," and that is about the best name for it.

Smoking and drinking and gambling are men's vices and therefore attract some boys, but this "beastliness" is not a man's vice; men have nothing but contempt for a fellow who gives way to it.

Some boys, like those who start smoking, think it a very fine and manly thing to tell or listen to dirty stories, but it only shows them to be little fools.

Yet such talk and the reading of trashy books or looking at lewd pictures, are very apt to lead a thoughtless boy into the temptation to self-abuse. This is a most dangerous thing for him, for should it become a habit, it quickly destroys both health and spirits; he becomes feeble in body and mind, and often ends in a lunatic asylum. . . .

Sometimes the desire is brought on by indigestion, or from eating too rich food, or from constipation. It can therefore be cured by correcting these, and by bathing at once in cold water, or by exercising the upper part of the body by arm exercises, boxing, etc.

It may seem difficult to overcome the temptation the first time, but when you have done so once it will be easier afterwards.

If you still have trouble about it, do not make a secret of it, but go to your scoutmaster and talk it over with him, and all will come right.[42]

That is clear as a bell, and *Scouting for Boys* would reprint the passage for many years. In the 1939 French translation, the passage was still there.[43]

When he addressed older scouts, the Rovers, in his *Rovering to Success* in 1922, Baden-Powell appealed to somewhat nobler ideas. Here, instead of the heading "Continence," we have "The Germ is a sacred trust for carrying on the race."[44]

Do not give in to temptation, he exhorted. Doing so, "just checks that semen getting its full chance of making you the strong man you would otherwise be. You are throwing away the seed that has been handed down to you as a trust instead of keeping it and

ripening it for bringing a son to you later on. The usual consequence is that you sap your health and brain just at the critical
time when you would otherwise be gaining the height of manly
health and intelligence."

To all appearances, let us repeat, the realm of scouting was thus
one in which the fight against masturbation long remained the
order of the day.

After the physicians, after the educators, there were the parents. How could they be expected to evolve rapidly while the mass
of physicians was evolving so slowly?

Stekel, writing in 1923 in Austria, described the attitudes he
observed around him:

> I know mothers who think the principal goal of education consists
> in protecting children against it [masturbation]. Who has not en-
> countered in his office distraught fathers who have brought in a
> masturbating son they would like to cure of his vice by force? All
> the sedatives are tried. The children are closely watched. They are
> tied up in the most illogical and grotesque fashions. The father is
> frantic. The mother already envisions her child as an idiot, shut up
> in an asylum. Other fathers force their child to confess every
> morning to see if he has masturbated, and if he has relapsed, they
> reprimand him or beat him until they turn him into a veritable
> Flagellant.[45]

Some parents borrowed the physicians' tactic of threats. Arthur
Koestler's mother threatened her son with "lingering illness and
death" if he touched himself.[46] Julien Green's mother, when she
learned that her son—a little boy of six—used his hand, screamed
in terror and ran to get a large knife that she brandished while
screaming: "I'll cut it off."[47]

In 1936, the British specialist Meagher deplored the fact that
"many well-intentioned" parents "threaten to amputate the penis
or hand of the young child."[48] Evidence of this type of threat is
available throughout the 1930s and beyond. Françoise Dolto,
writing in 1939, evoked the range of threats used by parents: the

threat to deliver the child into the hands of those perceived as the ultimate menace: "the black man," "the bogey-man," or "the policeman"; the announcement that he is going to be taken to the doctor who "will operate on him," or, as it is more crudely put, "will cut it off"; the warning that the guilty hand will dry out or will become paralyzed. Dolto stressed that the "beliefs in the dangers of masturbation, in illness, insanity, imbecillity, and even the softening of the spinal cord" remained widespread in certain circles.[49] As late as 1946, a Swiss (female) doctor wrote:

> How many parents threaten their child with taking him to the doctor to have his penis cut off! I can still see the expression of infinite distress on the face of a poor six year-old child whose mother brought him to my office so that I could explain to him that amputation would be the only recourse the next time he "pulled his puddin." . . . Another time, I saw a well-meaning grandmother drag a poor three-year-old tot, who was literally out of his mind from terror and whose piercing screams had drawn my attention, to a rabbit hutch. The grandmother explained to me that since he had "behaved like a little piggy with his willy, they were going to feed it to the rabbits."[50]

At the same period, somewhere in Flanders, a mother threatened to burn her young son, in the strategic spot, with a match.[51]

This persistence by physicians, educators, and parents meant that the suffering of children often persisted as well. When Montherland spoke, in 1939, of "poor kids they terrify about onanism,"[52] the word "terrify" was, in many instances, fully accurate.

Weatherhead, who played the dual role and had the double experience of pastor and psychoanalyst, evoked in 1931 the case of poor patients who accused themselves of being guilty of "the worst possible type of sin." In some cases, they were truly ill. Weatherhead said: "What has so often happened is that the practice has been so surrounded by feelings of guilt, shame, inferiority, self-loathing, horror and, above all, fear, that all sorts of pathological mental conditions have resulted. . . ."[53]

The resulting disorders could be varied. Brill, in 1916, claimed to have witnessed the development of a castration complex—resulting in sexual impotence—in the case of a young man whose father had threatened to "cut if off," as the turn of phrase went.[54] Freud generalized and considered such threats to be one of the classical origins of the castration complex.[55] Julien Green, whose mother had shown him a large knife, declared that the scene left him with deep and lasting psychological scars.[56] In the realm of the suffering of youth, a good portion of the twentieth century was simply a continuation of the nineteenth.

Our portrait of masturbation has been, it could be suggested, a bit impressionistic. We readily recognize it. However, how could it be otherwise?

There are nonetheless two studies that allow a much-needed statistical approach to the problem. They both came from the United States and were published in 1937 and 1938, respectively.

One of the studies, by Mabel Huschka in New York, evaluated 320 children aged 1 to 14.[57] These were "problem children" who had been referred for psychiatric consultation between 1935 and 1938. Huschka systematically questioned the parents, or the person who had brought the child, on the child's masturbatory history.

From this systematic questioning it was revealed that 142 out of the 320, or 44 percent, had been caught masturbating or were reported to have masturbated. This did not include all those—and there were doubtless many of them—who slipped through the net of surveillance. The figure of 44 percent clearly represented, if we are looking for the reality of masturbation, less than the actual total.

In the case of the 142 children reported to have masturbated, Mabel Huschka asked the parents what their reaction was and what they said to the child. In 128 cases out of 142, that is to say in nine-tenths of the cases, the parents admitted having scolded, punished, or threatened.

There were only 25 cases of mild censure—of the type expressed by "it isn't nice." In more than 100 cases out of the 128, the child was actually punished or threatened, or punished and threatened together.

The threats are particularly interesting to analyze. They fell into several categories. There was the grand warning about the danger, the various injuries that the guilty party risked; there was the threat of punishment; there was also the threat of surgical intervention.

"It will stunt your growth"; "you will become a cripple"; "you can die"; "they'll put you away where all the crazy people are"; "your penis will get full of germs"; "you won't be able to have a nice baby"; and "it will make you an idiot"—the whole range of threats, in a large number of cases, was vividly evoked.

The child was also menaced with harsh punishment if he did not stop. In 14 cases—that is 1 out of 10 masturbating children—the threat was directly physical; "they might have to cut it off," 12 little boys were told; another was told that the cat might bite it off and turn him into a girl; a little girl was threatened with having her vagina sewn up. In New York, during the years 1935–1938, "to cut it off" was a threat that hung continually over the young child.

The second statistical study, from 1937, is the work of a professor from Duke University in North Carolina, E. V. Pullias.[58] Pullias, in the course of interviews with students, was struck by the fact that certain young people believed their future to have been compromised, or their life ruined, because they had masturbated. To find out what was going on, he undertook a study of 75 freshmen, with an average age of 19. He basically asked them two questions: what have you been told about the effects of masturbation? What do you think?

Answers to the question about what the students had been told were revealing. Sixty-six students out of 75, or 8 out of 9, had been told—by their parents, a doctor, books, or another source—that masturbation had harmful, and sometimes very harmful, effects. Thirty-nine of them, that is to say, more than half, had been warned that masturbation could be a direct cause of mental illness.

Almost all these young students believed what they had been told or what they had read. Sixty-two out of 75 declared that they believed masturbation to be truly dangerous. The description of the possible damages varied greatly from student to student—ranging from a vague allusion to nervous disorders to a vision of total physical and mental destruction in the future—but the notion of masturbation's damage was shared by all.

Despite the fact that it was less statistically precise, a third study, undertaken also in an American university, is worth noting. It is the work of a physician employed in the student mental hygiene services at Yale University.[59] The study revealed the results of his practice over 16 years, from 1926 to 1942. The students who consulted him and who admitted to masturbation, he explained, "seemed uniformly to believe that masturbation was 'bad.'" It was what they had been taught to believe at home, where their parents had raised the specters of insanity and tuberculosis. These students exhibited constant feelings of anxiety. These feelings were particularly acute among those for whom masturbation constituted the sole sexual activity. Among nearly two-thirds of those in this group, the feelings of fear and of guilt tended to become obsessional.[60] These results, let us emphasize, were based on students who consulted the mental hygiene services.

A final study that is revealing, despite its lack of statistics, was made in 1961, taking Belgian students as its subjects.[61] Those who undertook the investigation noted that they were struck by the fact that as late as 1961, "university students still talk of going blind, having their growth stunted, of hair loss, weakening of the will, impotence, and of the great danger of divorce, sterility, the procreation of abnormal children, etc., in later life."[62] The authors noted that nearly all the students questioned believed that masturbation had negative psychological effects.[63]

It is clear to what point, even in educated circles—the students at Duke University, as Pulias stresses, came from the upper middle class, and the same was true for those at Yale—tradition endured. However, it was within these circles that thinking must have evolved the most quickly—more quickly, surely, than it did within the lower classes.

The problem of variations in the perception of masturbation among social classes is one to which we have devoted much thought. We've already noted, however, just how difficult it was to study. However, another American study—that of Kinsey in 1948—managed to shed some light. The upshot of Kinsey's investigation was that it was in the lower classes that the notion of masturbation's harm remained firmly entrenched for the longest time.[64] In the eighteenth century, it was undoubtedly the upper classes that had first accepted Tissot's ideas, seemingly the product of the new enlightened science. As science evolved and abandoned its old notions, it was also generally the upper classes that managed to readjust to the change in ideas. It was apparently the lower classes that continued to believe the teachings of earlier generations for far longer.[65]

Chapter Ten

Reflux into Disorder

The progressive fading, then the near disappearance of the ideas that had turned masturbation into the bogey, did not represent a linear phenomenon that could be clearly plotted. The impression that one gets, as one follows the decline of these notions that had been so firmly anchored for so long, is that of an army in retreat, and one whose retreat, in fact, had turned into a rout: great, very great confusion, troops withdrawing hastily while others obstinately continued to fire; officers who, here and there, were attempting to rally the troops were then forced to give up; disorder, great disorder—but the retreat continued and accelerated inexorably.

There were no great leaders directing this retreat. Tissot was, in his time, in the days of the offensive, a leader who had been followed. During the retreat, the orders no longer came from above.

There are, certainly, some figures who seem important, and who appear as if they could have served as authorities. Such is the case with Magnus Hirschfeld in Germany or Wilhelm Stekel in Austria. Magnus Hirschfeld, who was the most famous German sexologist of the first third of the twentieth century, adopted an extremely clear position in his *Sexualpathologie* in 1917. All that

had been written on the harm of onanism should be thrown over-
board, he said forcefully: it has never been shown to have any
harmful effects whatsoever on health.[1] Stekel, one of Freud's disciples (although Freud had broken off the relationship), was no
less clear in his book *Onanie und Homosexualität,* published the
same year as Hirschfeld's work.[2] This book, despite the fact that it
was published in wartime, which was hardly propitious, was a
great success.

However, it was neither Hirschfeld nor Stekel who led the
withdrawal. Their voices were merely heard among many others.
The withdrawal, we repeat, was accomplished in the absence of
any true leaders. Once traditional ideas had been undermined, the
doubt spread and became stronger; intellectual contagion came
into play. Everyone abandoned what were henceforth considered
"prejudices."

The abandonment would in certain cases be brusque, without
transition. We saw what the *Larousse médical illustré* wrote in
1912. The 1912 text, with its somber evocation of "a great physical weakening" and "a state of intense degradation," continued to
be reprinted in 1922.[3] Then, in 1924, it was replaced by an entirely
different text: "Parents are wrong to be alarmed at a habit which,
most often, has no serious drawbacks. . . . Onanism does not
merit the importance that some families wrongly give it."[4]

In other cases, the evolution was progressive. A striking example was the advice that the Children's Bureau of the American
government gave to parents in its manuals entitled *Infant Care.*
Here it was a question of masturbation in infancy. The 1914 edition of *Infant Care* warned American parents that children could
be "wrecked for life" by this "injurious practice." The latter must
be "eradicated" from the first moment it was detected. The recommended methods were "mechanical": during the night, for example, it might be necessary to restrain the baby's hands by
pinning the nightgown sleeves to the bed, or tying its feet to either side of the crib.[5] In the 1921 edition, mechanical means were
still advocated, but the warning was toned down: it was no longer

a question of children being "wrecked for life." The "injurious practice" had become a "habit" that was nonetheless necessary to combat.[6] In 1929, *Infant Care* no longer considered mechanical means to be of much value and warned parents against any treatment that could psychologically scar the child. The baby should instead be occupied and diverted; he might, for example, be given a toy to play with until he fell asleep. In the 1942 edition, mothers were told straight out not to worry about what their babies did naturally: "A wise mother will not be concerned about this." In 1951—the final stage—the "wise mother" was advised above all not to say "No, no" to her baby, which might confuse him. Masturbation was one topic for which American parents clearly needed to have the latest edition of *Infant Care*.

What evolved the fastest—we are referring obviously to what was written more or less seriously and not to ideas that were floating about in the mind of the general public—were notions relating to masturbation and physical health. Beginning in the thirties, those who continued to defend the old ways of thinking were merely isolated members of the rear guard. A traditionally minded Jesuit like Père Honoré still spoke in 1934 of "great disasters," "prostration," the "blank gaze," and the "sin which attacks the source of life,"[7] but he represented, in 1934, only a past that had disappeared almost entirely from view.

We've just proposed that the evolution in notions of the physical effects of masturbation was rapid, sometimes almost spectacularly so. Nevertheless, despite the withdrawal, one position continued to be heavily defended: it was the idea that while masturbation practiced without excess posed no health risks, excess, on the other hand, could be harmful. Dr. Albert Moll insisted on the innocuousness of masturbation, but in the case of excess, he cried: Danger! Excess, he said, could, among other things, lead to impotence.[8] Iwan Bloch wrote similarly: "At the present day all experienced physicians who have been occupied in the study of masturbation and its consequences hold the view that moderate masturbation in healthy persons, without morbid inheritance, has no bad results at all. It is only excess that does harm." But Bloch found himself obliged to admit: "The boundary line at which the harmless masturbation *(Onanie)* ceases and the injurious onanism *(Onanismus)* begins cannot generally be defined."[9] Therein lay the difficulty: the dangers of "excess" were easily enough evoked, but no one clearly was able to define where that excess begins. Some set the limit quite far out: excess, according to an *Encyclopédie des connaissances médicales* in 1929, occurs only when one masturbates "nonstop."[10]

Despite its longevity, the notion of the harm caused by "excess" would eventually be disparaged in turn. Wardell Pomeroy, Kinsey's closest collaborator, wrote in 1968: "No physical harm can result from it, contrary to the old beliefs, no matter how frequently it is done." Pomeroy added: "This was not generally understood until a comparatively short time ago."[11] Dr. Spock said the same thing to teenagers in 1971: "There is no truth in the statement some-times heard that masturbation is harmless only if practiced in moderation."[12]

The weight of tradition was, however, visible, in that even those who had ceased to believe in "excess," or its danger, remained ready in some cases at least to tip their hat in the direction of the old ways of thinking. The sexologist Oswald Schwartz was a man of energetic ideas. It was that energy that he exhibited in 1949, in his *Psychology of Sex:* "It can not be overemphasized that no harm, physical or mental, temporary or lasting, is caused by masturba-tion." But he wrote later: "Since it causes no harm, it is useless to attempt to oppose it with force: all that can be done is to warn the boy against excesses in this realm, with the thought that this has been done more to clear our conscience than in hopes of doing him some good."[13] "To clear our conscience": this meant that one avoided the necessity of making a total break with the conformity of the past.

Yet, if they had given up terrain on the issue of physical health, many physicians, psychologists, and educators remained en-trenched on the issue of masturbation's psychological impact. At times their judgments could be extremely harsh. It was on this ground that the battle continued.

There were, however, two ways of approaching the problem of the relationship between masturbation and psychological balance. Masturbation could be perceived as a dangerous and worrisome psychological symptom or, on the contrary, as a source of psychological damage.

The first approach was that of Dr. Chavigny, professor at the Strasbourg Medical School in 1921. Chavigny wrote: "Repeated masturbation indicates a predisposition to mental disorders. It translates a congenital state of unbalance. . . . When a young masturbator has been detected, he must be viewed as virtually an unbalanced person requiring treatment."[14] We quote this text for its value as a curiosity, given the date and the quality of its author, but all that can be said of it has been said earlier on the dark warnings of Père Honoré: it was already a relic in its own time.

On the other hand, the second theme, that of masturbation's psychological effects, inspired many writers—including many famous names—to heights of eloquence. The anthology of names that could be compiled on this topic, extending into the late twentieth century, would be quite extensive.

For Iwan Bloch, whom we quote because he is considered an enlightened, even advanced sexologist, the juvenile masturbator was destined to grow up to be morose, coldhearted, and egotistical. "The campaign against masturbation as a group manifestation is eminently a social campaign for altruism," Bloch wrote.[15] Elsewhere, for example in a *Pratique médico-chirurgicale,* we read of a "state of emotional nonchalance" and even of "serious neurotic consequences."[16] "The intellectual and moral ailments" of the masturbator, to borrow the terminology of a 1945 doctoral thesis in medicine, was a theme that will persist over several decades.[17]

Psychoanalysts would, more than once and in their own manner, jump into the fray. As we've already seen, this represented no betrayal of Freud. Hesnard, in 1933, described and denounced the presence of "all sorts of unfortunate character changes" in masturbators. They ranged from timidity, lack of initiative, and the fear of action to hypochondria.[18] In 1970, Dr. Dierkens spoke, clearly with greater restraint, of certain psychological "drawbacks" of masturbation; such as the "short-circuit between desire and satisfaction, which causes the young person to shy away from social contacts motivated by sexual tension—resulting in a tendency for isolation which was often already the basis of the masturbatory withdrawal."[19]

But it was Catholic authors—and especially those with a cause—who managed to come up with the most energetic turns of phrase. In 1946, Dr. René Biot thundered out against the "culture of sensuality" that "prevents the mind from opening itself to the great spiritual truths," which "hardens the heart, renders it less generous."[20] Dr. Niedermeyer, a Viennese specialist in "pastoral medicine," revealed in 1953 that the "habitual practice" of masturbation "engenders a dangerous disposition of the soul, characterized by the destruction of self-confidence, the loss of a sense of self-worth, to which is substituted a growing sense of inferiority"; the "ability to love" was replaced by "an increasingly narrow egocentrism."[21] Again, in 1967, a Catholic writer denounced masturbation as a veritable psychological "wound": it was "the school of abandon, of disgust for life or work."[22]

These notions became complicated by the frequent attempt to distinguish the different periods of masturbation. Many said that it was normal and of limited psychological harm in the child or the adolescent. But in the case of the adult, the warning was "Stop!": for adulthood was the period during which masturbation could become a quite worrisome symptom (and here we come back to the notion of masturbation as a symptom).

Meagher, one of the experts in the field between World War I and World War II, proposed as a basic thesis: "masturbation, while almost a normal phenomenon for the child and the adolescent, is not to be so regarded in the adult. When performed by the latter, it shows a failure of psycho-sexual development."[23] For Maurice Debesse in 1952, "it appears that masturbation is only truly dangerous when it persists beyond the start of puberty; . . . it becomes, in the case of the adult, a search for autosatisfaction which reveals an affective regression that is medical in nature."[24] If it continues into adulthood as a prime form of sexual satisfaction, wrote Odette Thibault in 1971, "it is to be treated as a sign of neurosis."[25] Oswald Schwartz, backed by his reputation, made the same distinction: "in the case of the adult, it is generally a neurotic symptom and consequently requires psychological treatment."[26]

But let us come back to youth. If one believed that masturbation could do young people psychological harm, was it necessary to attempt to deter them from it? The answer was simultaneously yes and no. There was considerable wavering on this point.

A growing number of physicians and psychologists believed that the greatest danger of masturbation lay, in fact, in the fear and sense of shame, in the guilt complex that it provoked. This was what could do the young person the most harm.

This idea was repeatedly stressed: "And we are all agreed that the fears do more harm than the habit itself," Meagher wrote in 1924.[27] Fifty years later, the *Petit Larousse de la Médecine,* after having spoken of the innocuousness of masturbation, emphasized: "It is in fact the strong sense of guilt tied to this act that is the most harmful to the emotional balance of the child and the adolescent."[28]

It was thus important to reassure the child, to remove the sense of fear and remorse, but it was also necessary to attempt to wean him of his habit. Psychologists and physicians became mired in this contradiction.

Mounier, for example—the great Emmanuel Mounier of *Esprit*—noted in 1947 in his *Traité du caractère* how "dangerous it is to arouse an overwhelming sense of guilt in this matter" which "can result in stigma as serious as those left by habitual masturbation. . . . Instead of throwing the adolescent into a state of moral terror and self loathing, it is more useful to point out to him the impasse into which he risks venturing."[29] What was that impasse? Mounier described it:

The masturbatory activity is an activity that deviates from its end and lacks the discipline of reality. He who becomes its slave acts henceforth without a goal, lacks control, perseverance and direction, his attention wanders, his will is destroyed. His emotional life is dominated by infantile components, egotism and destructive violence: his personality shifts suffice to denounce him. He reveals a brutal cynicism combined with an unhealthy timidity. The habit of an unmentionable secret life leads him to dissimulation, a habitual absence of candour, of clarity. . . . All this can end in neurasthenia or in various sexual anomalies.[30]

Was it by thus describing such an "impasse" to an adolescent, even in a toned-down version, that one really hoped to avoid provoking a sense of guilt?

One must, certain authors said, "be wary of two contrary excesses": "not taking it seriously" or "terrorizing the child by drawing a gloomy portrait of imaginary consequences." At midpoint between the two excesses was "adroitness"; "judicious, personalized advice, suitable for the child's age."[31] It was this midpoint, obviously, that was often difficult to define.

Dr. Gilbert-Robin, in 1948, advised warning, but with appropriate moderation: "The first precaution that must be taken," he wrote, "is not to terrify the child, not to draw him a hellish portrait of the damages caused by masturbation . . . , this would increase his anxiety." "The most simple and humane approach is *cautiously* to draw his attention to some of masturbation's physical and physiological drawbacks: fatigue, weight loss, rapid exhaustion [it is clear that Gilbert-Robin is a conservative], and above all the weakening of intellectual vigor, the diminution of educational capacity, principally in terms of memory and attention."[32] In spite of the author's care in emphasizing that this was to be done *cautiously*, it is difficult to see how his suggestions would avoid increasing the child's anxiety.

Some believed that the best method was to appeal to the child's self-respect and to his sense of pride. "It is through pride and not through shame that it is permissible to attempt to exert an influence," wrote Dr. Bergé in 1936. "Why not teach young boys (who are the most at risk in this business), from the time of puberty, that a certain part of their body is the seat of virility . . . The child can be shown that all plants, all beings which live and develop, live and develop all the more robustly when they are more greatly respected and less frequently touched."[33] Marie-Thérèse Van Eeckhout offered the same advice in 1961: "The appeal to strength of character, to will, to self-control or to religious sentiment can be very constructive. . . . It is less advisable to grossly overemphasize or focus solely on the question of guilt. Emphasizing the joy and the pride of the victory over himself and of his manly courage will be infinitely more positive and comforting."[34]

The range of thought is thus considerable even within the field of sexology. Arthur Koestler, who published an *Encyclopaedia of Sexual Knowledge* in 1934,[35] declared himself a partisan of a quite traditional form of "treatment": hygiene, appropriate diet, and physical exercise, which can assist the masturbator in stopping his habit. Subsequently the work was translated into English, and the British specialist who headed the translation, Norman Haire, held the entirely opposite opinion. "The treatment," he wrote, "is worse than the disease." Under the effect of all those "long and complicated directions," the patient "spends his whole time thinking of masturbation, wanting to masturbate, fighting against the temptation, at last succumbing to it, and then suffering from remorse until the cycle is completed once more." Haire's personal advice was far simpler: "I have found it much better to explain to the patient that masturbation will not do him any harm at all and that he can masturbate as often as he wants to." According to Haire, the frequency of the habit consequently diminished to moderate proportions.[36]

A divergence of opinion can even be seen, in 1973, within the same group of sexologists, or at least in their different publications. The team was that of Doctors Cohen, Kahn-Nathan, Tordjman, and Verdoux, who published in France a great *Encyclopédie de la vie sexuelle* in five volumes, designed for varied age groups.

What do we find in the manual designed for 10- to 13-year-olds? A dialogue between father and son. The son asks: "Is masturbation forbidden because it is dangerous?" The father answers: "No, masturbation is neither a vice nor a danger. But if a child gets a taste for it, it will be hard for him later to love someone else."[37]

In the volume for the 17- to 18-year-olds, the tone is different. It begins on a reassuring note: "For the adolescent, masturbation remains simultaneously both the most frequent and the most innocuous release mechanism for sexual instinct." Yet what follows certainly looks like a warning: "Masturbation reinforces egocentrism (the tendency to view everything in terms of self), the flight from reality, and so postpones the onset of a true relational life. . . . It poses no problem when it is only transitory . . ., it is psychologically dangerous, on the contrary, when it persists for too long."[38]

In the volume meant for adults, emphasis was placed on the notion of "disculpation." "The danger of masturbation resides in the adolescent's struggle with himself. It is the role of parents or educators to help him to overcome it and then to win it. They must never miss an opportunity to remove the guilt from this solitary pleasure by showing how widespread a practice it is."[39]

From volume to volume, the subtle and not-so-subtle shifts were visible. For the 10- to 13-year-olds, masturbation was not condemned, but an attempt was made nonetheless to dissuade them from it, by a bit of "blackmail for their own good."[40] In the case of the 17- to 18-year-olds, the word *danger* reared its head among the reassurances. For adults, on the other hand, the primary danger lay in giving the child a guilt complex. All of this is somewhat incoherent and inexact: it is the very image of a field that was still unsure of its positions.

Vocabulary in itself is an excellent gauge of changes in ways of thinking. The language of "curing" the child or the adolescent remained long entrenched, before being forced to surrender under successive assaults; we find it for the last time in 1967, in the text of a Catholic author.[41] "Bad habits" or "unfortunate habits" would resist for a long time; they reappeared in the writings of a leading educator like Freinet as late as 1962.[42] The words *vice* or *vicious habit* would continue to be used through the fifties and even sixties.[43] The word and the idea, of course, go hand in hand; as late as 1940 a candidate for admission to the Naval Academy at Annapolis was rejected when a doctor discovered he had masturbated.[44]

What did more than anything else to sweep away the language of "cure," "bad habit," and "vice," and what played a decisive role in the shattering not only of some traditional ideas relating to masturbation but also the near-totality of traditional thought on the subject, was the startling revelation that masturbation was an extremely common, widespread, and banal phenomenon. From common, banal, and widespread, there was a natural transition to the notion of what was normal.

This startling revelation came primarily from the Kinsey report, which profoundly marked the field. One might almost say—admittedly by grossly simplifying things—that our history of masturbation began with *Onania* and Tissot and ends with Kinsey.[45]

Well before Kinsey, however, there had been ample evidence and corroborating studies to demonstrate the widespread existence of masturbation. Experts quoted figures, and those figures were published in well-documented studies. Koestler, in his *Encyclopaedia of Sexual Knowledge,* cited percentages for male masturbation established by various researchers: 85 percent, 90 percent, 93 percent, 95 percent.[46] So did Gügler, in a systematic study published in 1942.[47] Yet those studies largely failed to reach or have much of an effect upon the general public. Kinsey, on the other hand, through the wide use made of his results, did—directly or indirectly—have an effect.

The Kinsey report—*Sexual Behavior in the Human Male*—was published in 1948 and, as we know, was a considerable success. The study, devoted to the United States, was huge and detailed. The figures were there. Kinsey wrote: "Ultimately about 92 percent of the total population is involved in masturbation which leads to orgasm.

More individuals (96 percent) of the college level and 95 percent of the high school group, are ultimately included, fewer (89 percent) of the males who never go beyond grade school. . . . In the present study we have examined the histories of 5,300 males, of which about 5,100 record experience in masturbation."[48]

Studies like Kinsey's in other countries did not produce such spectacular results, but they revealed percentages that were still quite striking. The Simon report in France noted that "three quarters of men questioned say they have practiced masturbation."[49]

Such statements had a widespread impact, even in popular reference works such as handbooks and encyclopedias. "According to numerous statistical reports, almost all young males have had a masturbatory experience," noted the *Myers Lexicon* in 1975.[50] The 1972 *Larousse de la Médecine* noted, for its part: "From puberty to adulthood, this behavior is so ordinary that it cannot be considered as pathological."[51]

"Ordinary": From "ordinary" the slip to "normal" would be natural. The notion of normality, and, when all is said and done, the law of normality, is set by the percentages. The notion of normality would gain terrain. "A perfectly normal way to relieve sexual desire," wrote the *Petit livre suédois d'éducation sexuelle.*[52] "Transitory masturbation is the rule," a French manual stated in 1971.[53]

From this new perspective, the abnormality ceased to be masturbation and became the absence of masturbation. Masturbation, two French sexologists note in 1970, "is the most frequent adolescent sexual activity, since, according to combined American and European statistics, its rate hovers around 90 percent for boys, versus 25 percent for girls. It thus represents a normal developmental stage in sexual physiology. . . . The inevitable conclusion is that the abnormality, if it exists, is to be found at the level of the 10 percent of inactive adolescents."[54] Two years later, the Simon report said the same thing: "It is a question of a normal stage in the psychological and emotional development of the individual. . . . It is the total absence of masturbation that can be, under certain conditions, worrisome."[55]

With ordinariness and normalcy, all the dangers attributed to masturbation could be completely swept away. The psychological dangers would increasingly be consigned to oblivion alongside the physical ones. Practically the only danger that remained, in this case, was the child's own reaction. "What is pathogenic is not masturbation itself, but the anxiety experienced by the subject following the act," according to the *Larousse de la Médecine*.[56] Barandier stated: "There are no physical consequences of masturbation whatsoever. . . . The sole pathological effects are the anguish, the fear and the guilt that are often associated with it."[57]

The only precautions to be taken, given these conditions, were to calm the child's fears, and above all to avoid doing anything to stir them up again. Repressive attitudes were mentioned only to be condemned as relics of the past. Even simple attempts at dissuasion by parents or educators were more and more often perceived as dangerous. "The danger of misguided educational concern," wrote Alsteens, "lies in aggravating, increasing the burden of guilt linked to masturbation."[58] Children should be left alone.

Young people's attitudes toward masturbation, moreover, were undergoing radical changes as well. Let us recall the results of Pullias's 1937 study: 82 percent of the freshman university students questioned by Pullias believed in the dangers of masturbation. In 1975, less than 40 years later, the proportions were reversed. Miller and Lief, in 1975, published the conclusions of a study of 556 American university students, most of whom were medical school students. During the study, students were asked to respond "true" or "false" to the proposition that "certain conditions of mental and emotional instability are demonstrably caused by masturbation." "False," responded nearly 84 percent of the students interviewed.[59] Compared to Pullias's study, this was not an evolution; it was a veritable revolution. Kinsey had played a role in it.

In this new atmosphere, moral notions changed as well. What we have here is a textbook case of morality adjusting to fit psychology.[60] How could what is now considered commonplace and normal continue to be condemned on moral grounds?

Here again, one study and its figures stand out. They came once again from the United States: in 1972 a study questioned a little over 2,000 Americans—a "reasonably good representation of American adult society"—on sexual problems. Subjects were asked to agree or disagree with the proposition "masturbation is wrong." Among males from 18 to 34, no more than 15 or 16 percent responded affirmatively in 1972. "Masturbation is wrong" elicited a "no" from four-fifths of 18- to 34-year-olds.[61] Some would suggest that the question was unclear, since "wrong" could be taken to refer to either physical or moral aspects, or to both. Yet ideas had unquestionably changed on both the moral and the physical levels.

The notion that masturbation was a sin had fallen by the wayside. Some Catholic authors would make a valiant effort to revive it, despite the fact that ways of thinking had evolved. "Sin, grievous sin against divine law," Vermeire wrote in 1959.[62] "Sin of unchasteness," Abbé Petitmangin said forcefully in 1967.[63] Even the abbot Marc Oraison, who was not known to have conservative leanings, continued in 1972 to hold the theoretical view that "the masturbatory act and the accompanying psychological state unquestionably constitute a material transgression. It is contrary to the ends of sexuality, that is to say to the love-union and to the creation of life. It is, properly speaking, an act that is beyond the bounds of nature, that is even unnatural.... [It] goes against God's plan for creation."[64] It is true that, later in the same book, Marc Oraison considerably attenuated the gravity of the sin on the practical level.

Yet alongside the Catholic authors who persisted in speaking of sin, there were many others who had ceased to use the term. For them, religious morality was a thing of the past. "On what basis" one of them even wondered, "will they now attempt to convince adolescents to give up this habit?"[65]

Those who abandoned the notion of sin generally did so simply by keeping quiet—totally quiet—on the subject. But there were also a moralist or two, a theologian or two—they were, however, very rare—who looked closely at the matter and wondered if there might not be cause to alter traditional ways of thinking. A Catholic moralist asked, in 1969: "Is the gravity of masturbation indisputable? Is it possible, in fact, to establish the objective value of an act without taking into account its meaning, its sense as an actual lived experience? . . . What we've been told [the moralist is referring here to the psychologists] about the meaning of adolescent masturbation . . . should perhaps lead us to more nuanced judgments of the objective gravity of a practice which is so widespread at that age."[66] A Dominican, Père A. Plé, expressed for his own part, in 1966, doubts about the validity of the arguments that had traditionally served to buttress the notion of mortal sin. These arguments, Father Plé wrote, "could be revised, it seems to me." In the light of modern biology, he noted, is it not difficult to continue to speak purely and simply, as was done in the past, of an "unnatural act"? On the other hand, threatening sin could be a very dangerous thing. "No greater educational blunder could be committed than to aggravate, through the fear of sin, the anguish and the mental guilt ordinarily associated with masturbation. One might as well shout *Danger!* to a man who suffers from vertigo: it is to give him a psychological shove and make him fall into the abyss which fascinates him." The moral lesson to be preached and inculcated, according to Plé, was not that of the "horror of vice" but rather the positive lesson of love and the virtues of chastity.[67] Father Plé took up these same ideas several years later, in the article *Masturbation,* written for the French dictionary *Catholicisme.*[68]

Many confessors, Plé wrote, "feel deeply uncomfortable" treating masturbation as a mortal sin.[69] They were often spared their unease, however, by their penitents, who no longer brought up the topic during confession. Abbé Petitmangin took particular note of this development in 1967: "These days, we encounter penitents who admit being sinners in many respects, except that of their auto-erotic behavior. Simply, they have come to accept their masturbatory habits as inevitable. They plainly think they can qualify their solitary satisfactions as perfectly insignificant acts."[70]

Faced with this indulgence, both practical and theoretical, Rome, it must be noted, reacted. It did so through the voice of the Congregation for the Doctrine of the Faith. The latter published, in 1976, a strongly worded declaration that attempted to apply the brakes to laxist tendencies in sexual matters. It simultaneously condemned homosexuality, sexual relations before marriage, and masturbation. On this last point, as on the others, it represented a refusal to bow to the evolution in thought, and, a reaffirmation of tradition.

"The traditional Catholic doctrine that masturbation constitutes a grave moral disorder is often called into doubt or expressly denied today," the Congregation for the Doctrine of the Faith wrote.

> It is said that psychology and sociology show that it is a normal phenomenon of sexual development, especially among the young. . . .
>
> This opinion is contradictory to the teaching and pastoral practice of the Catholic Church. Whatever the force of certain arguments of a biological and philosophical nature, which have sometimes been used by theologians, in fact both the Magisterium of the Church—in the course of a constant tradition—and the moral sense of the faithful have declared without hesitation that masturbation is an intrinsically and seriously disordered act. . . . whatever the motive for acting in this way, the deliberate use of the sexual faculty outside normal conjugal relations essentially contradicts the finality of the faculty.

The Congregation said strongly that Kinsey (whom it never names, however), cannot undermine morality. "Sociological surveys are able to show the frequency of this disorder according to the places, populations, or circumstances studied. In this way facts are discovered, but facts do not constitute a criterion for judging the moral value of human acts."[71]

All that was clear, very clear, but it was a wasted effort. In fact, the whole of the declaration from Rome, with its completely traditional approach to sexuality—marriage and nothing but marriage—was generally received with jeers, unease, or a shrug of the shoulders. "You'd think you were dreaming," wrote Odette Thibault in *Le Monde*. "Are we in 1976 or the Middle Ages?"[72] Henri Fesquet, also in *Le Monde*, emphasized that in making such a declaration, the Church "is going against the grain of the modern world." "It legislates for an ideal man who is practically nonexistent, and it turns up its nose at the most ordinary experience."[73] A certain number of theologians openly made their reaction known and declared that they "question the advisability and the validity of a statement whose definitive and preemptory tone, under the guise of defending absolute principles, condemns men of flesh and hope to the state of legal sinners."[74] "The text takes no account of the questions that men of today ask themselves" said Père René Simon, professor at the Catholic Institute in Paris. "The tragedy of the Church" he added, "lies in its repetition of ethical norms concerning sexuality, in the imperative mood, in a context that has rather radically modified our own notions of sexuality."[75] Like the dissenting theologians, Père Simon said out loud what a great number of bishops, in France and elsewhere, surely thought.

The largest Flemish newspaper in Belgium, which entitled its commentary: "A missed opportunity," wrote: "We fear that 90 percent of Catholics will fail to be guided by this document, as was the case, statistics reveal, for the encyclical *Humanae Vitae*."[76]

In attempting to predict public reaction to the 1976 declaration, the comparison to *Humanae Vitae* was not unreasonable. Yet in 1976, what occurred was less complicated. Paul VI's 1968 encyclical, with its ban on contraception, also went against the grain of the modern world. But since it was an encyclical, with all the authority of an official text, it caused no small amount of consternation. The various episcopates had to reach heights of cleverness in order to show the greatest respect for the Pope's words while at the same time finding a way to get around his orders. *Humanae Vitae* resulted in balancing acts. The Declaration of the Congregation for the Doctrine of the Faith, on the other hand, produced neither balancing acts nor consternation. Following the reception we outlined above, the text was simply buried and forgotten. The rear guard's battle had been in vain.

After 1976, no traces of Rome's declaration were to be found in the advice meted out within Catholic circles.

Take, for instance, the instructions on *L'Education affective et sexuelle à l'école maternelle et primaire* that came out of the Central Council for Belgian Catholic Primary Education. Masturbation was treated there under the title: "A Search, a Progression, a Risk." "A progression" it was explained, "is a transitional behavior, a new stage of masturbation on the route of heterosexuality; it is a moment of passage which carries with it the seed of heterosexual attraction, a stage towards adulthood." "The risk," however, was that if it became a habit, masturbation "endangers the evolution of the individual towards the opposite sex." "In this case, but only in this case, the moral gravity of masturbation becomes undeniable. It then becomes a sin against love."[77] "A sin against love": we are a long way from Rome's "intrinsically and seriously disordered act."

Or take the 1982 pamphlet on *Onanisme dans le discours médical* put out by the School of Public Health of the Catholic University of Louvain. We are often asked for advice on the topic of masturbation, the authors wrote. Their answer: "Would physicians perhaps not best handle their doubts by refraining from getting involved? . . . The acts of adolescents or adults in the realm of sexual pleasure need thus be neither condoned nor condemned."[78] Rome uttered not a word in response.

For his part, the religion columnist for *Le Monde*—a progressive Catholic, undoubtedly, but a perfectly orthodox one—calmly explained his way of seeing things the day following the declaration from Rome. He took exception to the document: "From the moment that it is acknowledged that neither 'wasting seed'—nature does it all the time—nor the search for pleasure are unnatural, why should masturbation be immoral? Would it not be wisest to say that most often, it has no moral connotation whatsoever?"[79]

The authority of Rome was, however, not so easily discouraged or ready to give up. In 1983, Rome spoke again, but with a much lower profile than it had taken in 1976.

New instructions were published in Rome on November 1, 1983. They came, this time, from the Congregation for Catholic Education. Their primary topic: sexual education. Traditional doctrine was unfailingly upheld: "According to Catholic doctrine, masturbation is a grave moral disorder." Yet the condemnation of the act does not preclude, it was emphasized, an attitude of considerable lenience toward the individual: "While taking into account the objective gravity of masturbation, prudence is called for in evaluating the subjective responsibility of the individual." This had an entirely new ring to it: obviously the Church was adapting. It was adapting as well by substituting the notion of positive help for that of repression:

> Perspicacious educators and advisors must try to understand the causes of the deviation, in order to help the adolescent move beyond the immaturity which underlies this habit. . . . So that the adolescent may be helped to feel welcome within a community of charity and relieved of his withdrawal into himself, the educator must de-dramatize masturbation and must not withhold his esteem or his kindness; he must help him to integrate himself socially, to open himself to others and to take interest in them, in order to succeed in ridding himself of this form of auto-eroticism by moving in the direction of an oblative love which is characteristic of sentimental maturity.[80]

The Roman congregation was apparently attempting—while still upholding the principles—to demonstrate a maximum degree of understanding. A fresher, more contemporary breeze had begun to blow over the hills of Rome.

The 1992 *Catéchisme de l'Eglise Catholique* leads us to the same conclusion. The catechism came out of Rome, where it had been meticulously formulated. It was issued by the Pope on October 11, 1992 in the form of an Apostolic Constitution and published in its original French in November of 1992. Masturbation certainly continued to be condemned (it is an "intrinsically and gravely disordered act"), but that said, the catechism quickly moved on to address the range of possible attenuating circumstances: "In order to form an equitable opinion of the moral responsibility of the individuals and to perform our pastoral duties we must take into account emotional immaturity, force of habit, a state of anguish, or other mental or social factors which lessen, indeed even extenuate the individual's moral guilt."[81]

Outside Catholic circles, we can see the last stage of the evolution. After the prohibition had come permissiveness. After permissiveness, praise. After having so long been an illness to be cured, it would now be described by some as a remedy.

This new positive outlook made its breakthrough appearance in the United States.[82] It was still basically an extension of the effect produced by Kinsey. How could something that is normal not also be, at least in some respects, good? Dr. Pomeroy, who had closely collaborated with Kinsey, presented "the pro side, the reasons for feeling free to masturbate," in his 1968 book *Boys and Sex:* "It is a pleasurable and exciting experience. . . . It releases tensions and is therefore valuable in many ways. . . . It provides a full outlet for fancy, for daydreaming, which is characteristic of adolescence. . . . In itself, it offers a variety which enriches the individual's sex life." And Pomeroy concludes: "it is not only harmless but is positively good and healthy, and should be encouraged because it helps young people to grow up sexually in a natural way."[83]

"It should be encouraged": the old world had been turned on its head.

Pomeroy was not an isolated case. McCary, in *Sexual Myths and Fallacies,* declared that, in terms of both adolescent sexual development and the release of certain adult sexual tensions, masturbation could be considered "a gift of God."[84] A popular encyclopedia, *Man's Body,* published in 1976, offered nearly the same praise of masturbation: "Nowadays, masturbation . . . is more generally accepted for what it is: part of our normal sexual experience. First, it has functioned (especially before the development of the Pill) as a way of diverting some of the sexual drive that otherwise would result in immature partnership commitments. Second, it releases acute tension due to an unsatisfactory sexual life or the temporary absence of a partner. Third, it alleviates the sexual loneliness of old age."[85]

In France in 1973, René Verdier launched a capable defense of masturbation in his *L'onanisme ou le droit au plaisir*. Masturbation was, for Verdier, "salutary and a part of mental hygiene," it was "beneficial in nature." Verdier analyzed its "functions," all of which were beneficial: maturing function, compensatory function, physiological function, ludic function. He made the case for "happy and liberated masturbation."[86]

These new views were consecrated in 1974 in the very serious *Encyclopaedia Britannica*, which took special note of them. "Many students of sexual behavior," in the words of the *Encyclopaedia Britannica*, "extol its virtues as being healthy, pleasurable, sedative, and a release of tension."[87]

On the women's side, Shere Hite, the author of the sensational *Hite Report*, based on letters sent in by some 3,000 American women, emphasized the pleasure that a considerable number of women declared they'd found in masturbation. As a good feminist, Shere Hite vigorously defended the right to this type of pleasure, "the right to enjoy masturbation."[88]

It goes without saying that these ideas had an impact on young people. We cited earlier the study of American students by Miller and Lief, the results of which were published in 1975. The students were asked to agree or disagree with the idea that "relieving tension by masturbation is a healthy practice." More than three-quarters of the students—76 percent—said that they agreed. A little under 15 percent said that they were undecided. A little under 10 percent indicated disagreement.[89] Thus, more than three-quarters of the students viewed masturbation in a positive light.

Where this evolution has taken us is still not, however, entirely clear. The old taboos have been knocked down, but they are far from gone. They find hardly any champions at all now in medical or pedagogical literature, but they have not completely died out among the general public. It makes sense to assume that some families must still be reading yesterday's books. No matter how much we emphasize the 76 percent in Miller and Lief's study, we can't overlook the 10 percent who seem to resist the evolution. Above all, what is striking is that in spite of Kinsey, in spite of the statistics, in spite of the opinion of specialists, masturbation still often provokes a feeling of discomfort, even of repulsion, which results in an attempt to hide it. Recently, a physician-sexologist wrote of her patients: "The word 'masturbation' is still whispered or said with lowered gaze, even to us, sexologists, labeled as people who are allowed to talk about sex. During one month I noted that one patient out of two felt obliged to 'apologize' for speaking to me about it."[90] An American author noted the same inhibition in 1972: "It is far easier to admit that one does not believe in God, or was once a Communist, or was born illegitimately, than that one sometimes fondles a part of his own body."[91] In the case of youth—children and adolescents—it is of course admitted that masturbation is normal. Yet, once the adolescent stage is over, normality in the eyes of many, undoubtedly in the eyes of most, can mean only one thing: heterosexuality. Masturbation, on this level, has not managed to join the ranks of normal sexual pleasures that are recognized as such. If it is pleasure-inducing, one keeps quiet, unless perhaps one decides to write to Shere Hite to let her know.[92] The taboo, in this sense, remains. Tissot has been entirely forgotten, the terror of old is gone, the Church and its moral theology have ceased to reverberate in the modern ear, yet a hint of the past, in spite of it all, continues to hang in the air.

Two examples of the tenacity of the past:

In the early 1990s in England, a study of the sexual habits of the English had to drop its questions on masturbation "because of the distaste and embarrassment it caused to respondents."[93]

In the United States, what happened in December 1994 is even more remarkable: it is the manner in which President Clinton demanded the immediate resignation of the surgeon general of the United States, Jocelyn Elders.

As surgeon general, that is to say as head physician and government spokesperson on matters of public health, Jocelyn Elders, the first African American woman to hold this position—and the highest-ranking African American woman in the Clinton administration—had already made conservatives uncomfortable by her liberal views on sexual education in school and the legalization of drugs. President Clinton nonetheless supported her. In December 1994, comments that she had made at a United Nations conference on AIDS were reported. Recalling her arguments for sex education in schools, and specifically on the topic of masturbation, Jocelyn Elders commented that in her eyes, masturbation was part of human sexuality and that it might be well if it were included in sex education courses in public schools. The reaction from the president was immediate: the president does not believe that is what schools are for, declared a White House spokesperson. Jocelyn Elders was dismissed on the spot.[94]

The famous medical journal *The Lancet* commented on the dismissal as follows: "Jocelyn Elders will go down in history as a distinguished pediatrician and clinical research worker, and a very courageous surgeon general who was dismissed for speaking the truth."[95]

BRIEF CONCLUSION

Indifference, total or partial. A quack who sounds the alarm and who, finding no serious scientific obstacles in his way, achieves some degree of success; a famous physician who, echoing the quack, supports the warning with the weight of his authority and thereupon builds a theory; a society that discovers in the theory an answer to some of its questions and so adopts it; a long period during which this theory reigns, with hardly any detractors, and spreads a climate of fear across Europe. Then opponents, rare at first, then numerous, who make no scientific discoveries but who simply note, one after another, that the theory doesn't hold water; now a reversal of opinions, first partial, then total; the acknowledgment that what had been taken as abnormal was in fact normal—that is roughly the cycle of masturbation that we've witnessed.

One question is inescapable: without the quack at the beginning, would any of this have happened? Without *Onania*'s author, would we have had a story to tell? It is a troubling question and one that will never be answerable with anything better than a tower of suppositions. Yet one thing seems clear to me: it is that the hypothesis according to which nothing would have happened without *Onania*'s author is not an absurd hypothesis at all.

One man, two men even, counting Tissot, played an essential role. But what they set in motion was a social mechanism in the true sense of the expression.

This mechanism basically had two components. One was the belief in onanism's harm, which, as it spread, tended to produce its own proof. Each time a physician or a patient found that masturbation offered an explanation for a condition that was otherwise hard to explain, this very explanation reinforced the notion that masturbation was a veritable scourge. It was the snowball effect.

The second component was the impression that one was faced with a scourge. This impression reinforced the notion that masturbation was a formidable vice, and this notion of vice began to find its place within society's value system. The social value system and medical notions then propped each other up, mutually reinforcing each other. From that point on, we were truly faced with a social phenomenon.

It is society as a whole, in this case, that was implicated, and not its supporting institutions. No institution, remarkably enough, seems to have played a particular role either during the formative period or during the period of stabilization. One might have expected the Church—whose condemnation of masturbation was of long standing—to exercise considerable influence. In fact, the Church accompanied the process, no more. Confessors do not seem to have been any harsher than doctors or educators.

In the decomposition and the eventual dissolution of the belief, the mechanisms began to work backwards. Each time the term *prejudices* was used to designate what had up until then been taken as the truth, it was the credibility of the entire theory that was shaken, leading to new doubts. The snowball effect this time was destructive. Each time prejudices were mentioned, moreover, the very notion of vice, based on now-contested medical notions, was shaken as well.

This decomposition was slow, very slow, and not without its fits and starts, but it continued inexorably. It seems almost over, and as far as anyone can predict, there will never be another Tissot.

The cycle nearly complete, the matter nearly settled once and for all, our reaction today tends to be one of surprise at this "great terror" that certainly existed, despite the fact that there was no good reason for it ever to have existed at all. Yet, as my daughter, Isabelle Stengers, who has studied the problem of drugs reminds me, there are clear parallels between the two issues. It may be that in fifty years or less, the West will have decriminalized the use of marijuana and other soft drugs, for the simple and logical reason that these substances will have been proved to be no more dangerous (and proved in fact less dangerous) than tobacco or alcohol, and the reaction will then be the same: surprise at the image of a bogey against which it had been necessary to declare "war."

The memories of police and judges arresting and punishing someone for possessing several grams of marijuana will appear, in retrospect, just as ridiculous and incomprehensible as the memory of a physician who announced to a young man that his "bad habits" would lead inexorably to deafness. The future, on this point, is easily forecast. We might perhaps attempt an even bolder prediction of the future, in the realm of both mental and physical health—a fluctuating and fragile realm, if there ever was one. Perhaps, in a day when psychoanalysis will have been totally discredited, people will have trouble understanding why, for so long, so many people in civilized societies spent their time lying on a couch.

NOTES

INTRODUCTION

1. W. Davenport, "Sex in Cross-Cultural Perspective," in *Human Sexuality in Four Perspectives*, ed. F. A. Beach (London and Baltimore: 1976), p. 152.

CHAPTER ONE

1. P.-J. Proudhon, *De la Justice dans la Révolution et dans l'Eglise. Nouveaux principes de philosophie pratique*, vol. I (Paris: 1858), p. 336.
2. *Grand Dictionnaire universel du XIXe siècle*, vol. X (Paris: 1858), pp. 1320–22.
3. See also, at about the same date, the entry *Onanisme* in *Dictionnaire de la Conversation*, which summarizes the "terrible consequences" of the vice (2nd ed., vol. XIII [Paris: 1872], p. 732.
4. Fournier and Béguin, entry *Masturbation* in *Dictionnaire des Sciences médicales*, vol. XXXI (Paris: 1819), p. 108.
5. *Hygiène et physiologie du mariage* (Paris: 1848), p. 226. Same in 57th ed. (Paris: 1872), p. 226.
6. Réveillé-Parise, "Traité d'hygiène appliqué à l'éducation de la jeunesse, par le Docteur Simon," *Revue médicale française et étrangère* (1828), vol. II, p. 93.
7. J.-B. de Bourge, *Le memento du père de famille et de l'éducateur de l'enfance, ou les conseils intimes sur les dangers de la masturbation*

(Mirecourt, 1860), p. 28. Dr. Demeaux similarly emphasized: "This vice is considered, by all who have studied the question with real care, as a true scourge of humanity . . . The evil has taken on the proportions of a huge epidemic." (J.-B. Demeaux, *Mémoire sur l'onanisme et sur les moyens d'en prévenir ou d'en réprimer les abus dans les établissements consacrés à l'instruction publique* (Paris: 1856), pp. 6–7.

8. J.-B. Fonssagrives, *L'éducation physique des garçons* (Paris: 1870), pp. 302 and 313. Fonssagrives was a professor in the Montpellier Medical School. On his ideas, see also G. Vigarello, *Le Corps redressé. Histoire d'un pouvoir pédagogique* (Paris: 1978), pp. 184–85.

9. P. J.-C. Debreyne, *Essai sur la théologie morale considérée dans ses rapports avec la physiologie et la médecine,* 4th ed. (Paris: 1844), pp. 64–67; 5th ed. (Brussels: 1846), pp. 68–71. On Debreyne, see the entries in the *Dictionnaire de Biographie française,* vol. X, col. 449, *Dictionnaire d'Histoire de Géographie ecclésiastiques,* vol. XIV, col. 143–44, and *Catholicisme,* vol. III, col. 498.

10. F. Devay, *Hygiène des familles ou du perfectionnement physique et moral de l'homme,* vol. II (Paris: 1846), p. 72.

11. Monsignor Dupanloup, *De l'éducation,* vol. III (Paris: 1897), pp. 437 and 451–53. The book was first published in 1862.

12. *Grand Dictionnaire universel du XIXᵉ siècle,* vol. XV (Paris: 1876), p. 235, under *Tissot.* In the preface to his *Essai sur la théologie morale,* cited earlier, Debreyne noted: "There are few, even among the clergy, who have not read this opuscule" (p. VI). In addition to the multiple reeditions of Tissot, there were also a significant number of enlarged editions and adaptations. For a very partial overview, see T. Tarczylo, *Sexe et liberté au siècle des Lumières* (Paris: 1983), pp. 293–94.

13. We know that Doussin-Dubreuil's work was particularly successful because it was republished in 1839, in a revised and enlarged edition, in the popular series, the *Manuels-Roret* (J.-L. Doussin-Dubreuil, *Nouveau manuel sur les dangers de l'onanisme, et conseils relatifs au traitement des maladies qui en résultent,* ed. J. Morin [Paris: 1839]).

14. Samuel La'Mert, *Self-Preservation* (Manchester: S. Gilbert, 1841), pp. 52, 48, 2. It was also published in French under the title: *La Préservation personnelle.* The 1860 edition (at the Bibliothèque Nationale in Paris) is announced as the 52nd edition, but the first French edition, in 1847, was already numbered as the

"22nd edition," given the fact that the translation was based on the 22nd English edition. Publicity in the press helped boost sales: see, for example, the announcements in the *Indépendence belge*, September and October 1849.

15. See the catalog entry in the Bibliothèque Nationale, *Le livre dans la vie quotidienne* (Paris: 1975), pp. 13–14.

16. A. Debay, *Hygiène et physiologie du mariage* (Paris: 1848), pp. 226 and 335.

17. P. H. Nysten, *Dictionnaire de médecine*, 7th ed. (Paris: 1839), p. 602; 10th ed., entièrement refondue par E. Littré et Ch. Robin (Paris: 1855), vol. II, p. 780.

18. See the catalog *Le livre dans la vie quotidienne*, cited above, p. 13, and D.-B. Weiner, *Raspail, scientist and reformer* (New York), pp. 146–47. First published in 1845, the *Manuel Annuaire* sold around 200,000 copies in five years. It was still popular a half-century later. Van Gogh, painting everyday objects in 1889—a candlestick, a bottle, his pipe—included Raspail's book among them (see P. Lecaldano, *Tout l'oeuvre peint de Vincent van Gogh*, vol. II (Paris: 1971), p. 217, no. 629.

19. F.-V. Raspail, *Manuel annuaire de la santé ou Médecine et pharmacie domestique* (Paris: 1845), pp. 211–12. The use of hygienic underwear with camphor had already been recommended by Raspail in his *Histoire naturelle de la santé et de la maladie chez les végétaux et chez les animaux en général*, vol. II (Paris: 1843), p. 507: "I know of no other more powerful way to banish all thought of solitary pleasures in children than to have them regularly wear, under one pretext or another, hygienic underwear, that is to say underwear having camphor powder in the area of the private parts. The powder is to be replaced nightly, if necessary; then camphor powder is also to be put on the bedsheets. It would be desirable for this practice to be adopted in secondary schools and boarding establishments." Raspail is indignant at the fact that animosity towards his ideas—of political origin—might prevent the adoption of such an effective procedure: "Those who carry political hatred to the point of proscribing, out of fear of having to pronounce an author's name, a medication capable of preserving our young generation from a vice which so sadly ravages its ranks, is guilty in our eyes, of an offence against parents and country." Camphor, given Raspail's passion for it, took on a symbolic role: it became the "republican medicine." See particularly on this

topic D. Ligou's preface to *François-Vincent Raspail ou le bon usage de la prison* (Paris: 1968), pp. 28–30.

20. *Le livre sans titre* (Paris: 1830); 2nd ed. (Paris: 1844). The author of the *Conseils sur les moyens de corriger les jeunes détenus de l'habitude de l'onanisme* (n.d.) highly recommends the *Livre sans titre* [*Untitled Book*] to young men in prison, where masturbation was rife: "The text of this work is mediocre," but "its usefulness lies entirely in the illustrations," which were capable of "inspiring great terror."

21. *Antidote moral contre les suites funestes d'un vice impur qui exerce les ravages les plus affreux sur le genre humain* (Tournai, n.d.), pp. 54–55. The Bibliothèque du Séminaire de Tournai has a copy.

22. *Précis historique, physiologique et moral des princiaux objets en cire préparée et coloriée d'après nature qui composent le Museum de J.-F. Bertrand Rival* (Paris: 1801), p. 309. See also J.-P. Aron and R. Kempf, *Le pénis et la démoralisation de l'Occident* (Paris: 1978), p. 189.

23. J.-L. Doussin-Dubreuil, *Lettres sur les dangers de l'onanisme*, 3rd ed. (Paris: 1825), p. 96. "I have heard," added Doussin-Dubreuil, "that M. Bertrand had moved it to Marseille." Another "medical museum" in Paris at the end of the century, with equally edifying figures, is mentioned in P. Bonnetain, *Charlot s'amuse*, 2nd ed. (Brussels: 1883), p. 268.

24. Letter of August 20, 1832, signed "Gaétan," published in the May 23, 1976, edition of *Le Monde*. Pierre Ordioni, who presented the document, did not identify the Gaétan in question, but the information he provided on his father—baron of the Empire, battalion leader of the 56th in 1832—allows us to identify him as Gaétan Viaris, born in 1812 (see A. Révérend, *Armorial du Premier Empire*, vol. IV [Paris: 1897], p. 365; *Almanach royal*, 1832).

25. Edmond and Jules de Goncourt, *Journal*, ed. Ricatte, vol. VI, *1863–1864* (Monaco: Imprimerie Nationale, 1956), p. 184 (entry for February 29, 1864)—Under the Restoration, the case of the duc d'Angoulême, whose deformities, tics, and manias were attributed to a "schoolboy vice," was cited (see J. Turquan, *Le dernier Dauphin. Madame, duchesse d'Angoulême* [Paris: 1909], pp. 132–33 and 136–37, and J. Cabanis, *Charles X, Roi ultra* [Paris: 1972], pp. 442–43). His case, which had struck a chord with the public, would continue to be cited in later years: see, for example, Gustave Flaubert, *Bouvard et Pécuchet*, ed. A. Cento (Naples-Paris:

1864), p. 568 ("it is claimed that the duc d'Angoulême did it"), and Henry Céard, preface by P. Bonnetain, *Charlot s'amuse*, 2nd ed. (Brussels, 1883), p. IX ("the onanical passion which the duc d'Angoulême, a prince, did not disdain").

26. *Journal*, vol. XVII, *1890–1891* (Monaco: 1956), pp. 24–25 (entry for March 28, 1890).

27. First and second editions (Brussels: Kistemaeckeers, 1883). Henry Céard had given the novel a preface in which he declared that Bonnetain, in his description of masturbation, was "moral like Tissot." On Bonnetain, see *Dictionnaire de Biographie française*, vol. VI, col. 1028–29.

28. The trial took place in December 1884, before the Assize Court of the Seine; see the reports in the *Journal des Débats* and *Temps*, December 29, 1884, and in *Indépendence belge*, December 30, 1884, as well as the lead piece in the new expanded edition published by Kistemaeckers in 1885; see also A. Zevaes, *Les procès littéraires au XIXe siècle* (Paris: 1924), pp. 236–38. The editor Kistemaeckers was also prosecuted for the publication of *Charlot s'amuse*, but in Belgium, and was also acquitted (see C. de Cruyenaere-Baudet, entry *Kistemaeckers* in *Biographie Nationale*, vol. XXXVIII, col. 421).

29. A. Debay, *Hygiène et physiologie du mariage*, 57th ed. (Paris: 1872), p. 228.

30. *Hygiène et physiologie du mariage*, p. 336.

31. M. Friedlander, *De l'éducation physique de l'homme* (Paris: 1815), pp. 402–403.

32. J.-B. Fonssagrives, *L'éducation physique du garçon* (Paris: 1870), p. 319.

33. C. Londe, *Nouveaux éléments d'hygiène*, 4th ed. (Brussels: 1840), p. 102.

34. Dr. Rozier, *Des habitudes secrètes ou des maladies produites par l'onanisme chez les femmes*, 3rd ed. (Paris: 1830), p. 217.

35. C. Pavet de Courteille, *Hygiène des collèges et des maisons d'éducation* (Paris: 1827), p. 36.

36. C. Londe, *Nouveaux éléments d'hygiène*, p. 102.

37. C. Crommelinck, *Le vrai trésor de la santé . . . Ouvrage adressé aux gens du monde*, 13th ed. (Brussels: 1875), p. 106.

38. C. Crommelinck, *Traité d'anthropologie à l'usage des gens du monde* (Brussels: 1855), p. 177. Crommelinck was particularly attached to his idea of parallel bars; he also discussed them in his

Vrai trésor de la santé, where he even took care to furnish a drawing of this instrument that he recommended "keeping within reach during the night."

39. *Hygiène des collèges et des maisons d'éducation,* p. 62.
40. *De l'éducation physique de l'homme,* p. 400.
41. *Traité d'anthropologie,* p. 178.
42. C. Londe, *Nouveaux éléments d'hygiène,* p. 101.
43. Dr. Rozier, *Des habitudes secrètes ou des maladies produites par l'onanisme chez les femmes,* p. 246.
44. *Traité d'anthropologie,* p. 177.
45. *De l'éducation physique de l'homme,* pp. 412–13.
46. Simon, *Traité d'hygiène appliquée à l'éducation de la jeunesse* (1827), p. 174. "Tying the hands during the night" is "quite suitable for this purpose," noted Fournier and Bégin in their article *Masturbation* in the *Dictionnaire des sciences médicales* in 1819 (vol. XXXI, p. 130).
47. *Lettres sur les dangers de l'onanisme,* 3rd ed. (Paris: 1825), p. 34.
48. J. Christian, entry *Onanisme* in *Dictionnaire encyclopédique des Sciences médicales,* ed. A. Decambre, 2nd series, vol. XV (Paris: 1881), p. 384
49. Fournier and Béguin, *Masturbation* in *Dictionnaire des sciences médicales,* vol. XXXI, p. 130.
50. See G. Jalade-Lafond, *Considérations sur la confection de corsets et de ceintures propres à s'opposer à la pernicieuse habitude de l'onanisme* (Paris: 1819) and, by the same author, *Considérations sur les hernies abdominales, sur les bandages herniaires rénixigrades et sur de nouveaux moyens de s'opposer à l'onanisme,* 2 vols. (Paris: 1821). See also Aron and Kempf, *Le pénis et la démoralisation de l'Occident,* pp. 191–92. Jalade-Lafond was convinced of the importance of his invention, for the stakes were high: "One could say without exaggeration," he said of onanism, "that here is no illness whose source cannot be found in these solitary and illicit pleasures" (*Considérations sur la confection de corsets . . . ,* p. 5).
51. Handbill for the surgical bazaar of the rue Neuve-des-Petits-Champs [Bazar chirurgical de la rue Neuve-des-Petits-Champs] (1860): Bibliothèque Nationale, Te–103–3.
52. Entry *Masturbation* in *Dictionnaire des sciences médicales,* cited earlier.
53. *L'éducation physique des petits garçons* (Paris: 1870), p. 320.
54. Gustave Flaubert, *Par les champs et par les grèves,* in *Voyages,* ed. R. Dumesnil, vol. I (Paris: 1948), p. 203.

55. See the critical edition by A. Cento (Naples-Paris: 1964), pp. 568–69.

56. The last three words ("croyant tout perdu"—"believing all was lost") appeared in the manuscript, but Flaubert later crossed them out (see A. Cento, p. 568): we have retained them for what they reveal of Flaubert's thinking.

57. The prices of instruments sold in 1860 in the surgical bazaar (see n. 51 above), ranged from 25 to 500 francs. "The difference in price," noted the handbill, "is based only on the materials from which the instruments are constructed. The 500-franc model is made of silver coat of mail."

58. J. Van Ussel, *Sociogenese en evolutie van het probleem der seksuele propaedeuse tussen de 16de en 18de eeuw, vooral in Frankrijk en Duitsland,* photocopied thesis (Gand: 1967), p. 240; from the same author: "'Vuile Manieren' en seksuele opvoeding," *Sextant* no. 11 (1968), p. 8 (drawing of the bench).

59. *L'éducation physique des garçons,* p. 312.

60. On Monsignor Bouvier and his *Dissertatio,* all references can be found in J. Stengers, "Les pratiques anticonceptionnelles dans le mariage au XIXe et au XXe siècle; problèmes humains et attitudes religieuses," in *Revue Belge de Philologie et d'Histoire,* vol. XLIX (1971), pp. 410 and cont.

61. Dr. Rozier, *Des habitudes secrètes,* p. 293.

62. *Le vrai trésor de la santé,* p. 110.

63. Entry *Masturbation* in *Grand Dictionnaire universel du XIXe siècle.*

64. Léopold I to Queen Victoria, May 30, 1853 (Windsor: Royal Archives and photocopies at Brussels, Archives des Palais Royaux). See also B. Emerson, *Léopold II of the Belgians, King of Colonialism* (London: 1979), p. 14.

Chapter Two

1. See, on Benedicti, the entries in the *Dictionnaire de Théologie catholique,* vol. II, col. 601–62, and the *Dictionnaire de Biographie française,* vol. V, col. 1439 (under *Benoît*). The first edition of the *Somme des péchez* was published in 1584. We have quoted the *Abregé de la Somme des péchez,* published in Liège in 1595 (Bibliothèque Royale, Réserve précieuse).

2. *Abregé de la Somme des péchez,* pp. 113–14.

3. See V. L. Bullough, *Sexual Variance in Society and History* (New York: 1976), pp. 358–59. "A thorough study of over sixty medieval penitentials," wrote John Benton, shows "that masturbation was usually classed as a mortal sin, often equivalent to the penance demanded to murder" ("Comment," in *History of Childhood Quarterly,* vol. I (1974), p. 587. However, there were other penitentials in which the penance imposed was far more lenient; see, for example, J.-L. Flandrin, *Le Sexe et l'Occident. Evolution des attitudes et des comportements* (Paris: 1981), p. 113.

4. On Thomas of Cantimpré, see most recently C. Renardy, *Les maîtres universitaires du diocèse de Liège, Répertoire biographique, 1140–1350* (Paris: 1981), pp. 453–54, and R. Godding, "Une oeuvre inédite de Thomas de Cantimpré, la 'Vita Ioannis Cantipratensis,'" *Revue d'Histoire ecclésiastique,* vol. LXXVI (1981), pp. 241 and cont.

5. *Bonum universale de apibus,* book II, chap. 30; Douai edition, 1627, pp. 324–25. See also the French translation, *Le bien universel ou les abeilles mystiques,* trans. V. Willart (Brussels: 1650), p. 228.

6. *Bonum universale de apibus,* Douai edition, p. 322; French trans., *Le bien universel ou les abeilles mystiques,* p. 227.

7. *Bonum universale de apibus,* Douai edition, p. 323; French trans., *Le bien universel ou les abeilles mystiques,* p. 227.

8. Jean Gerson, *De confessione mollitiei,* in *Oeuvres complètes,* ed. Monsignor Glorieux, vol. VIII, *L'oeuvre spirituelle et pastorale* (Paris: 1971), pp. 71–74. The attribution of the work to Gerson is not, we note, entirely certain. See, on this point, T. N. Tentler, *Sin and Confession on the Eve of the Reformation* (Princeton: 1977), p. 93. On *De confessione molittiei,* see Tentler, pp. 91–93; P. Ariès, *L'enfant et la vie familiale sous l'Ancien Régime* (Paris: 1960), pp. 109–10; J.-L. Flandrin, *Les amours paysannes. Amour et sexualité dans les campagnes de l'ancienne France (XVIᵉ-XIXᵉ siècle)* (Paris: 1975), pp. 162–63; and by the same author, *Le Sexe et l'Occident,* pp. 260–61.

9. *Opera omnia,* vol. X, *Secunda Secundae Summae Theologiae a quaestione CXXIII ad quaestionem CLXXXIX* (Rome: 1899), p. 244 (quaestio CLICV, art. 11); *Somme théologique. La Tempérance,* vol. I. trans. J.-D. Folghera (in fact, there was no French translation provided for question 54 "because of the delicate matters" that it treated) (Paris: 1928), p. 280.

10. *Secunda pars totius Summe majoris beati Antonini* (Paris: 1505), titulus V, cap. 4.

11. *Summula . . . de peccatis* (Anvers: 1575), pp. 455–56.

12. "Loquendo de eodem peccato ut subordinatur morosae delectationi aut desiderio aulterii, recipit etiam adulterii deformitatem; et ut subordinatur morosae delectationi aut desiderio incestus, admittit deformitatem incestus; et sic de aliis" (commentary by Cajetan on Saint Thomas's *Somme théologique,* in the edition of the *Summa Theologiae* cited earlier (Rome: 1899), p. 245.

13. *Abregé de la Somme des péchez,* p. 113. See also J.-L. Flandrin, *Le Sexe et l'Occident,* p. 263. Translator's note: since there is no single English equivalent, the Latin "mollities" has been retained in the English translation.

14. J.-B. Bouvier, *Dissertatio in sextum Decalogi praeceptum,* 7th ed. (Le Mans: 1836), p. 56.

15. *Jerusalem Bible* (Garden City, NY: Doubleday, 1966).

16. Jean Calvin, *Commentaire sur le premier livre de Moyse, dit Genèse* (Geneva: 1554), p. 418; modernized text in J. Calvin, *Commentaires sur l'Ancien Testament,* vol. I, *Le Livre de la Genèse,* ed. A. Malet (Geneva: 1961), p. 527. The Latin version of the commentary, published simultaneously, was equally explicit: "A coitu se data opera retrahere ut semen in terram decidat, duplex est monstrum . . ." (J. Calvin, *Opera,* vol. XXIII [*Corpus Reformatorum,* vol. LI] [Brunswick: 1882], col. 495).

17. *Coitus interruptus* would often be called "conjugal onanism" in the nineteenth century. In theological circles, however, it would sometimes be called simply "onanism" (see J. Stengers, "Les pratiques anticonceptionnelles dans le mariage," pp. 421–22). There are thus not only two parallel interpretations of "Onan's crime" but also two different meanings of the term "onanism." This, however, created no difficulties in the nineteenth century, for there was no interpenetration between specialized theological literature—the only realm in which "onanism" was used as a synonym of *coitus interruptus*—and lay vocabulary, in which onanism was invariably a synonym of masturbation.

18. *Abregé de la Somme des péchez,* p. 113. Translator's note: In the place of "mols," the *Jerusalem Bible* [Garden City: Doubleday, 1966] has "catamites," the Oxford *New Testament* [Oxford U. Press, 1981] and the *Holy Bible* from Eyre & Spottiswoode, Ltd

[Edinburgh, n.d.] have "effeminate." No single English term evokes the full range of the term "mol."

19. See particularly, among a wide range of sources, J. T. Noonan, *Contraception. A History of its Treatment by the Catholic Theologians and Canonists* (Cambridge, MA: 1965), pp. 34–36, and D. Daube, *The Duty of Procreation* (Edinburgh: 1977), pp. 4–5.

20. On this point see two articles by A. Plé: "La Masturbation," in *La Vie Spirituelle. Supplément* (May 1966), p. 261; and "Masturbation," *Catholicisme,* vol. VIII, col. 835–36.

21. *Summa Theologiae* (Rome: 1899), pp. 229–30 (quaestio CLIV, art. V); *Somme théologique. La Tempérance,* trans. Folghera, pp. 265–68.

22. "Utrum nocturna pollutio sit poena tantum vel etiam culpa," in *Doctor irrefragabilis Alexandri de Hales Summa theologica,* vol. III (Quarrachi: 1930), p. 268.

23. *Summula . . . de peccatis* (Anvers: 1575), pp. 455–56: the commentary on the *Somme théologique* in the edition of the *Summa Theolgiae* previously cited, pp. 230–31 ("Circa conclusionem principalem, scilicet: *Pollutio nocturna nunquam est peccatum, sed quandoque est sequlea peccati praecedentis,* dubium occurit . . .").

24. "Ex operatione daemonis . . . nequitia daemonis . . . Legitur de quodam quod semper in diebus festis pollutionem nocturnam patiebatur, hoc diabolo procurante, ut impeditur a sacra communione" (*Summa theologiae,* p. 230, trans. Folghera, p. 267).

25. Benedicti thus followed Saint Thomas on this point, but he was the last, let us emphasize, to do so: after Benedicti the role of the devil disappeared completely from theological literature on masturbation; beginning with the seventeenth century, masturbation was a matter in which the devil no longer intervened. There is no known case of exorcism used in an attempt to cure a victim of his pollutions. With all the irrationality that has always been associated with the demonic, one might well have thought that Saint Thomas would have continued to have some disciples, but theology first, then medicine, imposed their notions of rationality here.

26. *Abregé de la Somme des péchez,* pp. 114–16.

27. Th. Sanchez, *Disputationum de sancto matrimonii sacramento tomi tres,* vol. III (Anvers: 1614), book IX, disp. 17 and 45; P. Laymann, *Theologia moralis in quinque libros distributa,* 3rd ed. (Anvers: 1634), pp. 254–55; M. Bonacina, *Opera omnia,* vol. I

(Anvers: 1654), pp. 267–69; T. Tamburini, *Explicatio Decalogi* (Venice: 1678), pp. 224 and cont.; P. Sporer, *Theologia moralis sacramentalis* (Salzburg: 1690), pp. 610 and cont.; L. Habert, *Theologia dogmatica et moralis ad usum Seminarii Catalaunenis*, vol. VII (Paris: 1712), p. 755; *Collegii Salmaticensis FF. Discalceatorum . . . Cursus Theologiae Moralis*, vol. VI (Venice: 1755), p. 129; *Theologia moralis antehac breviter concinnata a R. P. Herm. Busembaum nunc pluribus partibus aucta a R. P. Cl. La Croix*, new edition, vol. II (Venice: 1734), pp. 220–22; C. Roncaglia, *Universa moralis theologia*, vol. I (Augsburg: 1736), pp. 441–46; P. Collet, *Continuatio praelectionum theologicarum Honorati Tournely sive Tractatus de universa theologia morali* (Paris: 1733–47), vol. III, pp. 563–66 and 708–11, and vol. VI, pp. 263–77; Alphonse de Liguori [Alfonsus de Ligorio], *Theolgia moralis*, ed. L. Gaude, vol. I (Graz: 1954), pp. 697–707.

28. In Saint Jean Eudes's confessional manual from the seventeenth century, the questions relating to "voluntary pollution" and pollution during sleep represent just two very brief questions among the 33 questions to be asked on the subject of sins of impurity. No details are given. See Jean Eudes, *Le bon confesseur ou Avertissemens aux confesseurs*, 4th ed. (Caen: 1673), p. 233.

29. The only text of note is the one published in 1700 by the prior of Sennely, in Sologne, in which he described his experience as the village pastor. He wrote: "Young people do not understand what we mean when we speak to them of the sins of *mollesse* and pollution, they need to have these things explained to them, and when their age and temperament lead us to assume they may have committed these sorts of impurities, they are to be questioned in the following way: Have you not thought of commerce with women; or have you been so unfortunate as to have spilled your seed?" (*Le Manuscrit du Prieur de Sennely 1700*, published by E. Huet in *Mémoires de la Société archéologique et historique de l'Orléanais*, vol. XXXII [1908], p. LXXXXIV [sic]; see also J.-L. Flandrin, *Les amours paysannes*, p. 162). There is a brief allusion as well, in 1744, in the statutes published by the Bishop of Boulogne on the occasion of a diocesan synod, in which confessors are advised to prudently question their penitents on the topic of sins against the sixth commandment, "specialiter de pollutione voluntaria, quam inter opera carnis comprehendi multi non intelligunt"—in other terms: many do not understand the gravity of

their sin (*Actes de la province ecclésiastique de Reims*, ed. T. Gousset, vol. IV [Reims: 1844]; see also J.-L. Flandrin, p. 164).

30. Philips Wielant, *Practijcke Criminele*, ed. A. Orts (Gand: 1872), pp. 128–29.

31. *Praxis rerum criminalium* (Anvers: 1555), p. 354. See also the French translation: Josse de Damhoudere, *La practicque et Enchiridion des causes criminellles* (Louvain: 1555), p. 208 ("to be punished by banishment or other extraordinary punishment").

32. "Remarques et observations sur la Coustume généralle d'Arthois" (Lille: Bibliothèque Municipale, Ms. 510, folio 2477 recto. On this text, see R. Muchembled, *Culture populaire et culture des élites dans la France moderne (XVᵉ-XVIIIᵉ siècles)* (Paris: 1978), pp. 236–37.

33. *Le procès criminel* (Rouen: 1619), pp. 40–41.

34. Wielant, *Practijcke Criminele*.

35. Wielant, *Practijcke Criminele*.

36. Wielant, *Practijcke Criminele*.

37. "Remarques et observations sur la Coustume généralle d'Arthois," folio 2477 recto.

38. *Secunda pars totius Summe majoris beati Antonini* (Paris: 1505), titulus VI, cap. 5.

39. F. Toletus, *De instructione sacerdotum et peccatis capitalibus libri VIII* (Anvers: 1609), pp. 710 and 712. This work was published for the first time in 1599, three years after Toledo's death (see the entry *Tolet [Toledo]* in the *Dictionnaire de Théologie catholique*, vol. XV, col. 1224). A French adaptation from 1628 is used by J.-L. Flandrin, *Le Sexe et l'Occident*, p. 263–64.

40. "Ad expellendum semen corruptum ac noxium, sanitatis causa." F. Rebellus, *Opus de obligationibus justitiae, religionis et caritatis* (Lyon: 1608), p. 366. The work was published the year of Rebellus's death (see *Dictionnaire de Théologie catholique*, vol. XIII, col. 1910–11).

41. *Disputationum de sancto matrimonii sacramento tomi tres*, vol. III, p. 224 (book IX, disp. 17). On Sanchez's treatise and its effect, see J. Stengers, "Les pratiques anticonceptionnelles dans le mariage," pp. 427–28.

42. "Et si sanitatis recuperandae, vitae conservandae, vel alia quacumque causa." Laymann, *Theologia moralis*, p. 254.

43. L. Beyerlinck, *Magnum theatrum vitae humanae*, vol. V (Cologne: 1631), p. 586. The work is posthumous, as Beyerlinck died in

1627 (see the entry in the *Biographie Nationale,* vol. II, col. 404–408).

44. *Opera omnia,* vol. I (Anvers: 1654), p. 268 (= *De matrimonii sacramento,* quaest. IV, punctum X).

45. "Vitam potius affectu caritatis profundere," *Opera omnia,* vol. I, p. 268 (= *De matrimonii sacramento,* quaest. IV, punctum X).

46. *Theologia moralis sacramentalis,* p. 614. Sporer, as one commentator puts it, is generally "plus quam par benignus" (see J. Stengers, "Les pratiques anticonceptionnelles dans le mariage," p. 431 and n. 2).

47. *Universa moralis theologia,* vol. I, p. 442.

48. *Secunda pars totius Summe . . . ,* titulus VI, cap. 5.

49. Martinus Azpilcueta, Doctor Navarrus, *Enchiridion sive Manuale Confessariorum et Poenitentium* (Anvers: 1601), p. 255 (cap. XVI, n. 7). On Navarrus, see the entries in the *Dictionnaire de Théologie catholique,* vol. I, col. 2119 (under *Aspilcueta*) and in the *Dictionnaire d'Histoire et de géographie ecclésiastiques,* vol. V, col. 1368–74 (*Aspilcueta*).

50. *Enchiridion,* p. 256.

51. *De instructione sacerdotum . . . ,* p. 710.

52. *Explicatio Decalogi,* p. 226.

53. See P. Collet, *Continuatio praelectionum theologicarum,* vol. III, pp. 563–64.

54. See the entries in *Dictionnaire de Théologie catholique,* vol. II, col. 1709–12; *Catholicisme,* vol. II, col. 527–8; and *New Catholic Encyclopedia,* vol. III, p. 99. See also K. Kranbbenhoft, "Pascal contre Caramuel," *XVIIe Siècle* (Oct.-Dec. 1981).

55. J. Caramuel, *Theologia moralis fundamentalis,* 3rd ed. (Lyon: 1657–1664), pt. II, vol. III, pp. 420–21, n. 1965–67.

56. J. Caramuel, *Theologia moralis fundamentalis,* pt. II, vol. III, pp. 420–21, n. 1965–67.

57. C. Duplessis d'Argentré, *Collectio judiciorum de novis erroribus,* vol. III (Paris: 1736), p. 350. On the 1679 condemnations, see the entry *Laxisme (Querelle du),* by E. Amann, in the *Dictionnaire de Théologie catholique,* vol. IX, col. 72–85.

58. See W. Krenkel, "Masturbation in der Antike," in *Wissenschaftliche Zeitschrift der Wilhelm-Pieck-Universität Rostock,* vol. XXVIII (1979), pp. 164–65.

59. Galien, *De locis affectis,* book 6, in *Claudii Galeni Opera omnia,* ed. C. G. Kuehn, vol. VIII (Leipzig: 1824), pp. 417–20; French

translation in *Oeuvres anatomiques, physiologiques et médicales de Galien,* trans. C. Daremberg, vol. II (Paris: 1856), pp. 687–89. English translation: Galen, *On the Affected Parts,* trans. Rudolph E. Siegel (Basel: S. Karger, 1976).

60. Notably, the passage is cited in the article *Manstupration* of the *Encyclopédie;* on this article, see chapter VI below.

61. *Onania examined and detected* (London: 1723), pp. 99–100; on this pamphlet, see chapter III below.

62. See L. Demaitre, "The Idea of Childhood and Child Care in Medical Writings of the Middle Ages," *The Journal of Psychohistory,* vol. IV, no. 4 (spring 1977), pp. 461–90. Professor Luke Demaitre has confirmed this silence in a detailed personal letter; he considered it significant.

63. See A. Castiglioni, *Histoire de la médecine,* French trans. (Paris: 1931), p. 346.

64. *De Decoratione,* cap. 9, in G. Falloppius, *Opera,* vol. II, ed. I. P. Maphaeus (Frankfurt: 1600), p. 339. See L. Demause, "The Evolution of Childhood," in *The History of Childhood,* ed. L. Demause (New York: 1974), p. 48.

65. Leonellus Faventinus de Victoriis, *Practica Medicinalis* (Ingolstadt: 1545), 2nd part, f° 44 v° to 45 v°. On Leonello Vettori, see *Biographisches Lexikon des hervorragenden Arzte aller Zeiten und Völker,* 2nd ed., vol. V, p. 743.

66. P. Forestus, *Observationum et curationum medicinalium Libri XXVI^mus et XXVII^mus* (Lyon: 1597), pp. 106–107; by the same author, *Observationum et curationum chirurgicarum libri quatuor posteriores* (Frankfurt: 1634), pp. 584–85. On Forestus, see *Biographisches Lexikon des hervorragenden Arzte aller Zeiten und Völker,* vol. II, p. 568, under *Foreest.*

67. *Observationum et curationum medicinalium* (1597), p. 109.

68. It was also, I feel, on religious and moral grounds and not on medical grounds that the Puritan Richard Capel argued when he eloquently denounced, in his *Tentations* of 1633, the abominations of acts of self-defilement committed "with ones self." In his eyes, acts committed with oneself were morally worse than those committed with others "as self-murther is worse than the murther of another." Capel inveighed: "This is a foule sinne much against nature, and therefore the worse, for the more unnatural the sin is, the greater the guilt is still in that respect, and whereas it is thought that there is not that wrong in it, as in taking away the

chastity of another, I urge that there is most wrong when a man doth wrong himselfe; and as the theefe doth in the candle, so these selfe defilements doe rot and weaken the body, by the curse of God exceedingly. And (as in all such inordiante practises) there is a secret kinde of murther; what, if not in the intention of the doer, yet in the condition of the thing done: God is much displeased with these kinde of sins, they are execrable in his sight; [they] . . . make people unfit for marriage without the great mercy of God ever after. I could wish people to marry on ever so poore termes, rather than to fall [into] such illicite, darke and abominable practises, which doe grieve the very principals of nature" (Richard Capel, *Tentations; Their Nature, Danger, Cure* [London: 1633], pp. 353–54; the same text, with slight spelling changes, appears in the 6th edition [London: 1658], pp. 210–11; "theefe" for example, becomes "thief": the "thief" has stolen a candle, which he quickly melts down.) "Rot and weaken the body," "make people unfit for marriage": this is strong language, but within the flood of Capel's imprecations, it is obviously more a question of divine retribution, "the curse of God," than it is of any natural physical consequences. On Capel, see the *Dictionary of National Biography,* vol. IX, pp. 17–18; on his *Tentations,* see K. F. Jacobs, *Die Entstehung der Onanie-Literatur im 17, und 18. Jahrhundert* (Munich: 1963 [Inaugural-Dissertation de la Faculté de Médecine]), pp. 8–20.

69. On Nicolas Venette, see the entries in Michaud's *Biographie universelle,* vol. XLVIII, pp. 134–35, and in Hofer's *Nouvelle Biographie Générale,* vol. XLV, col. 1079–80, as well as in P. D. Rainguet, *Biographie Saintongeaise* (Saintes: 1852), pp. 601–602. See also P. Darmon, *Le mythe de la procréation à l'âge baroque* (Paris: 1981), p. 263–64.

70. [Nicolas Venette], *Tableau de l'amour considéré dans l'estat du mariage* (Parma: 1696), p. 339.

71. *Tableau de l'amour considéré dans l'estat du mariage,* pp. 488–89. Venette makes frequent reference to Galen. Contrary to what Darmon said (*Le mythe de la procréation à l'âge baroque,* p. 29), he did not denounce the dangers of masturbation; he only dealt with the harmful consequences that "over-frequent caressings of women" can have (p. 226 and cont.).

72. M. Etmüller, *Opera Medica Theorico Practica* (Geneva: 1736), pp. 419–20. On Ettmüller, see *Biographisches Lexikon der . . . Ärzte,* vol. II, pp. 443–44.

73. *The History of Cold Bathing: Both Ancient and Modern,* 2nd ed. (London: 1706), 2nd part, *Treating of the Genuine Use of Hot and Cold Baths,* by Edward Baynard, pp. 68–69. On Baynard, see *Dictionary of National Biography,* vol. III, p. 453.

74. J.-F. Ostervald, *Traité contre l'impureté* (Amsterdam: 1712), pp. 90, 154 and cont.

75. L. Stone, *The Family, Sex and Marriage in England, 1500–1800* (London: 1977), p. 512.

76. On this journal, only parts of which have been published, see H. Himmelfarb, "Un journal peu ordinaire," in *Nouvelle Revue de Psychanalyse,* no. 19 (1979), pp. 269–79. The interest of the passages relating to Louis XIII has been noted by P. Ariès, *L'enfant et la vie familiale sous l'Ancien Régime* (Paris: 1960), pp. 102–105; O. Ranum, "Comment," in *History of Childhood Quarterly,* vol. II (1975), pp. 181–87; and L. Stone, *The Family, Sex and Marriage in England, 1500–1800* (London: 1977), pp. 507–510. A remarkable new edition of the journal has been published under the direction of M. Foisil, *Journal de Jean Héroard,* 2 vols. (Paris: 1989). On the subject under discussion, see the introduction to vol. I, pp. 109–110.

77. *Journal de Jean Héroard sur l'enfance et la jeunesse de Louis XIII,* ed. E. Soulie and E. de Barthelemy, vol. I (Paris: 1868), pp. 31, 34, 35, 38, 45, 68–9, 76, 80, 81, 100, 137, et al.

78. Charles Sorel, *Histoire comique de Francion,* ed. E. Roy, vol. II (Paris: 1926), pp. 48–49.

79. *Le Cabinet secret du Parnasse. Pierre de Ronsard et la Pléiade,* ed. L. Perceau, vol. IV (Paris: 1935), pp. 123–24.

80. *Le Cabinet secret du Parnasse,* vol. III (Paris: 1932), pp. 34–35.

81. *The Diary of Samuel Pepys,* ed. R. Latham and W. Matthews, vol. VIII, 1667 (London: 1974), p. 588, entry for Dec. 24, 1667. Plumb thought that Pepys relates this episode "with considerable pride" (J. H. Plumb, "The New World of Children in Eighteenth-Century England," *Past and Present* [May 1975], p. 92). Plumb's interpretation, I think, twists the meaning of the text.

82. J.-L. Flandrin, *Le Sexe et l'Occident,* p. 262.

83. "Est adeo universale ut crediderim maximam patem damnatorum hoc infici peccato" (F. Toletus, *De instructione sacerdotum,* p. 712).

84. *Sermons de Saint Vincent de Paul, de ses coopérateurs et successeurs immédiats pour les missions des campagnes,* ed. abbé Jeanmaire, vol. II (Paris: 1859), p. 435. See J. Delumeau, *Le péché et la peur.*

La culpabilisation en Occident (XIIIe- XVIIIe siècles) (Paris: 1983), p. 495.

85. P. d'Outreman, *Le pédagogue chrestien,* new revised edition (Mons: 1650), vol. I, p. 148. See also J. Delumeau, *Le péché et la peur,* p. 495. Latin translation: *Paedogogus Christianus,* trans. J. Broquardt (Mayence: 1654), p. 187. On this work, see the entry on Philippe d'Oultreman in the *Dictionnaire de Spiritualité ascétique et mystique,* vol. XI, col. 1068–69.

86. "A lewd fellow-servant led me to practise a sin, which too many young men are guilty of, and look upon as harmless, tho' God struck Onan dead in the place for it" (J. H., *The Life of the Reverend Mr Geo. Trosse, late minister of the City of Exon . . . written by himself* [Exeter: 1714], p. 19). Trosse's text refers to a period during which he was living in Portugal, but his reflection obviously concerns the psychology of young men as he understood it in England. Trosse, born in 1631, finished his autobiography—he said it himself—in February of 1693 (see p. 103). On Trosse, see the Dictionary of National Biography, vol. LVII, pp. 250–52. The passage relating to masturbation was first noted by P. Delany, *British Autobiography in the Seventeenth Century* (London: 1969), p. 71.

CHAPTER THREE

1. It is perhaps a copy of that first edition (there is no way to be sure; however, it might have been the second or the third) that was part of the British Library collection and appeared in the printed catalog (*British Museum. General Catalogue of Printed Books,* vol. 175 [London: 1963], col. 617). It was destroyed during World War II. The catalog gives 1710 as the date, with a question mark. The date 1710 subsequently entered the literature on the history of masturbation. See, for example, J. Van Ussel, *Histoire de la répression sexuelle* (Paris: 1972), p. 198; J. Solé, *L'amour en Occident à l'époque moderne* (Paris: 1976), p. 110; L. Stone, *The Family, Sex and Marriage in England,* p. 514. The date is clearly incorrect. The only reliable indicator of correct chronology we have, is a passage from the 4th edition of *Onania,* published in November 1718. Its author noted: "I had finished this little Treatise almost three years ago" (p. 62).

2. *The Weekly Journal or Saturday's Post,* February 16, 1716, p. 5 (Cambridge Univ. Library). It cannot be the first edition, as the announcement indicates that the book includes "many considerable additions" and that "the additions may be had by themselves."

3. The date is reasonable, given the fact that following the 3rd edition, the author receives a letter from a reader dated June 1717 (see 4th edition, pp. 65–66).

4. Announced as "just published" in the *Weekly Journal or Saturday's Post* in the November 22, 1718 (British Library) and December 6, 1718 (Cambridge Univ. Library) issues. The British Library and the New York Public Library have copies of this 4th edition.

5. S. Tissot, *L'Onanisme* (Lausanne: 1760), pp. 25 and 47 ("Dr. Bekkers' collection"); 3rd ed. (Lausanne: 1764), pp. 27 and 61. The name of "Dr. Bekkers" regularly appears today in the literature on the subject; see, for example: K. F. Jacobs, *Die Entstehung der Onanie-Literatur,* pp. 30 and cont.; A. and W. Leibrand, *Formen des Eros. Kultur- und Geistesgeschichte der Liebe,* vol. II (Munich: 1972), pp. 419–24.

6. He never makes any reference to any type of professional medical experience whatsoever. He says he consulted a physician on the prescriptions for the medicines (see the passage cited below).

7. The claim has been made, for example by A. Comfort, *L'origine des obsessions sexuelles,* French trans. (Verviers: 1969), p. 89; L. Stone, *The Family, Sex and Marriage in England,* p. 514, etc.

8. "Ignorant Empiric," "His profession of Quackism" (*Onanism display'd,* 2nd ed. [London: 1719], pp. VI, 13); "This author has, for some time or other, quacked" (Philo-Castitatis, *Onania examined and detected* [London: 1723], p. 62). In 1728, the *Chambers Cyclopaedia* includes the author of *Onania* among the ranks of the "emperics" (see beginning of chapter IV, below).

9. *Onania,* preface, p. III.

10. *Onania,* p. 11.

11. *Onania,* p. 18.

12. *Onania,* pp. 20–21.

13. *Onania,* p. 19.

14. *Onania,* p. 29.

15. *The Original Weekly Journal with fresh Advices, foreign and domestick,* July 28-August 4, 1716 (London), pp. 561–62 (Cambridge Univ. Library).

16. *The Weekly Journal or Saturday's Post*, May 24, 1718, p. 454 (Cambridge Univ. Library).

17. On eighteenth-century English quacks and their success, see the excellent chapter by W. C. Sydney, *England and the English in the Eighteenth Century*, vol. 1, 2nd ed. (London: 1892), chap. X: "Concerning Quacks and Quackery."

18. *The Weekly Journal or Saturday's Post*, December 26, 1719, p. 6 (British Library).

19. See the letter from a reader, dated May 1, 1722, in the 8th edition. The reader claimed to have just seen an advertisement for the 6th edition of *Onania* in the press.

20. *The Weekly Journal or Saturday's Post*, January 19, 1723, p. 6 (British Library). The notice reads: "There having been sold near 10,000 of the former editions." The Bibliothèque de l'Arsenal in Paris has a copy of the 7th edition.

21. *The Weekly Journal or Saturday's Post*, May 4, 1723, p. 6 (British Library), "Above 12,000 of the former editions having been sold." The British Library and the National Library of Scotland in Edinburgh have copies of the 8th edition.

22. *The Weekly Journal or Saturday's Post*, September 14, 1723, p. 6 (British Library), "above 15,000 of the former editions having been sold." This edition can be found at the Countway Library of Medicine (Massachusetts). Advertisements for the 12th edition in 1727 made it as far as the English provincial press. See G. A. Cranfield, *The Development of the Provincial Newspapers, 1700–1760* (Oxford: 1962), pp. 222–23.

23. The British Library has a copy.

24. Copies in the British Library, the Edinburgh University Library (copy used by Robert MacDonald in his "The Frightful Consequences of Onanism: Notes on the History of a Delusion," *Journal of the History of Ideas*, vol. XXVIII (1967), pp. 423 and cont.; the library of the Catholic University of Louvain (Louvain-la-Neuve), and, in the United States, the Library of Congress and the Center for Research Libraries in Chicago. The number of existing copies suggests that a fairly substantial number of copies of the 16th edition were printed.

25. See *Onania, National Union Catalog*, vol. 430.

26. Entry *Onan*, in *Questions sur l'Encyclopédie* (see chapter VI below).

27. Second edition (London: 1719). The title indicates "Made English from the Paris Edition," but this is certainly a fabrication designed to impress the public, for there is no trace of a French edition. The only copy of this 2nd edition is held in the collection of the National Library of Medicine in Bethesda, Maryland. We have not found a copy of the first edition. It would likely date from 1717 or 1718, since it was published after the 3rd edition of *Onania*, which we've already placed in early 1717 (see on this point *Onania*, 8th edition, p. vii).

28. *Onanism display'd*, p. 2.

29. *Onanism display'd*, p. 3.

30. *Onanism display'd*, p. 38.

31. *Onanism display'd*, preface, p. VI.

32. *Onania*, 8th ed., pp. VII-VIII.

33. The only known copy is at the British Library (call no. 1173.b.9.1.). It bears the date 172 . . . , the last figure being illegible. We can date it to around 1720, by comparing the advertisement on page 40 of the pamphlet with newspaper ads from 1720 (see, for example, *The Weekly Journal or Saturday's Post*, June 18, 1720, p. 6). The date of 1724 furnished by the British Library's printed catalog (under *Onan*) is probably incorrect. The attribution was likely based on the fact that *Eronania*, with which it is bound, is dated 1724.

34. *Of the crime of Onan*, pp. VIII, 5, 11, 26.

35. The Library of the Royal Society of Medicine in London has the only known copy.

36. See *A Supplement to the Onania*, 6th ed. (1730), pp. 8–44.

37. At the British Library.

38. See *Onania*, 8th ed., pp. 117–18; 15th ed. (1730), p. 97.

39. *The Little Review or an Inquisition of Scandal*, Aug. 3, 1705, p. 71.

40. The first edition of the *Supplement* is announced in the 8th edition of *Onania* (1723), p. 197.

41. Fifteenth ed. (1730), pp. 160–61.

42. Fifteenth ed. (1730), pp. 161–62.

43. *Supplement*, 6th ed. (1730), pp. 76–78.

44. See 8th ed. (1723), pp. 136–37.

45. S. Tissot, *L'Onanisme* (Lausanne: 1760), pp. 24–29; 3rd ed. (Lausanne: 1764), pp. 26–31. Tissot admits that he has been warned about *Onania*, but he trusts it nonetheless: "Even though it may include some suppositions, and some passages do look that way,

it is nonetheless proven that the majority of facts are only too real" (1760 ed., pp. 24–25; 3rd ed., p. 27).

46. See 7th ed. (1723), p. 197.
47. *Onania examined and detected,* preface ("a mercenary principle which made his pen go for money") and p. 62 ("to draw gain").

Chapter Four

1. *Onania examined and detected* (London, 1723), p. 1
2. *Chambers Cyclopaedia,* vol. II (London: 1728), p. 662.
3. *Chambers Cyclopaedia,* vol. II, p. 848.
4. *Encyclopaedia Britannica,* 1st ed. (Edinburgh: 1771), vol. III, p. 414.
5. *A Short Treatise on Onanism or the Destestable Vice of Self-Pollution, by a Physician in the Country* (London: 1767). The preface is signed W. Farrer. On this pamphlet, see T. Tarczylo, *Sexe et liberté au siècle des Lumières* (Paris: 1983), pp. 131 and 282.
6. Trans. A. Hume (London: 1766).
7. It would perhaps be more correct to say Tissot "launched" the term. It was employed for the first time in 1721 by an obscure writer and seems to have gone largely unnoticed. In *La religion des Mahométans exposée par leurs propres Docteurs . . . tiré du latin de M. Reland* (La Haye: 1721), the author spoke of a "detestable onanism," adding in a note: "I ventured this word, following the Englishman who calls this crime *Onania*" (p. 62). See, on this text, R. Arveiller, "Cinq notes de lexique," in *Mélanges de langue et de littérature françaises offerts à Pierre Larthomas* (Paris: 1985), p. 18). The word was thus "ventured" as early as 1721, without being subsequently adopted by anyone prior to Tissot.
8. "There is a treatise on masturbation," he wrote in his foreword. "Its author discusses the physical aspects and deadly consequences of this crime. I will attempt to examine the moral aspects and to show the full extend of their horror" (p. 1). What follows is a sermon from the pulpit, full of biblical references. Dutoit-Membrini is the only pastor to resuscitate the notion of diabolical intervention so cherished by Saint Thomas and Benedicti: onanism is inspired by Satan, by the "enemy," by the "Prince of Darkness" (*passim* and p. 171). On this point, he would have no

intellectual posterity. On Dutoit-Membrini, see J. Chavannes, *Jean-Philippe Dutoit. Sa vie, son caractère et ses doctrines* (Lausanne: 1865).

9. Strikingly, he would not be cited even once in the many works on onanism published after 1760. We will thus not return to this stillborn work.

10. See chapter VI below.

11. On Mandeville, see the *Dictionary of National Biography*, vol. XXXVI, pp. 21–22.

12. *A Treatise of the Hypochondriack and Hysterick passions* . . . (London: 1711), pp. 142–45.

13. *A Modest Defence of Publick Stews, or an Essay upon Whoring* (London: 1724), pp. 30–31. On this work see L. Stone, *The Family, Sex and Marriage in England, 1500–1800* (London: 1977), p. 617.

14. *A Modest Defence of Publick Stews*, p. 31–32.

15. *Onania oder die erschreckliche Sünde des Selbst-Besteckung* (Leipzig: 1736). Translation of the 15th English edition.

16. Züllichau: 1740. On this work, see F. X. Thalhofer, *Die sexuelle Pädagogik bei den Philanthropen* (Kempten-Munich: 1907), p. 5. We consulted the copy in the Harvard University Theological Library.

17. Vol. XXXVI (Leipzig-Halle: 1743), col. 1586–90. On Zelder's huge *Universal Lexicon aller Wissenschaften und Künste*, see B. Kossmann, "Deutsche Universallexika des 18. Jahrhunderts," *Archiv für Geschichte des Buchwesens*, vol. IX (1969), col. 1563–94.

18. See J. Roger, *Dictionnaire universel de médecine traduit de l'anglais de Robert James*, in Diderot, *Oeuvres complètes*, vol. I, *Le modèle anglais* (Paris: 1975), pp. 153–63.

19. R. James, entry *Mastupratio*, in *A Medicinal Dictionary*, vol. II (London: 1745). French trans., *Dictionnaire universel de médecine*, trans. Diderot, Eidous, and Toussaint, vol. IV (Paris: 1747), col. 1186.

20. R. James, entry *Amaurosis*, in *A Medicinal Dictionary*, vol. I. French trans., *Dictionnaire*, vol. I (Paris: 1746), col. 954.

21. R. James, entry *Mastupratio*, in *A Medicinal Dictionary*, vol. II.

22. R. James, entry *Mastupratio*, in *A Medicinal Dictionary*, vol. II.

23. The same goes for the general remarks on the effects of masturbation. James, under the entry *Amaurosis* (cited above), also bor-

rowed an example from the German physician Hoffmann. We will come back to this example later (see chapter V below).

24. Entry *Gonorrhea*, in *A Medicinal Dictionary*, vol. II. Besides James, there is another anonymous English pamphlet that shows *Onania*'s influence. It is entitled *A Practical Essay upon the Tabes Dorsalis in the way of Aphorism and Commentary* (London: 1748). Tissot would attribute this pamphlet to a certain Lewis, although we have no way of knowing if this attribution is founded (see chapter V, note 31 below). Its author denounced masturbation as the source of Tabes dorsalis: "That abominable practice of school-boys, a practice which I cannot describe in terms odious enough, *Pollutio sui* . . . Here lies, I say, very often, the original and almost unconquerable cause of deplorable effects, and from this source, highly criminal in a religious view, springs the debilitated condition of the tabid patient" (p. 13).

James would be heavily borrowed from in both France and England. In his *Dictionnaire portatif de médecine*, J.-F. Lavosien copied James word for word: "a vice not decent to name, but productive of the most deplorable and generally incurable disorders," vol. I (Paris: 1764), p. 426.

25. *Confessions*, Book II, in *Oeuvres complètes*, vol. I (Paris: La Pléiade, 1959), pp. 66–67.

26. *Confessions*, Book III, in *Oeuvres complètes*, vol. I, p. 109.

27. See the important study by P. Lejeune, "Le 'dangereux supplément.' Lecture d'un aveu de Rousseau," *Annales. Economies, sociétés, civilisations* (July-August 1974), pp. 1009 and cont.

28. *Emile*, Book IV, in *Oeuvres complètes*, vol. IV, p. 663.

29. See Tissot's July 8, 1762, letter to Rousseau in A. François, "Correspondance de Jean-Jacques Rousseau et du médecin Tissot," *Annales de la Société Jean-Jacques Rousseau*, vol. VII (1911), pp. 21–22; and in J.-J. Rousseau, *Correspondance complète*, ed. R.-A. Leigh, vol. XI (Geneva: 1970), pp. 238–39.

30. Rousseau to Tissot, July 22, 1762, in A. François, "Correspondance . . . ," pp. 22–23; and in *Correspondance complète*, pp. 82–83.

31. (M. Procope-Couteaux), *L'Art de faire des garçons* (Montpellier, n.d.), 2nd pt., pp. 119–20: new edition, *L'Art de faire des garçons ou Nouveau tableau de l'amour conjugal* (Montpellier: 1755), p. 135. On the attribution of his work, see J.-M. Querard, *La France littéraire*, vol. VII, p. 350.

CHAPTER FIVE

1. Among the many dictionary entries on Tissot, we note the following: R. Desgenettes, *Dictionnaire des sciences médicales, Biographie médicale*, vol. VIII (Paris: 1825), pp. 341–43; A. de Montet, *Dictionnaire biographique des Genevois et des Vaudois*, vol. II (Lausanne: 1878), pp. 566–68; E. Olivier, *Médecine et santé dans le pays de Vaud au XVIIIe siècle*, vol. II (Lausanne: 1939), pp. 1060–62. See also C. Eynard, *Essai sur la vie de Tissot* (Lausanne, 1839); A. Vinet, *Littérature et histoire suisses*, ed. H. Perrochon (Lausanne: 1932), pp. 206–34 (article from 1839) and 235–41 (article from 1840); E. Cochet, *Etude sur S. A. Tissot* (doctoral thesis, Paris: 1902); M. and Mme. W. de Severy, *La vie de société dans le pays de Vaud à la fin du XVIIIe siècle*, vol. II (Lausanne-Paris: 1911), pp. 159–95, and cont.; M. and Mme. W. de Severy, *Le comte et la comtesse Golowkin et le médecin Tissot* (Lausanne: 1928); A. Guisan, E. Olivier, Mme. W. de Severy, and G.-A. Bridel, "Le deuxième centenaire du Docteur Tissot," *Revue historique Vaudoise* (August-September, 1928); H. Bucher, *Tissot und sein Traité des nerfs. Ein Beitrag zur Medizingeschichte der schweizerischen Aufklärung* (Zurich: 1958). Note that Tissot's first name is Samuel-Auguste, not Simon-André, as it is often mistakenly written. Two important recent works on Tissot are: A. Emchderiaz, *Tissot, Physician of the Enlightenment* (New York: 1992) and L. Benaroyo, *"L'avis au peuple sur sa santé" de Samuel-Auguste Tissot (1728–1797): la voie vers une médecine éclairée* (Zurich, 1988).

2. See in particular the report in the *Journal des Sçavans* (May 1756), p. 310: "This work seems to us to be one of the most instructive that has ever been published on the subject of innoculation."

3. *Correspondance littéraire . . . par Grimm, Diderot, Raynal, Meister, etc.*, ed. M. Tourneux, vol. VII (Paris: 1879), pp. 245–46.

4. (A.-F. J. Masson de Pezay), *Les soirées helvétiennes, alsaciennes et francomtoises* (Amsterdam: 1771), pp. 398–99.

5. A. Vinet, *Littérature et histoire suisses*, p. 206.

6. Numerous letters have been preserved, particularly in the Fonds Tissot of the Bibliothèque cantonale et universitaire de Lausanne, Manuscript Dept.

7. Isabelle de Charriere/Belle de Zuylen, *Oeuvres complètes*, vol. VIII (Amsterdam-Geneva: 1980), p. 145. Originally published in 1785.

8. A. Vinet, *Littérature et histoire suisses,* p. 239.
9. In P. Morren, *La vie lausannoise au XVIIIe siècle* (Geneva: 1970), p. 322.
10. P. Morren, *La vie lausannoise au XVIIIe siècle,* p. 322.
11. See on this point the long lists of clients cited in the works of: M. and Mme. W. de Severy (*La vie de société dans le pays de Vaud à la fin du XVIIIe siècle* and *Le comte et la comtesse Golowkin et le médecin Tissot*); P. Morren (*La vie lausannoise au XVIIIe siècle*); and A. Guisan ("Le livre de malades du Dr. Tissot," *Revue médicale de la Suisse romande,* vol. XXXI [1911]). We mention, as an example, the report of a consultation in J.-G. Sulzer, *Journal d'un voyage fait en 1775 et 1776 dans les pays méridionaux de l'Europe,* French trans., new ed. (Rotterdam: 1789), pp. 44–45.
12. (J.-B. de la Borde), *Lettres sur la Suisse. par un voyageur françois en 1781,* vol. I (Geneva: 1783), p. 269. As is to be expected, Tissot is frequently mentioned in texts relating travel in Switzerland. Another example is found in *Lettres de M. William Coxe à M. W. Melmoth sur l'état politique, civil et naturel de la Suisse,* French trans., vol. II (Paris: 1781), pp. 145–46.
13. A. Vinet, *Littérature et histoire suisses,* p. 240.
14. See A. Galante Garrone, *Gilbert Romme. Histoire d'un révolutionnaire (1750–1795),* French trans. (Paris: 1971), p. 100; Cl. Manceron, *Les hommes de la liberté,* vol. II (Paris: 1975), p. 453.
15. Reeditions in Louvain, 1760 and Lausanne, 1780 and 1790.
16. See the beginning of chapter VI below.
17. See the annotation on the copy in the collection of the Bibliothèque Nationale in Paris (call no. 8-TD.124.1.d): "This edition was made in Paris: it is the first in this city."
18. Tissot refers to Baynard in his *Tentamen de morbis ex manustupratone,* 1758 ed., p, 237; 1760 ed., p. 172; 1764 ed., p. 194. References to Ettmüller: 1760 ed., p. 223–24 and 225; 1764 ed., pp. 259–60 and 261.
19. In *Opera omnia physico-medica,* vol. IV (Geneva: 1740), pp. 294–95.
20. *Tentamen de morbis ex manustupratone,* 1758 ed., pp. 189, 195 and 232; 1760 ed., pp. 10–11, 29 and 110–11; 1764 ed., pp. 13–14, 31, and 129.
21. *Tentamen de morbis ex manustupratone,* 1758 ed., pp. 197–98; 1760 ed., p. 33; 1764 ed., pp. 35–36. ("The disorders which I have seen the most often are: 1. A total disturbance of the stomach, indicated

in some by loss of appetite or irregular appetite, in others by sharp pains, especially during digestion, by repeated vomiting, which resists all remedies as long as the patient continues his bad habits; 2. A weakening of the organs of respiration, which produces dry coughs, nearly always hoarseness, weak voice and shortness of breath as soon as the patient undertakes any brusque movement; and 3. Total disruption of the nervous system.")

22. *Tentamen de morbis ex manustupratone,* 1758 ed., p. 198; 1760 ed., p. 34; 1764 ed., p. 37.

23. *Tentamen de morbis ex manustupratone,* 1758 ed., p. 199 (letter "ante biennium conscripta"); 1760 ed., p. 36; 1764 ed., p. 39.

24. *Tentamen de morbis ex manustupratone,* 1758 ed., pp. 195–97; 1760 ed., pp. 29–33; 1764 ed., pp. 32–35.

25. See *Tentamen de morbis ex manustupratone,* 1758, *Proémium.* This volume is mentioned in the catalog of his library; see Papiers Tissot, no. 71, "Catalogue de la Bibliothèque de M. le Professeur Tissot commencé à Lausanne le 10 juin 1812," p. 124: "*Onania,* London, 1752." Copies of this 17th edition are preserved at the University of Gand Library, the Library of Congress, and the Library of the College of Physicians in Philadelphia.

26. *Tentamen de morbis ex manustupratone,* 1758, *Proémium.*

27. 1760 ed., p. 29; 1764 ed., pp. 31–32. Earlier in the *Tentamen,* 1758, p. 179.

28. *Journal des sçavans* (July, 1758), pp. 490–93.

29. *Journal de médecine, chirurgie, pharmacie, etc.* by M. Vandermonde (June 1760), pp. 483–94; reprinted in *Gazette salutaire* (de Bouillon), (1761), nos. XXV, XXVI, and XXVII.

30. Preface to the 1760 ed., p. VIII; 1764 ed., p. XI.

31. This is also the case of the *Practical Essay upon the Tabes dorsalis,* which we cited earlier (see note 24 in chapter IV above). Tissot, in the 1758 ed. of *Tentamen,* regretted not having known of this book, attributed, as he indicates, to Cl. Lewis, of whom he has heard much good ("quod laudari et Cl. Lewis tribui video": *Proemium*). He had read it in 1760, when he was writing *L'Onanisme* (see p. 117). Thereafter he would cite it abundantly, mentioning not only the passage on masturbation, but also several others (see 1764 ed., pp. 19–20, 135, 137, 171, 173, 174, 176, 192, 193, and 194). He refers each time to "M. Lewis"—we have no way of knowing, however, if the attribution is founded or who the Lewis might be. I warmly thank H.-J. M. Symons, of the

Wellcome Institute for the History of Medicine in London, who helped me unravel the problem of "M. Lewis."

32. On the following discussion, see the 1764 ed., pp. 2, 2–3, 73, 75–76, 78–79, 79–80, 87, 98–99, 101–103, 104–105, 106–10, 111, 113, 114–15, 116, 117–20, and 219–20. On the "humors" in Tissot's writings, see T. Tarczylo, "'Prêtons la main à la nature': *L'Onanisme* de Tissot," *Dix-huitième siècle*, vol. XII (1980), pp. 81–82.

33. E. Guyenot, *Les sciences de la vie aux XVIIe et XVIIIe siècles. L'idée d'évolution* (Paris: 1941), pp. 161, 163, 165, and 187.

34. 1764 ed., pp. 199 and 200–203. Tissot was a great proponent of the waters of Spa; see, for example, his 1776 consultation in "Une consultation du Dr. Tissot," *Revue médicale de la Suisse romande*, vol. LXIX (1949), pp. 916–18. He himself went to Spa in 1779—Spa, he said, is "a place inhabited by Englishmen where other nations are tolerated." See M. and Mme. W. de Severy, *La vie de société dans le pays de Vaud à la fin du XVIIIe siècle*, vol. I, pp. 216–17.

35. 1764 ed., p. 219.

36. 1764 ed., pp. 219–20.

37. C. Daremberg, *Histoire des sciences médicales*, vol. II (Paris: 1870), p. 1207. Daremberg wrote elsewhere with nearly the same ferocity: "Tissot, distinguished practitioner, all the rage in Switzerland as well as in France, was a sensible man, with some wit, who held a good rank among those second or third-rate writers who have an easy style and provide some amusement" (*La Médecine, Histoire et doctrines* [Paris: 1865], p. 353).

38. J. Christian, entry *Onanisme* in *Dictionnaire encyclopédique des sciences médicales*, ed. A. Dechambre, 2nd series, vol. XV (Paris: 1881), p. 360. F. Mortier, W. Colen, and F. Simon attempted to rehabilitate Tissot as the author of *L'Onansime* in their study "Inner-Scientific Reconstructions in the Discourse on Masturbation (1760–1950)," *Paedogogica Historica. International Journal of the History of Education*, vol. XXX (1994). These authors feel it is an error to judge Tissot in terms of current science. For them, "measured by 18th-century physiological and biological standards, Tissot's work was sound science" (p. 846). I could not remain more unconvinced. By the same logic, the physicians whom Fontenelle mocks for discoursing on the Silesian child who grew a gold tooth would also have to be considered as performing

"sound science." (See Fontenelle, *Histoire des oracles*, ch. IV.) Tissot's "method" differs little from theirs: his own "gold teeth" are the "magnificent observations" he finds in *Onania*.

39. Letter from Rossary to Tissot, June 13, 1774; Lausanne, Fonds Tissot, no. 144 (11).

Chapter Six

1. The catalogs of the Bibliothèque Nationale and the British Library and the National Union Catalog alone show editions dating from 1765, 1766, and 1768 to 1788 (yearly without exception), 1780, 1781, and 1782. See also T. Tarczylo, *Sexe et liberté au siècle des Lumières*, pp. 291–92.

2. See C. G. Kayser, *Vollständiges Bücher-Lexikon*, vol. V (Leipzig: 1835), p. 451.

3. *Le Conservateur de la santé ou Avis sur les dangers qu'il importe à chacun d'éviter, pour se conserver en bonne amitié et prolonger sa vie* (Paris: 1763), pp. 320–35. The Bibliothèque Royal in Brussels possesses an identical edition that bears, however, the imprint "La Haye, 1763." Le Bègue de Presle's text is summarized and significant sections are reproduced in 14 succeeding issues of the *Gazette salutaire* (de Bouillon), from May 12 to August 11, 1763. Le Bègue de Presle was, as the title page of his book indicates, "Doctor-Regent of the Medical School in Paris and Censeur Royal." On Le Bègue de Presle, see the entry in Höfer's *Nouvelle Biographie Générale*, vol. V, col. 157–58.

4. J.-H. S. Formey, *Emile chrétien* (Berlin: 1764), p. 183.

5. *Encyclopédie ou Dictionnaire raisonné des sciences, des arts et des métiers*, vol. X (Neuchâtel: 1765), pp. 51–54. The article is unsigned, but the author of the article *Mariage*—who is Ménuret de Chambaud—claimed it was his. See J. Lough, *Essays on the Encyclopédie of Diderot and d'Alembert* (London: 1968), p. 482. Jean Mayer's attribution of the article to Hugues Mayet in his *Diderot homme de science* (Rennes: 1959), p. 343, is erroneous. On Ménuret de Chambaud, see J. Roger, *Les sciences de la vie dans la pensée française du XVIIIe siècle*, 2nd ed. (Paris: 1971), pp. 631–34.

6. *Encyclopédie*, vol. XI, p. 290.

7. *Oeuvres complètes*, vol. XX (Paris: 1879), pp. 133–35.

8. *Le Rêve de d'Alembert,* ed. G. Maire (Paris: 1921), pp. 1733–37; ed. P. Vernière (Paris: 1951), pp. 154–57; ed. J. Varloot (Paris: 1962), pp. 96–99.

9. *Mémoires pour Catherine II,* ed. P. Vernière (Paris: 1966), p. 223.

10. *Mémoires pour Catherine II,* ed. P. Vernière (Paris: 1966), p. 133.

11. Contencin, *Consultation sur un onanisme, avec complication de plusieurs accidents vénériens* (Paris: 1772), p. 21.

12. *Traité des maladies des voies urinaires,* 2nd pt. (Paris: 1791), p. 18. On Chopart, see *Dictionnaire de Biographie française,* vol. VIII, col. 1249.

13. G. Buchan, *Médecine domestique.* Trans. (from English) by J.-D. Duplanil, 4th ed. (Paris: 1788), vol. 4, pp. 507–508 (Duplanil's addition).

14. Reproduced in C. G. Salzmann, *Ueber die heimlichen Sünden der Jugend* (Leipzig: 1785), pp. 304–307. See, on Le Clerc, *Dictionnaire de Biographie française,* vol. VIII, col. 1469 (under heading Clerc [Le]).

15. *L'Enfer de la Bibliothèque Nationale,* vol. 1, *Oeuvres érotiques de Mirabeau* (Paris: 1984), pp. 514–15.

16. See F. Laurentie, *Louis XVII d'après des documents inédits* (Paris: 1913), p. 41. See also, among the numerous texts on this subject, G. Lenôtre, *Le Roi Louis XVII et l'énigme du Temple,* 3rd ed. (Paris: 1921), pp. 173–83.

17. *Réimpression de l'ancien Moniteur,* vol. XVIII (Paris: 1841), p. 90 (October 12, 1793 issue).

18. *Réimpression de l'ancien Moniteur,* vol. XVIII, p. 124 (October 16, 1793 issue).

19. *Réimpression de l'ancien Moniteur,* vol. XVIII, p. 139 (October 18, 1793 issue).

20. *Réimpression de l'ancien Moniteur,* vol. XVIII, p. 146 (October 19, 1793 issue).

21. *Précis historique . . . des principaux objets . . . qui composent le Museum de J.-F. Bertrand-Rival* (Paris: 1801), p. 310.

22. See, for example, Thomas Beddoes, *Hygeia: or Essays Moral and Medical on the Causes Affecting the Personal State of our Middling and Affluent Classes,* vol. I (Bristol: 1802), pp. 40 and cont. On Beddoes, see *Dictionary of National Biography,* vol. IV, pp. 94–95.

23. *Encyclopédie,* 2nd ed. (1781), vol. VII, pp. 5741–42; 3rd ed. (1797), vol. XIII, pp. 213–14; 4th ed. (1810), vol. XV, pp. 144–45

(slightly abridged); 5th ed. (1817), vol. XV, pp. 144–45; 6th ed. (1823), vol. XV, pp. 144–45.

24. In the discussion to follow, our analysis (when not followed by a specific reference) is largely based on the books by F. X. Thalhofer, *Die sexuelle Pädagogik bei den Philanthropen* (Kempten-Munich, 1907) and J. Hentze, *Sexualiät in der Pädagogik des späten 18. Jahrhunderts* (Frankfurt: 1979), as well as on the works by J. Van Ussel: *Sociogenese en evolutie van het probleem der seksuele propaedeuse tussen de 16de en 18de eeuw, vooral in Frankrijk en Duitsland. Bijdrage tot de studie van de burgerlijke seksuele moraal,* photocopied thesis (Gand: 1967); *Geschiedenis van het seksuele probleem* (Meppel: 1968); *Histoire de la répression sexuelle,* French trans. (Paris: 1970). On the pedagogical experts, the work by A. Pinloche remains fundamental, despite its age: *La réforme de l'éducation en Allemagne au dix-huitième siècle. Basedow et le Philanthropinisme* (Paris: 1889).

25. *Ueber die heimlichen Sünden der Jugend* (Leipzig: 1785), p. 59; see also p. 73.

26. *Ueber die heimlichen Sünden der Jugend,* p. 56.

27. *Ueber die heimlichen Sünden der Jugend,* p. 68.

28. *Ueber die heimlichen Sünden der Jugend,* pp. 139, 147, 154.

29. *Ueber die heimlichen Sünden der Jugend,* pp. 164–65.

30. *Ueber die heimlichen Sünden der Jugend,* pp. 165, 167.

31. *Ueber die heimlichen Sünden der Jugend,* pp. 213–14.

32. *Ueber die heimlichen Sünden der Jugend,* pp. 212–13.

33. *Ueber die heimlichen Sünden der Jugend,* see pp. 162, 204–205, 257–58.

34. *Ueber die heimlichen Sünden der Jugend,* see esp. pp. 40, 74, 77, 315, 339.

35. *Ueber die heimlichen Sünden der Jugend,* pp. 54–55

36. *Ueber die heimlichen Sünden der Jugend,* pp. 74–75.

37. In Thalofer, *Die sexuelle Pâdagogik,* p. 21.

38. On Campe, see Van Ussel, *Geschiedenis van het seksuele probleem,* p. 256, and *Histoire de la répression sexuelle,* p. 230. On Vogel, see E. J. Dingwall, *Male infibulation* (London: 1925), pp. 51–52.

39. I. Kant, *Ueber Pädagogik,* in *Gesammelte Schriften,* vol. IX (Berlin-Leipzig: 1923), pp. 497–98. We have generally consulted the French translation: E. Kant, *Eléments métaphysiques de la doctrine de la vertu, suivis d'un Traité de pédagogie,* trans. J. Barni (Paris: 1855), pp. 246–47. The reedition of this translation in E. Kant,

Traité de pédagogie, trans. J. Barni (Paris: 1886) omits the passage on masturbation (see p. 118). This omission persists in later editions of the work (see, for example, the 5th edition, [Paris: 1931], p. 118)

40. Salzmann, *Ueber die heimlichen Sünden der Jugend,* pp. 98–99.
41. *Le pénis et la démoralisation de l'Occident* (Paris: 1978), p. 160.
42. Interview in *Nouvel Observateur,* Oct. 23, 1978, p. 104.
43. Interview in *Nouvel Observateur,* Oct. 23, 1978, p. 104.
44. "Le 'dangereux supplément'," *Annales* (July-August 1974), p. 1015.
45. *Histoire de la répression sexuelle,* p. 191. Théodore Tarczylo also spoke of the "arcana of the bourgeois social imaginary" (preface to Dr. Tissot, *L'Onanisme* [Paris: 1980], p. 13). Tarczylo expresses rather different views in his *Sexe et liberté au siècle des Lumières* (Paris: 1983), in which he emphasizes the "revolution in sexual values."
46. *Avis au peuple sur sa santé,* 6th ed. (Lausanne: 1774–75), vol. I, pp. 84–85, 86, 120–21, 325; vol. II, pp. 233–40. In M. and Mme. W. de Severy, *La vie de société dans le pays de Vaud à la fin du XVIIIᵉ siècle,* we find a concrete example of bloodletting performed by Tissot, vol. II, p. 235.
47. A solid study on the history of bloodletting, within the framework of medical conceptions, was long lacking. The thesis by L. Delattre, *Essai sur l'histoire de la saignée* (Paris: 1886), is now quite dated, and the overview by T. W. Thorndike, "A History of Bleeding and Leeching," *Boston Medical Journal,* vol. 197 (1927–28), pp. 473–77, is superficial. Useful details are to be found in A. Davis and T. Appel, *Bloodletting Instruments in the National Museum of History and Technology* (Washington: Smithsonian Institution Press, 1979). On bloodletting in France, A. Franklin (*La vie privée d'autrefois,* vol. XIV, *Variétés chirurgicales* [Paris: 1894], pp. 1–29); and Dr. Cabanès (*Moeurs intimes du passé,* 6th series [Paris: 1920], pp. 1–85: *Le cérémonial de la saignée*), treat the topic primarily from an anecdotal perspective. There are interesting pages in F. Lebrun, *Se soigner autrefois. Médecins, saints et sorciers aux XVIIᵉ et XVIIIᵉ siècles* (Paris: 1983), pp. 62–65. Luckily, there are two excellent recent works: J. Héritier, *La sève de l'homme. De l'âge d'or de la saignée aux débuts de l'hématologie* (Paris: 1987); and J. Léonard, "A propos de l'histoire de la saignée (1600–1900)," in *Affaires de sang,* ed. A. Farge (Paris: Collection *Mentalités,* 1998).

48. *Encyclopédie*, vol. XIV, p. 501. On the entry written by Louis, see P. Astruc, "Les médecins collaborateurs de l'Encyclopédie," *Revue d'Histoire des Sciences*, vol. IV (1951), pp. 363–65.

49. *Encyclopédie*, vol. XIV, p. 509.

50. *A Medicinal Dictionary*, heading *Phlebotomia*.

51. *Encyclopédie, Saignée*, p. 511.

52. *Encyclopédie, Saignée*, p. 505.

53. *A Medicinal Dictionary*, heading *Phlebotomia*.

54. *Avis au peuple sur sa santé*, vol. II, pp. 236–38.

55. On the use of leeches, see H. Brabant, *Esculape chez Clio*, vol. III (Brussels: 1982), pp. 145 and cont.

56. On Broussais, see especially the remarkable pages by Henri Mondor, *Grands médecins presque tous* (Paris: 1943), pp. 179 and cont.; J. Léonard, *La France médicale: médecins et malades au XIXᵉ siècle* (Paris: 1978), pp. 130–31; H. Brabant, *Esculape chez Clio*, pp. 155 and cont. Castiglioni calls Broussais "the bloodiest of all the physicians" in *Histoire de la médecine*, French trans. (Paris: 1931), p. 571.

57. Quoted in A. Davis and T. Appel, *Bloodletting Instruments in the National Museum of History and Technology*, p. 5.

58. John Mortimer, "London Diary," *New Statesman* (May 27, 1977), p. 709.

59. Letter of December 13–18, 1800 in Heinrich von Kleist, *Sämtliche Werke und Briefe*, vol. II (Munich: 1961), pp. 559–61. See also R. Ayrault, *Heinrich von Kleist* (Paris: 1934), p. 27. We are leaving aside here the question of Kleist's own sexual habits, a most obscure problem that has already produced a flood of ink. Rank considered him "the poet who fought against masturbation with the greatest effort and the least success" (*Les premiers psychanalystes. Minutes de la Société psychanalytique de Vienne*, ed. H. Nunberg and E. Federn, French trans., vol. II (Paris: 1978), pp. 198–99.

60. *Journal de Médecine, Chirurgie, Pharmacie, etc.*, vol. XXXVIII (Jan. 1768).

61. *Tableau des variétés de la vie humaine*, vol. I (Paris: 1786), pp. 300–301 and 308–45.

62. Jacques Casanova, *Histoire de ma vie*, vol. I (Weisbaden-Paris: 1960), pp. 127–28.

63. We can cite, along the same lines, a letter "written by an experienced master in one of the most famous English public schools"

quoted by Havelock Ellis: "the more the severities," he wrote of the school's crusade against masturbation, "the more rampant the disease. I thought to myself that the remedy was creating the malady, and I heard afterward, from an old boy, that in those days they used to talk things over by the fireside, and think there must be something very choice in a sin that braved so much. " Havelock Ellis, *Studies in the Psychology of Sex*. Vol. I: *The Evolution of Modesty, the Phenomena of Sexual Periodicity, Auto-Erotism* (New York: [1937–42]), p. 242.

CHAPTER SEVEN

1. Tissot, *L'Onanisme*, new ed., Dr. E. Clément (Paris: 1875), preface, p. 5.
2. *La Sonate à Kreutzer*, trans. O. Sidersky (Paris: 1922), pp. 25–26. First published 1889.
3. *La Sonate à Kreutzer*, p. 27.
4. August Strindberg, "The Reward of Virtue," in *Getting Married*, trans. Mary Sandbach (London: Victor Gollanz, 1972), pp. 67–68. French trans.: "Le salaire de la vertu," in *Les Mariés. Douze caractères conjugaux* (Lausanne-Paris: 1885), pp. 42–45. On the writing of the short stories in this collection, see E. Poulenard, *Auguste Strindberg, romancier et nouvelliste* (Paris: 1962), pp. 198 and cont. On "The Reward of Virtue," see in particular V. J. McGill, *August Strindberg. The Bedeviled Viking* (London: 1930), pp. 42–44; P. Schepens, *August Strindberg. Leven en werken*, vol. I (Anvers: 1931), p. 270; and A. Berendsohn, *August Strindberg. Der Mensch und seine Unwelt* (Amsterdam, 1974), pp. 322–23.
5. A French translation was again published in France in 1871 (*L'art de prolonger la vie ou la macrobiotique*), new French ed., with notes by Dr. J. Pellagot (Paris: 1871) and is reprinted in 1896.
6. C.-G. Hufeland, *L'art de prolonger la vie humaine*. Trans. from the 2nd German ed. (Lausanne: 1809), pp. 161 and 163–64. The 2nd German edition was published in Iena in 1798.
7. *L'art de prolonger la vie humaine*, pp. 240–44.
8. According to the preface to the 80th edition, in the Dutch translation: O. Retau, *De zelfbewaring* (Leipzig, n.d.), p. XIV. Wilhelm Stekel, recalling his youth—he was born in 1868—wrote that

"thousands of copies" of Retau's work had been read by young men (W. Stekel, *Lettres à une mère,* French trans. [Paris: 1939], p. 190). "Who has not heard of the *Selbstbewahrung* of Retau, the prototype of this dangerous literature," noted Iwan Bloch, as well, (*The sexual life of our time,* English trans. [London: 1908], p. 421). The work was translated into Czech, Danish, French, Dutch, Italian, Polish, Russian, and Swedish. See *Gesamtverzeichnis des deutschsprachigen Schrifttums,* 1700–1910, vol. 116, p. 340.

9. M. Ryan, *Prostitution in London* (London 1839), p. 253.

10. See W. Acton, *A Practical Treatise on Diseases of the Urinary and Generative Organs,* 2nd ed. (London: 1851), pp. 222 and cont. See also Steven Marcus, "Mr. Acton of Queen Anne Street or the Wisdom of our Ancestors," *Partisan Review* (Spring 1974), pp. 218–33.

11. See J. Gathorne-Hardy, *The Public School Phenomenon* (London: 1977), pp. 84–93.

12. See the entry in the *Dictionary of National Biography, Supplement 1901–1911,* vol. II, pp. 9–12.

13. Quoted in A. N. Gilbert, "Doctor, Patient and Onanist Diseases in the Nineteenth Century," *Journal of the History of Medicine* (July, 1975), p. 217.

14. Gilbert, "Doctor, Patient and Onanist Diseases in the Nineteenth Century," p. 218.

15. See H. T. Engelhardt, "The Disease of Masturbation: Values and the Concept of Disease," *Bulletin of the History of Medicine,* vol. XLVIII (1974), pp. 234 and cont.; V. L. Bullough, *Sexual Variance in Society and History* (New York: 1976), pp. 542–47; G. P. Parsons, "Equal Treatment for All: American Medical Remedies for Male Sexual Problems, 1850–1900," *Journal of the History of Medicine,* vol. XXXII (1977), pp. 61–67; R. Hamowy, "Medicine and the Crimination of Sin: 'Self-Abuse' in Nineteenth Century America," *Journal of Libertarian Studies,* vol. 1, no. 3 (Summer 1977), pp. 229–70.

16. A. Jacobi, "On Masturbation and Hysteria in Young Children," *American Journal of Obstetrics and Diseases of Women and Children,* vol. VIII (1875–1876), pp. 597–99. On Jacobi, see *Dictionary of American Biography,* vol. V, pp. 563–64.

17. Cited in the anthology by D. Milsted, *The Guinness Book of Regrettable Quotations* (Einfeld: 1995), p. 182. On Rush's personality and reputation, see the *Dictionary of Scientific Biography,* vol. XI, pp. 616–18.

18. O.S. Fowler, *Creative and Sexual Science, or Manhood, Womanhood and their Mutual Interrelations . . . as Taught by Phrenology and Physiology* (1875), pp. 801–802. On Fowler, see the *Dictionary of American Biography*, vol. VI, pp. 565–66.

19. The classic work on this subject is E. H. Hare's "Masturbatory Insanity: The History of an Idea," *Journal of Mental Science* (January 1962), pp. 1–25.

20. W. C. Ellis, *A Treatise on the Nature, Symptoms, Causes and Treatment of Insanity* (London: Samuel Holdsworth, 1838), pp. 336–37. French trans.: *Traité de l'alénation mentale*, trans. T. Archambault (Paris: 1840), pp. 223–24.

21. H. Maudsley, "Illustrations of a Variety of Insanity," *Journal of Mental Science* (July, 1868), pp. 152 and cont. (quote found on p. 161); partially reproduced in V. Skultans, *Madness and Morals. Ideas on Insanity in the Nineteenth Century* (London: 1975), pp. 86–94.

22. W. Griesinger, *Traité des maladies mentales. Patholigie et thérapeutique*, French trans., 2nd ed. (Paris: 1865), pp. 206–207. The question here is one of degree. The notion of "masturbatory insanity" was present, it goes without saying, in Europe. Each year, a good number of individuals were confined to the great insane asylum of Lyon, L'Antiquaille, their insanity attributed to "onanism" in the hospital records: there were as many as 24 of them in 1857, 44 in 1860, 62 in 1862 and 1863, and even 71 the following year. See G. Bollenot, "Les fous à Lyon au XIXe siècle. Enfermement et thérapeutique," *Cahiers d'Histoire*, vol. XXVI (1981), p. 235, no. 20.

23. *Précis historique . . . des principaux objets . . . qui composent le Museum de J.-F. Bertrand-Rival* (Paris: 1801), pp. 343–44.

24. M. Platen, *Livre d'Or de la Santé*, trans. and expanded by Dr. L. Deschamps, *Volume spéciale* (Paris: n.d. [1902]), p. 602. The date of 1902 was furnished by the catalog of the Bibliothèque Nationale.

25. Letter from Sabatier quoted in Marc-Antoine Petit, *Onan ou le tombeau du Mont-Cindre. Fait historique présenté en 1809 à l'Académie des Jeux Floraux de Toulouse* (Lyon-Paris: 1809), p. 94.

26. J. Millar, *Hints on Insanity* (1861), reproduced in V. Skultans, *Madness and Morals. Ideas on Insanity in the Nineteenth Century*, pp. 57–58. On Millar, see F. Boase, *Modern English Biography*, vol. VI (London: 1965), col. 209.

27. We are following here the interesting views advanced by J.-F. De-larue, *L'onanisme dans la littérature médicale jusqu'au XIXe siècle*, photocopied medical thesis (Marseille: 1981), p. 33.

28. *Bulletin de la Société de Chirurgie de Paris pendant l'année 1864*, 2nd series, vol. V (1865), pp. 10–15.

29. Lecture by Dr. Yellowlees at the March 3, 1876 meeting in Glasglow of the Medico-psychological Association, in *The Journal of Mental Science*, vol. XXII (1876–1877), pp. 336–37.

30. Entry *Masturbation* in *Dictionary of Psychological Medicine*, pub. under the direction of D.-H. Tuke, vol. II (London: 1892), p. 785.

31. See especially Ch. Mauriac, art. *Onanisme* in *Nouveau dictionnaire de médecine et de chirurgie pratiques*, pub. under the direction of Dr. Jaccoud, vol. XXIV (Paris: 1877), p. 537; J. Duffy, "Masturbation and Clitoridectomy. A Nineteenth-Century View," *Journal of the American Medical Association*, vol. 186 (1963), pp. 246–48; R. A. Spitz, "Authority and Masturbation," *Psychoanalytic Quarterly*, vol. XXI (1952), pp. 502–504.

32. *Masturbation* in *Dictionary of Psychological Medicine*, pp. 785–86.

33. Mentioned in A. N. Gilbert, "Doctor, Patient and Onanist Diseases in the Nineteenth Century," *Journal of the History of Medicine*, pp. 230–31.

34. J. L. Milton, *On the Pathology and Treatment of spermatorrhoea*, new ed. (London: 1887), pp. 127–35.

35. Acton, *A Practical Treatise on Diseases of the Urinary and Generative Organs*, p. 248.

36. Article *Abus de soi-même* in *Encyclopédie méthodique, ou par order de matières. Médecine*, vol. I (Paris: Panckoucke, 1787), p. 44.

37. *Notes* (dated January 31, 1812) in Tissot, *Oeuvres complètes*, ed. J.-N. Hallé, vol. III (Paris: n.d.), p. 496. Several letters by Doussin-Dubreuil aptly illustrate this psychological process. "My imagination was struck by the prognosis revealed in that work (a work on masturbation), and, knowing my own state, I awaited death," wrote a young man (J.-L. Doussin-Dubreuil, *Lettres sur les dangers de l'onanisme*, 3rd ed. [Paris: 1825], p. 28). See also another striking letter on p. 58.

38. Henri-Frédéric Amiel, *Journal intime*, eds. B. Gagnebin and P. Monnier, vol. I, *1839–1851* (Lausanne: 1976). Much has been written on Amiel. I consulted in particular B. Halda's unsparing study *Amiel et les femmes* (Lyon-Paris: n.d. [1963]).

39. *The Gladstone Diaries,* vol. 1, ed. R. D. Foot (Oxford: 1968), p. 351.

40. P. J.-C. Debreyne, *Essai sur la théologie morale considérée dans ses rapports avec la physiologie et la médecine,* 4th ed. (Paris: 1844), p. 74.

41. J. B.-F. Descuret, *La médecine des passions, ou les passions considérées dans leurs rapports avec les maladies, les lois et la religion,* 3rd ed. (Liège: 1844), p. 291.

42. F. Devay, *Hygiène des familles,* vol. II (Paris: 1846), pp. 73 and 75.

43. A. Forel, *La question sexuelle,* 2nd ed. (Paris: 1906), p. 253. See also, from the same period, a striking observation—the case of a young man who developed an "insane terror" at the thought of the terrible effects of his masturbation—in F. Raymond and P. Janet, *Les obsessions et la psychasthénie,* vol. II (Paris: 1903), pp. 341 and cont. (observation 157): see also Th. Zeldin, *Histoire des passions françaises, 1849–1945,* vol. V, *Anxiété et hypocrisie,* French trans. (Paris: 1979), pp. 102–103.

44. W. Stekel, *Onanisme et sexualité,* French trans. (Paris: 1951), p. 34 (the 3rd German edition, on which the translation is based, was published in 1923). Stekel quoted a typical letter sent to him by a 18-year-old man: "During the second semester of school last year, I began to indulge the vice that is onanism and I continued up until a month ago because . . . I had begun to have back pains and I came across a book by I.-H. Tranke-Wortmann according to whom whoever contracts this vice is destined for a softening of the brain, phthisis of the bone marrow and other horrible things. The page I attach . . . reduced me to the deepest despair. To that were added . . . weakness in the feet, involuntary trembling of my extremities, as well as weakening of vision . . . I am in despair and am thinking of killing myself. Save me" (p. 146). Stekel also recalled his own personal experience in his *Lettres à une mère* (Paris: 1939), pp. 190–91. On Stekel, see chapter X below.

45. O. Rank, in *Les premiers psychanalystes,* vol. II, p. 197. Stekel wrote similarly that "many suicides, during this critical stage when the soul is torn between joy and disgust of life, can be explained as a futile battle against onanism" (*Lettres à une mère,* pp. 191–92). See also a page on this topic in G. Stanley Hall, *Adolescence,* vol. I (New York: 1908), p. 452.

46. A. C. Kinsey, W. B. Pomeroy, and C. E. Martin, *Sexual Behavior in the Human Male* (Philadelphia: W. B. Saunders, 1948). French

trans.: *Le comportement sexuel de l'homme* (Paris: 1948), pp. 289 and 648–49.

47. *Onanisme et homosexualté*, pp. 84–85.

48. The connection is made by A. N. Gilbert, "Doctor, Patient and Onanist Diseases in the Nineteenth Century," pp. 228–29.

49. Georges Claes, *Dissertatio medica inauguralis De Onania* (Liège: 1821), p. 16. At the Liège University library in the series *Dissertationes inaugurales medicae Universitatis Leodiensis anni 1820–1821*, call no. XIV-28-2; reprinted in G. Claes, *Recueil d'un mémoire couronné, d'une thèse inaugurale et d'une traduction des Aphorismes d'Hippocrate* (Saint-Trond, n.d.), p. 91 (for the passage mentioned above). On Claes, who was born in Looz in 1795, and was later burgomaster of his city, see the limited biographical data in *Bibliographie Nationale, 1830–1880*.

50. René Hénoumont, in *Pourquoi pas?* (Brussels), May 6, 1985, p. 178.

Chapter Eight

1. Entry *Onanisme* in *Dictionnaire de médecine*, pub. under the direction of Adelon, etc., vol. XV (Paris: 1826), pp. 426–27.

2. See, on Paget, the *Dictionary of National Biography. Supplement*, vol. III, pp. 240–42. "Name that is justly renowned," wrote the author of the preface to one of his books (J. Paget, *Leçon de clinique chirurgicale*, French trans. [Paris: 1877], p. VII, introduction by Verneuil). On Paget's disease, see J.-A. Lièvre, "Maladie osseuse de Paget," in *Traité de médecine*, eds. A. Lemierre, Ch. Lenormant, et al., vol. XVII (Paris: 1953).

3. J. Paget, "Sexual Hypochondriasis," *Selected Essays and Addresses* (London: 1902). We have quoted this last edition.

4. J. Paget, "Sexual Hypochondriasis," *Selected Essays and Addresses*, p. 47.

5. J. Paget, "Sexual Hypochondriasis," p. 48.

6. J. Paget, "Sexual Hypochondriasis," p. 48.

7. J. Paget, "Sexual Hypochondriasis," p. 49.

8. See chapter VII above. Charles Dana also wrote, in his *Textbook of Nervous Diseases*, "I do not believe it right for the physician to

prescribe fornication" (4th ed. [London: 1898], p. 530). There
were thus doctors who did.

9. J. Paget, "Sexual Hypochondriasis," pp. 52–53.

10. On Charles Mauriac (1832–1905), see *Grand Dictionnaire universel du XIXe siècle*, vol. XVII (2nd Supplement), p. 157; G. Thibierge, "Charles Mauriac," *Annales de dermatologie et de syphilligraphie* (1905), pp. 497–502; *Biographisches Lexikon der hervorragenden Ärzte*, 2nd ed., vol. IV, p. 124. On his description of *syphilitic erythema nodosum*, see *Traité de médecine*, eds. Lemierre et al., vol. I (Paris: 1948), p. 507.

11. *Titres and travaux scientifiques du Docteur Charles Mauriac* (1881), p. 43, no. 30.

12. Mauriac, entry *Onanisme* in *Nouveau dictionnaire de médecine et de chirurgie pratiques*, vol. XXIV, p. 518.

13. Mauriac, entry *Onanisme* in *Nouveau dictionnaire* . . . p. 525.

14. Mauriac, entry *Onanisme* in *Nouveau dictionnaire* . . . p. 525.

15. Mauriac, entry *Onanisme* in *Nouveau dictionnaire* . . . pp. 512, 513, 518–19, 526–29.

16. Mauriac, entry *Onanisme* in *Nouveau dictionnaire* . . . pp. 521, 524–25, 534.

17. On Jules Christian (1840–1907), see *Dictionnaire de Biographie française*, vol. VIII, col. 1287–88, and R. Semelaigne, *Les pionniers de la psychiatrie française avant et après Pinel*, vol. II (Paris: 1932), pp. 222–29.

18. *Dictionnaire encyclopédique des sciences médicales*, 2nd series, vol. XV, p. 360.

19. J. Christian, *Epilepsie et folie épileptique* (Brussels: 1890), p. 15.

20. *Dictionnaire encyclopédique des sciences médicales*, p. 361.

21. *Dictionnaire encyclopédique des sciences médicales*, p. 374.

22. *Dictionnaire encyclopédique des sciences médicales*, pp. 375–76.

23. *Meyers Konversations-Lexicon*, 2nd ed., vol. XII (1866), pp. 301–302.

24. *Meyers Konversations-Lexicon*, 3rd ed., vol. XII (1877), pp. 316–17.

25. *Meyers Konversations-Lexicon*, 5th ed., vol. XIII (1896), pp. 184–85.

26. The Brockhaus, during this period, remained far more conservative. There, masturbation was still described in 1903 as having "einen abschwächenden, oft zerrüttenden Einfluss auf Körper

und Geist" (*Brockhaus' Konversations-Lexikon*, 14th ed., vol. XIII [1903], p. 595, heading *Onanie*).

27. C. Lasègue, Etudes médicales, vol. II (Paris: 1884), pp. 808–809. On Lasègue, see *Grand Dictionnaire universel du XIXe siècle*, vol. XVII (2nd Supplement), pp. 1502–1503; *Biographisches Lexikon der hervorragenden Arzte*, 2nd ed., vol. III, pp. 683–88; and the introduction to C. Lasègue, *Ecrits psychiatriques*, ed. J. Corraze (Toulouse: 1971).

28. *Etudes médicales*, vol. II, p. 347; reproduced in *Ecrits psychiatriques*, p. 127.

29. See E. H. Hare, "Masturbatory Insanity," p. 7.

30. See, on Ellis: *Dictionary of National Biography*, vol. 1931–1940, pp. 258–60; and especially note two biographies: V. Brome, *Havelock Ellis, Philosopher of Sex. A Biography* (London: 1979); and P. Grosskurth, *Havelock Ellis. A Biography* (London: 1980). See also a harsh review of Brome's book by D. MacRae in the *New Statesman* (April 13, 1979).

31. Havelock Ellis, *Studies in the Psychology of Sex*. Vol. I: *The Evolution of Modesty, the Phenomena of Sexual Periodicity, Auto-Erotism* (Philadelphia: F. A. Davis: 1910), pp. 249, 280. Translator's note: the ordering of volumes is occasionally altered in different editions of this work.

32. Ellis, *Studies in the Psychology of Sex*. Vol. I: *The Evolution of Modesty . . .* , p. 250.

33. Ellis, *Studies in the Psychology of Sex*. Vol. I: *The Evolution of Modesty . . .* , p. 256.

34. Ellis, *Studies in the Psychology of Sex*. Vol. I: *The Evolution of Modesty . . .* , pp. 257–58.

35. Ellis, *Studies in the Psychology of Sex*. Vol. I: *The Evolution of Modesty . . .* , pp. 258–59.

36. See E. H. Hare, "Masturbatory Insanity," pp. 9 and 12.

37. Ellis, *Studies in the Psychology of Sex*. Vol. I: *The Evolution of Modesty . . .* , p. 266.

38. Ellis, *Studies in the Psychology of Sex*. Vol. I: *The Evolution of Modesty . . .* , pp. 269–70.

39. Ellis, *Studies in the Psychology of Sex*. Vol. I: *The Evolution of Modesty . . .* , p. 282.

40. Ellis, *Studies in the Psychology of Sex*. Vol. I: *The Evolution of Modesty . . .* , p. 283.

CHAPTER NINE

1. *Die Masturbation. Eine Monographie für Aerzte und Pädagogen* (Berlin, 1899).

2. *Die Masturbation,* pp. IV, V, 3, 4, etc.

3. A. Nyström, *La vie sexuelle et ses lois,* French trans. (Paris: 1910), p. 38. The original Swedish version dates from 1904; the work was subsequently translated into German (Berlin: 1904) and English.

4. A. Forel, *La question sexuelle,* 2nd ed. (Paris: 1906), p. 252. On Forel, see the entries in *Neue Deutsche Biographie,* vol. V, pp. 298–99, and *Dictionary of Scientific Biography,* vol. V, pp. 73–74.

5. H. B. Morris, *Injuries and diseases of the genital and urinary organs* (London: 1895), p. 38. From 1910 to 1912, Morris would be the President of the Royal Society of Medicine (see *Who Was Who, 1916–1918*).

6. G. Stanley Hall, *Adolescence: Its Psychology and its Relation to Physiology, Anthropology, Sociology, Sex, Crime, Religion and Education,* vol. I (New York: 1908), p. 444. The work was first published in 1904. On Hall, see *Dictionary of American Biography,* vol. IV, pp. 127–30. On his views on masturbation, see R. P. Neuman, "Masturbation, Madness and the Modern Concepts of Childhood and Adolescence," *Journal of Social History* (Spring 1975), pp. 14–16.

7. See *Les premiers psychanalystes. Minutes de la Société psychanalytique de Vienne,* ed. H. Nunberg and E. Federn, French trans., vol. II, *1908–1910* (Paris: 1978), pp. 528–56; vol. III, *1910–1911* (Paris: 1979), pp. 311–18, 326–35, 345–55; vol. IV, *1912–1918* (Paris: 1983), pp. 38–46, 55–63, 78–83, 90–105, 116–21 (Translator's note: the English translation, *Minutes of the Vienna Psychoanalytic Society,* eds. H. Nunberg and E. Federn, 4 vols. [NY: 1962–75], will be cited below); B. Dattner, P. Federn, et al., *Die Onanie, Vierzehn Beiträge zu einer Diskussion der Wiener Psychoanalytischen Vereinigung* (Weisbaden: 1912). On these discussions, see particularly A. Reich, "The Discussion of 1912 on Masturbation and our Present-Day Views," in *The Psychoanalytic Study of the Child,* vol. VI (New York: 1951), pp. 80 and cont., and A. Alsteens, *La masturbation chez l'adolescent* (Bruges: 1967), pp. 34–40. On Freudianism and masturbation, see chapter III of D.-J. Duché's *Histoire de l'onanisme* (Paris: Collection *Que sais-je?,* 1994).

8. "By and large . . . the majority of speakers have supported the view that masturbation is harmless," Stekel stated during the June 8, 1910 meeting (*Minutes of the Vienna Psychoanalytic Society*, vol. II, p. 572).

9. *Minutes of the Vienna Psychoanalytic Society*, vol. II, p. 61 (meeting of Nov. 18, 1908); Freud's contribution to *Die Onanie*, in *Gessamelte Werke*, vol. VIII (London: 1943), pp. 334 and cont., and in English translation in *Standard Edition of the Complete Psychological Works*, ed. J. Strachey, vol. XII (London: 1958), pp. 245 and cont.

10. *Gessamelte Werke*, vol. VIII, p. 342; *Standard Edition*, vol. XIII, p. 251.

11. See K. J. Zucker, "Freud's Early Views on Masturbation and the Actual Neuroses," *Journal of the American Academy of Psychoanalysis*, vol. VIII (1979), pp. 15–32.

12. *Standard Edition*, vol. XIII, p. 252; *Minutes of the Vienna Psychoanalytic Society*, vol. II, p. 561; *Gessamelte Werke*, vol. VIII, p. 343.

13. *Minutes of the Vienna Psychoanalytic Society*, vol. II, p. 61.

14. *Minutes of the Vienna Psychoanalytic Society*, vol. II, p. 561.

15. *Minutes of the Vienna Psychoanalytic Society*, vol. II, pp. 61 and 561. We note that on this point, as on many others, other members of the Vienna circle vigorously argued with Freud: see, for example, Stekel in the June 1, 1910 session, in *Minutes of the Vienna Psychoanalytic Society*, vol. II, p. 541.

16. *Minutes of the Vienna Psychoanalytic Society*, vol. II, pp. 561–62.

17. Freud later added an argument that seems to be built upon particularly base notions. Our only source, however, is the summary of the debates, which may have made his words seem harsher than they were: "The opinion that masturbation is harmful," he declared in the February 7, 1912 discussion, "finds support in observations made by an absolutely objective critic who traced back the later stultification of Arab youths to their masturbation, which was excessive and totally uninhibited" (*Minutes of the Vienna Psychoanalytic Society*, vol. IV, p. 41).

18. *Minutes of the Vienna Psychoanalytic Society*, vol. II, p. 563.

19. *Gessamelte Werke*, vol. VIII, p. 343; *Standard Edition*, vol. XII, p. 252. See also *Minutes of the Vienna Psychoanalytic Society*, vol. II, p. 563.

20. It is striking that after 1912, Freud devoted little discussion to masturbation. The subject, obviously, was not one of his favorites.

We encounter, in a 1935 text, a revealing expression. "I am rather happy" ("*ich bin vielmehr froh*"), he said in his *Nouvelles conférences sur la psychanalyse,* not to have to speak of masturbation, which would be "a long and difficult task" (*Gessamelte Werke,* vol. XV, 3rd. ed. [Frankfurt: 1961], p. 136; French trans. *Nouvelles conférences sur la psychanalyse* [Paris: 1936], p. 174). It was not a subject dear to his heart.

21. J. Rengade, *La vie normale et la santé. Traité complet de la structure du corps humain* (Paris: 1881), pp. 94–95.

22. A. Clerc, *Hygiène et médecine des deux sexes,* vol. I (Paris: 1885), pp. 352 and cont. On the author, see *Dictionnaire de Biographie française,* vol. VIII, col. 1465.

23. Garnier, *Onanisme,* 9th ed. (Paris: 1896), p. 3.

24. E. Monin, *L'hygiène des sexes* (Paris: 1890). We have quoted from the new edition, 10° mille (Paris; n.d.), pp. 56–57.

25. G. Surbled, *Le vice solitaire* (Paris: 1905).

26. Entry *Onanisme,* p. 811. The same text appears in Dr. Galtier-Boissière, *Dictionnaire illustré de médecine usuelle,* 52° mille (Paris: n.d. [1913]), p. 334, entry *Onanisme.* We can also cite the 1902 entry *Onanisme* in the *Nouveau Larousse illustré. Dictionnaire universel encyclopédique,* vol. VI (Paris: n.d. [1902]): "Onanism causes troubles that are often very serious: it involves considerable nervous expenditure; resulting in digestive problems, muscular weakness, loss of intelligence, stunted growth, etc."

27. *Onanisme,* in *Larousse médical illustré.*

28. *The Lancet* (January 12, 1901), p. 108; see also P. Grosskurth, *Havelock Ellis,* p. 222. Typical as well is the manner in which the *British Medical Journal* spoke of masturbation without actually naming it: "Dangerous Quack Literature: The Moral of a Recent Suicide," *British Medical Journal* (October 1, 1892), p. 753.

29. A. A. Brill, "Masturbation, its Causes and Sequellae," *The American Journal of Urology,* vol. XII (1916), p. 215. "It is sad to state that most doctors entertain similar ideas," Brill repeated later on p. 217.

30. "Masturbation, its Causes and Sequellae," p. 217.

31. W. R. Miller and H. I. Lief, "Masturbatory Attitudes, Knowledge and Experience," in *Archives of Sexual Behavior,* vol. V (1976), p. 448.

32. I. Bloch, *The Sexual Life of Our Time,* English trans. (London: 1908), p. 427.

33. André Gide, *Si le grain ne meurt,* 24th ed. (Paris: 1928), pp. 67–69. On this episode, see J. Delay, *La jeunesse d'André Gide,* vol. I (Paris: 1956), pp. 246–48, and P. de Boisdeffre, *Vie d'André Gide,* vol. I (Paris: 1970), pp. 62–63.

34. F. Brémond, *Les passions et la santé* (Paris: 1893), p. 149. On Brémond, see *Dictionnaire de Biographie française,* vol. VII, col. 202.

35. Julien Blanc, *Seule la vie . . . I. Confusion des peines* (Paris: 1947), pp. 57–58.

36. A. Comfort, *L'origine des obsessions sexuelles,* French trans. (Verviers: 1969), p. 112.

37. Jules Payot, *L'éducation de la volonté,* 27th ed. (Paris: 1907), p. 218.

38. *L'éducation de la volonté,* p. 211.

39. A. Langelez, *Notions d'hygiène générale. Applications à l'hygiène scolaire et à l'inspection médicale des écoles* (Luttre: 1916), pp. 190–91; 2nd ed. (Luttre: 1922), p. 291.

40. Dr. Lomry, *Les Ennemis de la santé. Conférences données au corps enseignant des écoles primaires du Luxembourg* (Arlon: 1928), p. 52; 2nd ed. (Brussels: 1936), p. 87.

41. Marcel Liebman, *Né juif. Une enfance juive pendant la guerre* (Paris-Gembloux: 1977), p. 161. Along similar lines, Pierre Debray-Ritzen's *Petite histoire naturelle de la sexualité infantile expurgée des jobardises* (Lausanne: 1982), depicts a French provincial religious establishment during the thirties (pp. 113–14).

42. R. Baden-Powell, *Scouting for Boys,* 9th ed. (London: C.A. Pearson, 1920), pp. 203–204. French translation: *Eclaireurs. Un programme d'éducation civique,* 9th ed. (Neuchâtel-Paris: 1939).

43. *Eclaireurs. Un programme d'éducation civique.*

44. *Scouting for Boys* (1930), pp. 104–106.

45. W. Stekel, *Onanisme et homosexualité,* French trans. (Paris: 1951), p. 168.

46. Arthur Koestler, *Arrow in the Blue: An Autobiography* (NY: 1957), p. 57. French trans.: *La corde raide* (Paris: 1978), p. 81.

47. Julien Green, *Oeuvres complètes,* vol. V (Paris: La Pléiade, 1977), pp. 656–57. See J. P.-J. Piriou, *Sexualité, religion et art chez Julien Green* (Paris: 1976), pp. 53–54. This occurred around 1906.

48. J. F. W. Meagher, *A Study of Masturbation and the Psychosexual Life,* 3rd. ed. (London: 1936), p. 96.

49. Françoise Marette, *Psychanalyse et pédiatrie* (Paris: 1939, Doctoral thesis in medicine), pp. 75–76; new edition under her married name, Françoise Dolto (Paris: 1971), pp. 70–72.

50. J. Stephani-Cherbuliez, *Le sexe a ses droits. Instruction et éducation sexuelle* (Brussels: 1946), p. 28.

51. See J. Kruithof and J. Van Ussel, *Jeugd voor de muur. Vlaamse studenten over hun seksuele problematiek* (Anvers: 1962), p. 94.

52. *Les lépreuses* (Paris: 1939), p. 153.

53. L. D. Weatherhead, *The Mastery of Sex Through Psychology and Religion* (London: Student Christian Movement Press, 1931), pp. 127 and 126. French trans.: *La maîtrise sexuelle (psychologie et reglion)* (Paris: 1933). On Weatherhead, who, as both a Methodist pastor and pioneer of psychoanalysis in England, was an interesting figure; see the obituary notice in the *Times*, January 5, 1976.

54. A. A. Brill, "Masturbation, its Causes and Sequellae," p. 221.

55. S. Freud, "Neue Folger der Vorlesunger zur Einführung in die Pschoanalyse," in *Gessamelte Werke*, vol. XV, 3rd ed. (Frankfurt: 1961), p. 93. Freud had described a case of this type in 1909 in his famous analysis of little Hans; see *Cinq psychanalyses*. French trans., 3rd ed. (Paris: 1967), p. 95.

56. Julien Green, *Oeuvres complètes*, vol. V, pp. 656–57. Again in 1968, Dr. Pomeroy, Kinsey's closest collaborator, wrote: "Every doctor who deals with young boys still encounters those who are as pale and fearful and trembling as their nineteenth-century predecessors and who finally confess that they are masturbating and are frightened by the vague old wives' tales they have heard about it" (*Boys and Sex* [New York: Dell Publishing, 1968], p. 33; French trans.: *Les garçons et le sexe* [Paris: 1971], p. 52).

57. M. Huschka, "The Incidence and Character of Masturbation Threats in a Group of Problem Children," *Psychoanalytic Quarterly*, vol. VII (1938), pp. 338–56.

58. E. V. Pullias, "Masturbation as a Mental Hygiene Problem. A Study of the Beliefs of Seventy-Five Young Men," *Journal of Abnormal and Social Psychology*, vol. XXXII (1937), pp. 216–22.

59. C. C. Fry and G. Rostow, *Mental Health in College* (New York: 1942), esp. pp. 99–101 and 117–19. The physician who related his experience at Yale is Dr. Fry.

60. The work also cited specific cases, including, of course, the classic case of a young man who had read a book on masturbation—a book, as it happens, from 1896—and who saw himself condemned to the various evils predicted by the book (see p. 118).

61. J. Kruithof and J. Van Ussel, *Jeugd voor de muur*, pp. 88–97.

62. J. Kruithof and J. Van Ussel, *Jeugd voor de muur*, p. 88.
63. J. Kruithof and J. Van Ussel, *Jeugd voor de muur*, p. 88.
64. A. C. Kinsey, W. B. Pomeroy and C. E. Martin, *Sexual Behavior in the Human Male* (Philadelphia: 1948), pp. 375–77 and 508–509. French trans.: *Le comportement sexuel de l'homme* (Paris: 1948), pp. 488–92 and 641.
65. In 1960, in France, Dr. Le Moal noted that "in some simple milieux" parents can still be heard telling their children "If you continue, I'll cut it off." P. Le Moal, *Pour une authentique éducation sexuelle* (Lyon-Paris: 1960), p. 135. Julien Green's mother would not have continued to use the same language in 1960.

CHAPTER TEN

1. M. Hirschfeld, *Sexualpathologie. Ein Lehrbuch fur Ärzte und Studierende*, vol. I, *Geschlechtliche Entwicklungsstörungen mit besonderer Berücksichtigung der Onanie* (Bonn: 1917). On Magnus Hirschfeld, who caused a stir in his day, see V.-L. Bullough, *Sexual Variance in Society and History* (New York: 1976), pp. 644 and cont.; *Handbook of Sexology*, pub. under the direction of J. Money and J. Musaph (Amsterdam-London: 1977), pp. 34–38.
2. *Onanie und Homosexualität* (Berlin: 1917), 2nd and 3rd eds., Berlin: 1921 and 1923. French trans. based on the 3rd ed., *Onanisme et homosexualité* (Paris: 1951). On Stekel, see H.-E. Ellenberger, *A la découverte de l'inconscient. Histoire de la psychiatrie dynamique*, French trans. (Villeurbanne: 1974), pp. 493–95, and his *Autobiography*, ed. F. A. Gutheil (New York: 1950). On his relationship with Freud, see in particular S. Freud, *Correspondance, 1873–1939*, French trans. (Paris: 1979), pp. 379–80 (Letter of January 13, 1924).
3. 1922 edition, p. 811, heading *Onanisme*.
4. *Larousse médical illustré* (Paris: 1924), p. 857, heading *Onanisme*.
5. M. West, *Infant Care* (Washington: U.S. Dept. of Labor, Children's Bureau: 1914), p. 62.
6. *Infant Care* [no author], (Washington: 1921), pp. 45–46. The same text appears in the 1922 edition, pp. 45–46. On the later evolution of the handbook, see M. Wolfenstein, "Trends in Infant

Care," *American Journal of Orthopsychiatry*, vol. XXIII (1953), pp. 120–22.

7. L. Honoré, *Elle . . . et toi, jeune homme!*, French adaptation of the work by J. Schilgen, 2nd ed. (Paris-Tournai: 1934), pp. 67 and cont.; same in the 4th ed. (Paris-Tournai: 1938), p. 67 and cont.

8. A. Moll, *Das Sexualleben des Kindes* (Berlin: 1909), pp. 164–65, 168–69, and 175. On Albert Moll, see *Handbook of Sexology*, eds. Money and Musaph, pp. 24–27.

9. I. Bloch, *The Sexual Life of Our Time*, English trans. (London: 1908), pp. 421–22. Iwan Bloch was a reputed sexologist: see *Handbook of Sexology*, eds. Money and Musaph, pp. 38–41.

10. *Tout le corps humain. Encyclopédie illustrée des connaissances médicales*, vol. IV (Paris: 1929), p. 108 (chapter on children's illnesses by Dr. Babonneix).

11. W. B. Pomeroy, *Boys and Sex* (New York: 1971), p. 33. French trans.: *Les garçons et le sexe* (Paris: 1971), p. 54.

12. Benjamin Spock, *A Teenager's Guide to Life and Love* (New York: 1970), p. 136.

13. O. Schwartz, *Psychologie sexuelle*, French trans. (Paris: 1952), pp. 27 and 34. On Schwartz, see the introduction by F. Duyckaerts, pp. v–xxv.

14. *Psychologie de l'hygiène* (Paris: 1921), p. 142.

15. I. Bloch, *The Sexual Life of Our Time*, p. 423.

16. *Pratique médico-chirurgicale*, eds. A. Couvelaire, A. Lemierre and Ch. Lenormant, 3rd ed., vol. VII (Paris: 1931), pp. 1082–83.

17. P.-E. Matignon, *Puberté et déterminisme sexuel* (Bordeaux: 1945), p. 62.

18. A. Hesnard, *Traité de sexologie normale et pathologique* (Paris: 1933), pp. 541–43.

19. J. Dierkens, *L'amour à 18 ans* (Paris: 1970), pp. 86–87. Also appears in Odette Thibault, *A la découverte de la sexualité. Cous d'éducation sexuelle destiné aux élèves des classes terminales des lycées* (Paris: 1971), p. 49.

20. *Education de l'amour* (Paris: 1946), p. 172.

21. A. Niedermeyer, *Précis de médecine pastorale*, French trans. (Mulhouse, 1955), p. 130. The German original was published in 1953.

22. C. Prudence. Preface by M. Petitmangin, *La Masturbation. Etudes clinique, morale, pastorale* (Paris-Liege: 1967).

23. J. F. W. Meagher, *A Study of Masturbation and Its Reputed Sequelae*, 2nd ed. (London: 1924), p. 63; nearly the same language in the 3rd rev. ed., *A Study of Masturbation and the Psychosexual Life* (London: 1936), p. 139.

24. *Les étapes de l'éducation* (Paris: 1952), p. 61

25. *A la découverte de la sexualité*, p. 49.

26. *Psychologie sexuelle*, p. 34.

27. *A Study of Masturbation and Its Reputed Sequelae*, p. 29.

28. *Petit Larousse de la Médecine* (Paris: 1976), p. 479, heading *Masturbation*.

29. E. Mounier, *Traité du caractère*, new rev. edition (Paris: 1947), p. 152.

30. *Traité du caractère*, pp. 152–53.

31. P. Sedallian and P. Monnet," Hygiène scolaire," in A. Rochaix, P. Sedellian and R. Sohier, *Traité d'hygiène*, vol. I (Paris: 1946), p. 244.

32. Dr. Gilbert-Robin, *La guérison des défauts et des vices chez l'enfant. Guide pratique d'éducation* (Paris: 1948), pp. 431–32.

33. A. Bergé, *Education familiale* (Paris: 1936), p. 139.

34. *Savoir élever les enfants*, vol. III (Paris: 1961), p. 180.

35. See Arthur Koestler, *The Invisible Writing*, vol. II of *Arrow in the Blue* (NY: 1954), ch. XIX. Koestler described it as "the only book of mine that met with an unanimously friendly reception" (p. 213). French trans. *Hiéroglyphes*, vol. II (Paris: 1978), pp. 87 and cont.

36. A. Costler, A. Willy, et al. *Encyclopaedia of Sexual Knowledge*, pub. by N. Haire, 3rd ed. (London: 1937), p. 95. Koestler was never able to resolve this quarrel with Haire, since, as he tells us himself, he never met him (*Hiéroglyphes*, vol. II, p. 101).

37. J. Cohen, J. Kahn-Nathan, G. Tordjman, and C. Verdoux, *Encyclopédie de la vie sexuelle de la physiologie à la psychologie*, vol. 10/13 *ans* (Paris: 1973), p. 84.

38. G. Tordjman, C. Verdoux, J. Cohen and J. Kahn-Nathan, *Enyclopédie . . .* , vol. 17/18 *ans* (Paris: 1973), pp. 155–57.

39. J. Cohen, J. Kahn-Nathan, S. Masse, G. Tordjman, and C. Verdoux, *Enyclopédie . . .* , vol. for adults (Paris: 1973), p. 145.

40. "Chantage au bonheur": an expression coined by Tony Duvert in his pamphlet *Le bon sexe illustré* (Paris: 1974), p. 79.

41. M. Petitmangin, *La Masturbation*, p. 75.

42. Elise and Celestin Freinet, *Vous avez un enfant* (Paris: 1962), p. 324. The authors asserted that the methods of the Freinet School

would eliminate masturbation in students, while any return to former pedagogical practices would cause "the reappearance of the deplorable tendencies" (p. 327). On Freinet, see G. Piaton, *La pensée pédagogique de Célestin Freinet* (1974).

43. See, in particular, M. Debesse, *Les étapes de l'éducation*, 1952, p. 61 ("the vicious habit"); M.-T. Van Eeckhout, *Savoir élever les enfants*, vol. III (1961), p. 180 (also "vicious habit").

44. See Kinsey, Pomeroy, and Martin, *Sexual Behavior in the Human Male*, p. 513.

45. Kinsey, Liam Hudson justly remarked, "did more than any other person to undermine Victorian prejudices about masturbation" ("Eros observed," *Times Literary Supplement*, Oct. 22, 1976, p. 1318).

46. A. Costler, A. Willy, et al., *Encyclopaedia of Sexual Knowledge*, pp. 72–73.

47. A. Gügler, *Die erziehliche Behandlung jugendlicher männlicher Onanisten* (Fribourg: 1942), pp. 61–62.

48. Kinsey, Pomeroy, and Martin, *Sexual Behavior in the Human Male*, p. 514.

49. P. Simon, J. Gondonneau, L. Mironer, and A.-M. Dourlen-Rollier, *Rapport sur le comportement sexuel des Français* (Paris: 1972), p. 262.

50. *Myers Lexicon*, 9th ed., vol. XV (1975), p. 734.

51. *Larousse de la Médecine, Santé, hygiène*. vol. II (Paris: 1972), p. 299.

52. J. Takman, *Le petit livre suédois d'éducation sexuelle*. French trans. (Paris: 1970), p. 113. See also another Swedish sex education manual cited in B. Linner, *Sex and Society in Sweden* (New York: 1972), p. 163: "Self-gratification is completely natural and harmless." The key word here is "natural."

53. M. Poissonnier, C. Sentilhes, C. Vesin, and P. Vesin, *Guide pratique ilustré des parents. L'Information sexuelle* (Paris: 1971), p. 101. "Practiced by mammals and all ethnic groups, masturbation appears to be natural, physiological, and should be accepted as such" (P. Debrary-Ritzen, *Petite histoire naturelle de la sexualité infantile expurgée des jobardises* [Lausanne: 1982], p. 32).

54. J. Kahn-Nathan and G. Tordjman, *Le sexe en question. Une expérience d'éducation sexuelle dans la région parisienne* (Paris: 1970), pp. 169–70.

55. P. Simon, J. Gondonneau, et al., *Rapport sur le comportement sexuel des Français*, p. 261.

56. *Larousse de la Médecine,* p. 299.
57. M. Barandier, *La sexualité de l'adolescent* (Paris: 1974), p. 78. Foster wrote in 1969: "It is definitely known today that the only real harm connected with masturbation is the guilt and anxiety that may be produced by adult attitudes toward it" ("Guidelines for Parents," in *Sex Education in a Changing Culture,* eds. G. P. Powers and N. Baskin [London: 1969], p. 305).
58. A. Alsteens, *Dialogue et sexualité* (1969), p. 231.
59. W. R. Miller and H. I. Lief, "Masturbatory attitudes, knowledge and experience: Data from the Sex Knowledge and Attitude Test (SKAT)," *Archives of Sexual Behavior,* vol. V (1976), pp. 454–55 (paper presented in 1975).
60. P. Druet, "Psychologie et morale dans la conscience contemporaine," *Nouvelle Revue Théologique* (Jan.-Feb., 1980), pp. 53–54.
61. Morton Hunt, *Sexual Behavior in the 1970s* (Chicago: 1974), pp. 16, 22, and 73–74.
62. J. Vermeire, *Hygiène sexuelle* (Kasterlee: 1959), p. 137.
63. M. Petitmangin, *La masturbation,* pp. 90 and cont.
64. Marc Oraison, *Vie chrétienne et problèmes de la sexualité* (Paris: 1972), p. 87.
65. A. Alsteens, *Dialogue et sexualité,* p. 231.
66. P. de Locht, "Le point de vue moral," postscript to A. Alsteens, *La masturbation à l'adolescence: un problème éducatif* (Brussels: Centre d'Education à la Famille et à l'Amour, 1969), p. 28.
67. A. Plé, "La masturbation. Réflexions théologiques et pastorales," in *La Vie Spirituelle, Supplément* (May 1966), pp. 270, 290, and 292.
68. *Catholicisme,* vol. VIII, col. 838–42. The text was published in part 36 of the dictionary in 1979 but was certainly written before the declaration of the Congregation for the Doctrine of the Faith in 1975.
69. A. Plé, "La masturbation," *La Vie Spirituelle,* p. 270.
70. M. Petitmangin, *La masturbation,* pp. 112–13.
71. Sacred Congregation for the Doctrine of the Faith [Congregatio pro Doctrina Fidei], *Declaration on Certain Questions Concerning Sexual Ethics.* December 29, 1975 (Washington, D.C.: United States Catholic Conference, 1976), pp. 9–10. French translation published in the French weekly *L'Osservatore Romano* on Jan. 23, 1976.
72. "L'ordre et le péché," *Le Monde,* Jan. 24, 1976.

73. "Une morale pour notre temps," *Le Monde*, Feb. 7, 1976. Jacques Cordy, in the Brussels newspaper *Le Soir*, spoke of the "rather awkward attempt by the Church to definitively pronounce upon a subject where questions abound, where moralists hesitate, and where scientific observation often makes no headway" (*Le Soir*, Jan. 17, 1976).

74. Declaration signed by 46 theologians and published in *Le Monde* on Jan. 25, 1976.

75. Interview in *Le Nouvel Observateur*, Feb. 9, 1976, p. 35.

76. "Une occasion manquée," *De Standaard*, Jan. 16, 1976.

77. "Une recherche, un cheminement, un risque," pamphlet from the Conseil central de l'Enseignement primaire catholique, series "Animation des Ecoles," no. 7 (1977), p. 31. See the commentary on this text by Henri Janne, "Education et sexualité," *Le Soir*, Jan. 6, 1978.

78. Ph. Van Meerbeek and A. d'Alcantara, *De L'Onanisme dans le discours médical* (Université Catholique de Louvain. Ecole de Santé Publique. Séminaire de Médecine scolaire: Feb. 1982, no. LXXXVIII), p. 5.

79. Henri Fresquet, "Une morale pour notre temps."

80. *Orientations éducatives sur l'amour humain. Instruction de la Congrégation pour l'Education catholique*, Nov. I, 1983 (Paris: 1984) (*Les Grands textes de la Documentation Catholique*, no. 49), p. 14–15.

81. *Catéchisme de l'Eglise Catholique* (Paris: 1992), pp. 478–79.

82. On this subject, see in particular T. Szasz, *Sex: Facts, Frauds and Follies* (Oxford: 1981), and the interesting review of this book by S. Sutherland, "The Disease of Dissatisfaction," *The Times Literary Supplement*, Aug. 14, 1981.

83. W. B. Pomeroy, *Boys and Sex*, pp. 32, 44.

84. J. L. McCary, *Sexual Myths and Fallacies* (New York: 1971), p. 113.

85. *Man's Body* (New York: Paddington Press), sec. K32. French trans.: *Le corps de l'homme* (Lausanne: 1977).

86. *L'onanisme ou le droit au plaisir*, pp. 103–25.

87. *New Encyclopaedia Britannica. Micropaedia*, vol. VI (1974), p. 682, entry *Masturbation*.

88. Shere Hite, *The Hite Report: A Nationwide Study of Female Sexuality*, new ed. (New York: 1977), p. 62.

89. Miller and Lief, "Masturbatory attitudes, knowledge and experience," *Archives of Sexual Behavior*, p. 463.

90. Dr. Marie Chevret-Measson, in N. Grafeille, M. Bonierbale, and M. Chevret-Measson, *Les cinq sens et l'amour* (Paris: 1983), p. 177.

91. Morton Hunt, *Sexual Behavior in the 1970s,* pp. 66–67.

92. "A man may boast to his friends of the pleasures he has taken with a woman, but he never describes the delights of his onanistic fantasies" (Donald Gould, "Understanding Everywoman," *The New Statesman,* April 30, 1971). See also the remarks by J.-R. Verdier, *L'onanisme ou le droit au plaisir* (Paris: 1973), p. 40.

93. "The Politics of Masturbation," *The Lancet* (Dec. 24, 1994), p. 1714.

94. See the *Sunday Times,* Dec. 11, 1994; the *International Herald Tribune,* Dec. 12, 1994; *Libération,* Dec. 12, 1994; and *The Lancet,* Dec. 17, 1994, p. 1695.

95. "The Politics of Masturbation," *The Lancet* (Dec. 24, 1994), p. 1715.

Index